W9-BUD-069

The publisher and the University of California Press Foundation gratefully acknowledge the generous support of the George Gund Foundation Imprint in African American Studies.

You Can't Stop the Revolution

You Can't Stop the Revolution

*Community Disorder and Social Ties
in Post-Ferguson America*

ANDREA S. BOYLES

University of California Press

University of California Press
Oakland, California

Library of Congress Cataloging-in-Publication Data

Names: Boyles, Andrea S., 1973– author.
Title: You can't stop the revolution : community disorder and social ties
  in post-Ferguson America / Andrea S. Boyles.
Description: Oakland, California : University of California Press, [2019]
  | Includes bibliographical references and index. |
Identifiers: LCCN 2019002897 (print) | LCCN 2019015884 (ebook) |
  ISBN 9780520970502 (ebook) | ISBN 9780520298323 (cloth : alk. paper)
  | ISBN 9780520298330 (pbk. : alk. paper)
Subjects: LCSH: Police-community relations—United States—
  21st century. | Police brutality—United States—21st century. | African
  Americans—Violence against—United States—21st century. | Protest
  movements—United States—21st century.
Classification: LCC HV7936.P8 (ebook) | LCC HV7936.P8 B695 2019 (print)
  | DDC 363.2/3—dc23
LC record available at https://lccn.loc.gov/2019002897

Manufactured in the United States of America

28 27 26 25 24 23 22 21 20 19
10 9 8 7 6 5 4 3 2 1

And yet her legacy lives . . .

I dedicate this book to my late mother, Brenda, who embodied immeasurable resilience through life and death, and to my children, Prentis Jr., Anaiah, and Faith, as the next generation of hope, determination, and accomplishment.

I also dedicate this book to the innumerable black citizens, volunteers, community and grassroots organizers, and leaders of color in general, who selflessly and innovatively work in the trenches and on the front lines of disparity, with little to no resources or fanfare, in service to disproportionately destitute, oppressed populations and places.

Contents

Illustrations

Acknowledgments

This is my second book. The fact that I raised the stakes to compete against myself made this journey even more tedious than the first one. The idea had been to work more innovatively, furthering theoretical implications, evidence-based data, and opportunity for provoking social change. However, this venture was compounded by the unimagined intricacies of an emerging twenty-first-century black social movement. As a black female St. Louisan sociologist and critical criminologist, from the outset my mission was to accurately and holistically account for the Ferguson civil unrest and uprising—both events and interactions. I wanted to get things right, wanted to capture the realness of events and experiences from the perspectives of those closest to, most subject to, and most affected by them. Further, my goal was to do this from within the movement, alongside my fellow black citizens. Our lives meant and continue to mean more than a series of headlines or evolving news cycles. No pressure from me for me (sarcasm), but I felt obligated to work in tandem with the drive and commitment of the people. Black citizens went hard immediately following Mike Brown Jr.'s death. Therefore, it was in this spirit that my three-year journey began. Only hours after Brown's death on August 9, 2014, I responded to an empirical call to action, influenced by community organizers, and I stayed the course, with a twofold agenda centered on black victimization. This course of action meant fully yielding to examinations and explanations while immersed in a steady flux of social conflict and a nonnegotiable demand for social change—locally, nationally, and internationally.

Accomplishing this feat meant that I needed and would have to rely on a sizable support system. Given the far-reaching implications and effects of civil unrest in the region, I would like to begin by first thanking Lindenwood University—both the Belleville and St. Charles campuses. Administrators, colleagues, and students alike were supportive of my research and writing agenda, pre- and post-Ferguson. I am grateful to the administrators and colleagues who regularly checked on me while I was immersed in protests (i.e., direct action). I am also appreciative of administrators, faculty, and staff with the Hammond Institute, who provided incentives for participants as well as research assistants. Since many interview participants resided in disadvantaged neighborhoods, I badly wanted to give back to them for their time spent giving to me; some of the most sensitive, indelible experiences and stories were shared through voluntary interviews. Likewise, I am grateful to my research and student assistants, Melissa Allen, Alyssa Flynn, Quinisa Grant, and Arron Whitt, for transcribing some field notes and interviews, (re)reading transcripts and materials for accuracy, and assisting with other relevant tasks. For years I juggled the interchangeable and overlapping demands of fieldwork and campus work. More specifically, I personally acquired all 125 of my citizen contacts through participant observation, in-depth interviews, and focus groups. I also coded most of the data and completed most of the research process by myself. Therefore, I wholeheartedly appreciated course releases, flexibility, and patience. I am also thankful to my colleague Trisha Prunty for continuously providing institutional review board assistance and to campus graphic artist Lennon Mueller for his assistance with the images in the book.

Further, I am appreciative of Rod Brunson. Rod has always been an objective, avid supporter of my research agenda and a critical reviewer of my work. I am grateful to him for being a mentor, colleague, and friend, whose work ethic and discipline have been exemplary for me. Since the beginning of my academic career, I have increasingly found myself adopting some of his catchphrases and approaches while navigating research and publishing. Unbeknown to him, I routinely deferred to his wisdom while working on this project. Our periodic conversations and his advice encouraged and strengthened me in my resolve and my commitment to this study. Fieldwork proved especially physically, mentally, and emotionally exhausting. His availability and willingness to be a sounding board and academic safe space for my critical and perhaps racing (LOL) thoughts and ambitious ideas and actions have been invaluable. His expertise and camaraderie provided much-needed support, particularly during tumultuous events and exchanges across the St. Louis region. It has meant the world to me that throughout the duration of this study, he allowed me to decompress or debrief without judgment following direct action, community events, interviews, and more. For that and more, Rod, I extend to you much gratitude.

I am also grateful to the University of California Press, especially my editor, Maura Roesner. I appreciate that we have developed a wonderful working relationship over the years. Maura respects and trusts my expertise, my professional and personal intuitiveness, and my ability to navigate timely, critical issues and terrain innovatively and effectively. I value that she has always been superexcited about my work. This has mattered most at times when I risked the ability to appreciate the depth of the study while intently concentrating on process (e.g., data collection, analysis, deadlines). I am thankful for Maura's uncanny ability to bring me full circle—how you, Maura, would meticulously say and do things that rejuvenated and reinvigorated my sense of the mission—to reach and complete the underlying goals and agenda of the study.

Similarly, I am thankful to my former professor, Robert Schaefer, as well as to supporter Torry Dickinson. I reached out to Robert sporadically—sometimes perplexed, overwhelmed, railing or rambling (I imagine), asking questions, and so forth. Sometimes I was so pressed that I had to forgo otherwise welcome conversations. However, it mattered that Robert made time for me. It has also meant a lot that he and Torry follow my career and continue to be ardent supporters. Even when we do not talk, Robert and Torry, I have appreciated knowing that you were and continue to be just an email or phone call away. I am grateful for having that connection and do not take your expertise and encouragement for granted.

I have also fully appreciated Queen Ford's consistent motherly prayers and inspirational conversations. They were needed and timely. Life happened, and there were times when I felt gut-punched due to an unexpected, often unyielding turn of events that distracted me or delayed me from working. These instances included but certainly were not limited to my own zealousness (e.g., perfectionism), the long-lasting impact of direct and indirect encounters and exchanges during protests of police responses to black citizens, and the emotional weight of participants' interviews and stories. Disorder and disparity in their rawest forms are overwhelming, and accounting for them intently often left me worn out and frustrated. Again, I desperately wanted to rightly attend to, analyze, and report the experiences of those whose daily existence afforded them little or no social reprieve, especially when compared to mine. I often worked single-mindedly, and therefore it was noteworthy when others took an interest in my research—that is, in the experiences of black citizens who otherwise might not have had a platform for divulging them. As an example, the fact that Billy and Kristy Jamison were intrigued and supportive enough to travel a long distance to support me, attending community events among many other things, was humbling. This was selflessness on display, and I felt honored. Part of my quest hinged on paying it forward and working toward the education and overall betterment of the black community in particular and across all populations in general. I appreciated that they supported me in those efforts.

As I mostly focused on others' well-being and advancement, I often inadvertently neglected to carve out much-needed time for my own self-preservation. I am thankful to my circle of sister-friends, who thought of, attended to, and obliged me in ways that advanced me. They creatively and sometimes spontaneously engaged my needs, which varied depending on where I was in the data collection and writing process. Simply put, I was stressed and stretched thin *a lot* and appreciated that they considered me—included, encouraged, influenced, offered, accompanied me—generally in ways and at times that added to my well-being and advancement. They were my endorsers, and I needed and valued that in ways that I cannot begin to explain. Since black women disproportionately face devaluation—overlapping discrimination and oppression—positive reinforcement and expressions of care mattered very much coming from my sister-friends of color. Given your own successful lives and heavy schedules, it is important that you know I did not take your kindness, efforts, or time for granted. Timing is everything, and I am extremely grateful for how each of you provided what I needed in unique ways that helped me regroup, refresh, and reactivate for focusing and working with even more dedication. As an example, Amy Hunter would sometimes make wake-up and check-in calls to me, especially when I pulled all-nighters. She even offered to bring me coffee and food so that I could work uninterrupted. She was also the second person to review my manuscript. It meant a lot that she felt honored to do so. Meanwhile, Lorez White was part of my everyday interaction. Rain or shine, she hung tight with me—figuratively and literally—providing constant affirmation and encouragement among other things. Others who extended themselves in diverse ways to keep me grounded were LaRhonda Wilson, Stefanie Strong, Monica Graham, Cherron White, Netra Taylor-Nichols, Shonda Young, Shinita Hishaw, Jacqueline (Jackie) Hayes-Dickson, and Antona Brent Smith. Good looking out! To you, I extend much respect, honor, and thanks.

I am also thankful to reviewers Peter Kraska and Jason Williams for taking the time and great care to read my manuscript. They too are academics with innumerable tasks and projects and I am grateful for their critical feedback, as it advanced the analysis and overall quality of my manuscript. Also, to Waverly Duck for his quick list of copy editors—thank you! I also want to thank JMT and community groups, organizers and organizations, media, and countless persons throughout the St. Louis region and beyond who embraced me. They variously afforded me space to volunteer or participate in community programming, as well as to promote my work or meet safely with participants. I have chosen not to disclose their names but instead have assigned them pseudonyms throughout this project. My goal was to attend to the post-Ferguson experiences and responses of black citizens and their efforts for advancing black life in general. The names were no more necessary to this goal than were those of participants. I made exceptions only where needed for contextualizing.

Further, I am thankful for my children's patience with me. At times I was short-tempered, running late, or forgetful due to stress and exhaustion. In other instances I needed to work uninterrupted or take a break from everyone and everything. They obliged. I appreciated that you stepped up and made up the difference by running errands, grabbing food, and managing other tasks as needed.

Finally, I am indebted to the black citizens who trusted me with their experiences. Despite depictions of them, and of other black citizens in general, that are so often stereotypically negative, I found many participants regularly engaging in selfless actions regardless of their own lack of support and their often complex circumstances. They were still cognizant of the plights surrounding them, as the participants were constants in their neighborhoods and the broader community. Many participants lived in desolate places or contended with unremittingly bleak situations, in which there are no "open or closed" hours or "9-to-5" shifts per se to counter or escape disorder and its effects. Yet they were innovative in countering disparity and gave back in ways that motivated me to increase my community service. For all of them and more, I am truly humbled and appreciative. Their altruism was representative of the interactions of *the majority* of the black minority. I am thankful that they allowed me to account for them, empirically and uniquely.

Introduction

We gotta use this as a starting point.

FERGUSON ORGANIZER, August 9, 2014

FADE IN:

CANFIELD GREEN APARTMENTS—INNER CRIME SCENE—DAY ONE, NOON
Police kill an unarmed black male teen. Black citizens gather. Snippets of information are released.

On Saturday, August 9, 2014, a little after noon, eighteen-year-old Michael Brown Jr. and his friend Dorian Johnson were on their way back from a local store, Sam's Meat Market, walking in the middle of the street that runs through the Canfield Green apartment complex. Ferguson police officer Darren Wilson pulled up and allegedly told them to "get the F on the sidewalk."[1] Apparently, words were then exchanged between Wilson and Brown, and a struggle ensued at the squad car, putting Brown on the run, with Wilson firing at him. Johnson then took cover, and Brown reportedly stopped running, put his hands up, and faced Wilson. At this point, Wilson shot Brown in the head, killing him. Wilson later described Brown as having charged him.[2]

Canfield Green Apartments—where Brown was killed and where his body lay for more than four hours in the middle of the street—for now should be understood as the "inner crime scene" (the immediate area surrounding the scene of a crime and the victim's body). It was from this location that the initial outcry from citizens emerged. This was the scene where citizens witnessed the shooting, commenced giving their accounts, and ultimately took to the streets. They expressed outrage against perceived police action and inaction. Furthermore, it was from here that the first descriptions of Brown's murder would spread throughout St. Louis. More important, this is also the place where his family would first encounter the body of their beloved son, also known as Big Mike or Mike-Mike.

CUT TO:

THE LIBRARY—TWENTY MINUTES AWAY—SAME DAY, EARLY AFTERNOON
I am reviewing the final edits for my book Race, Place, and Suburban Policing: Too Close for Comfort. *I receive a text about a party. Then I receive a phone call about Brown and about protesters gathering.*

What had begun as a relatively uneventful day for me took a sudden, unexpected turn. I had already spent much of the day tucked away in a local university library roughly twenty minutes from the inner crime scene, Canfield Green Apartments, where Brown had been killed and his body now lay, and where initial citizen action had occurred, along with the trickling out of scant information.

It was a little after 2:00 p.m. when I received both a text inviting me to a party and a phone call alerting me that a teen (Brown) had been killed by Ferguson police. The caller mentioned protesters gathering, asked me if I knew about it—I did not—and suggested that I check into local media online and maybe even drive by the scene. I agreed to do both. Given that I had been researching conflict between black citizens and police in the suburbs of St. Louis for years, I was curious and interested in learning more about this shooting and what appeared to be an instantaneous and personal response from black citizens. I immediately packed up my things, thinking I would merely drive by the scene to observe it en route to the party.

CUT TO:

THE INTERSECTION OF WEST FLORISSANT BOULEVARD AND CANFIELD DRIVE—
OUTER CRIME SCENE, "GROUND ZERO"—SAME DAY, LATE AFTERNOON
Hours have passed since Brown's death. Roughly two and a half blocks from the scene of the shooting, the street is blocked. No access. Some police, protesters, and media are held back at this intersection. It is now a second site. I stay and start documenting.

I was attempting to reach Canfield Green Apartments—the inner crime scene. However, as I drove up, I noticed that the street was blocked by crime tape and police. I then saw a group of protesters and media, unable to get in, anxiously waiting alongside a militarized police vehicle. An officer stood atop it with a very visible high-powered rifle. All were stark visuals that coalesced into an eerie scene in the middle of the street. This was not my first time at a homicide scene in St. Louis. However, as I approached, I noticed that this one was overtly different—from its already heavy multidepartmental, militarized police show of force to its audible, angry group of protesters. Just a few hours in, it seemed clear that an extraordinarily hardened and combative line of opposition had already been drawn by both sides—black citizens and police.

I never made it to the party. I parked at the back of a nearby car wash, got out, and walked straight into the intersection of West Florissant Boulevard and Canfield Drive. This intersection—or rather crossroads, literally and figuratively—was roughly two and a half blocks from where the shooting occurred, or the inner crime scene, and right in front of Red's Barbeque restaurant. The intersection had become a new, or rather a second, location for collective action that day. This place should also be understood as the "outer crime scene" (an exterior and more distant perimeter, quarantining the "inner crime scene"). Later, in the heat of civil unrest, it came to be known as "ground zero" and became the locale for much of the direct action by citizens and the site most often used for riot police formations, the deployment of tear gas, and the firing of rubber bullets on citizens (see figure 1).[3]

LAP DISSOLVE TO:
SAME PLACE—THE INTERSECTION—OUTER CRIME SCENE, GROUND ZERO— SAME DAY, LATE AFTERNOON

Crime tape is still up. More protesters gather. The media presence increases. State and local elected officials arrive. Only limited or no information is being received. Tension thickens. Brown's mother and other family members appear to emerge from the inner crime scene. Group prayers and condolences are offered. I wait for the inner and outer crime scenes to be opened.

As more and more protesters gathered at ground zero, bits of information continued to trickle from the inner to the outer crime scene. It was difficult to truly know whether Brown's body was still lying on the ground. Standing at the outer crime scene perimeter, we were unable to see his body, yet all signs (information coming from the inner crime scene, the crime tape, the blocked street) indicated that he was indeed still lying in the street. This further infuriated the protesters, and they demanded answers. Given that there had been some indication that Brown was killed while attempting to surrender, the protesters were adamant about learning who the shooting officer was and whether he would be held accountable. Both concerns were exacerbated by the apparently callous treatment of Brown's remains.

By now it had been well over four hours since Brown was killed, and the armored vehicle with an armed officer standing atop it, the visible

FIGURE 1. Day one, the outer crime scene. This is the intersection of Canfield Drive and West Florissant Boulevard, roughly two and a half blocks from where Mike Brown Jr. was killed. It is also where I arrived and noticed the armored vehicle, with a crowd gathering. This location and the stretch along West Florissant Boulevard came to be known as "ground zero." Photo by author.

high-powered weapons, the police line, and the crime scene tape had become symbolic. They had become constant, overt reminders of black vulnerabilities and the persistently aggressive, now-militarized policing of black citizens. For protesters, this hard-line police stance was tactless, inhuman, and indicative of institutional arrogance and a blatant disregard for what had just occurred—all factors the protesters believed to be consistent with the lack of real explanations being given for the shooting and perhaps symptomatic of a police cover-up getting under way. Protesters were increasingly enraged by this seemingly antagonistic show of force. It was intimidating— what appeared to be an observable readiness to inflict violence again, this time against the protesters. Subsequently some protesters became more aggressive, yelling, "Fuck you!" and other expletives at the police and then following up with questions: "Now what? You gon' shoot me, too?" This prompted other protesters—almost all at once—to warn and instruct some of their fellow protesters not to escalate the situation:

MALE PROTESTER 1:   Hey, hey, hey, hey, hey! Don't go to jail; . . . [D]on't' provoke 'em [police] like that.

FEMALE PROTESTER 1: [Angrily interrupts, yelling] How?!? We ain't said shit *towards* 'em!

MALE PROTESTER 1:   I'm just sayin'. . . . Don't cuss 'em! You can talk all you want, but don't cuss 'em. . . . Anything they can get on you [they will use].

Moments later two more protesters who had been listening to this conversation walked over and chimed in, offering similar advice. One of them spoke as if he were a brother to one young man who was yelling obscenities:

MALE PROTESTER 2:   [Taking the young man off to the side] Use better words than that, bruh. . . . You better than that.

A third male protester then spoke proactively and reactively to the entire group, not all of whom had been yelling. He wanted them to think more broadly about the perceived direction and possible consequences of their actions when interacting with law enforcement. Through this frame of reference he encouraged the group to act and respond accordingly. Here is what he said:

MALE PROTESTER 3:   Check this: . . . be intelligent. . . . [You] know what I'm sayin'? Be intelligent when you put 'em [police] in check 'cause when you ignorant, they treat you ignorant . . . for real . . . [A male voice in the background: "So they can lock you up!"] . . . But y'all know the game. . . . All of y'all out here *know* the game. . . . Y'all know it's [the criminal justice system] set up against us.

Meanwhile, as the agitated protesters continued to wait for official word that Brown's body had been removed, they paced, stood, and sat near the intersection and had additional fiery exchanges with each other and with law enforcement (see figures 2 and 3). In many instances these activities led to passing *more* time venting about what they believed had happened to Brown, their distrust of the police, and an overall suspicion of the criminal justice system. Male protester number 3 continued to call for protesters to "check game," as he called it, or rather to consider the entire

FIGURE 2. Day one, the outer crime scene from a different angle. Protesters are waiting outside the crime tape and police are waiting inside it. Photo by author.

situation—what had just happened to Brown as well as their own positions and experiences (direct and indirect) when interacting with law enforcement. Here is what he said:

> [Talking to protesters:] Y'all betta check game! [To police:] Cuz y'all wrong . . . in y'all heart! [Male voice in background: "Yeah, they wrong!"] Y'all gettin' a check. . . . ALL y'all gettin a check . . . [Female voice: "They don't give a fuck about that!"] . . . and y'all know that shit [Brown's death] was wrong! Y'all know it . . . in y'all heart!

The police watched quietly, a few with apparently sad and confused facial expressions and others "sit'n [standing] up there with the mean mug," as one female protester described them. Nevertheless, the third male protester called attention to their checks (i.e., their jobs as civil servants) and hearts (i.e., consciences). It was as if in doing so, he hoped to evoke clear empathy from them—that is, some reaction to corroborate what he and others were feeling—to mitigate the crowd's perception of them as a seemingly unsympathetic police line and a militarized display of aggression.

This was the situation just before sunset: protesters both indiscriminately calling the police and each other out for what they believed to be improprieties and perceptively redirecting one another's behaviors in an

FIGURE 3.   Day one, protesters waiting for the crime tape to come down. The location is the same as in figures 1 and 2. Photo by author.

effort to avoid what appeared to be looming violent confrontations with law enforcement. Furthermore, amid the waiting and mounting tension, Brown's mother appeared at the intersection. She had made her way from the inner crime scene to the outer, where we were, and was visibly shaken, now pacing the intersection with everyone else and calling for calm. The game had changed, and now we were waiting *with* some members of Brown's family—the protesters were now having to deal directly with the visible pain of the family, still checking one another's words and actions and generally trying hard to be respectful and patient, mostly for the sake of the family. Thus, consoling Brown's mother and other family members immediately took precedence over everything else. Several black state legislators, a city council member, and a pastor were on the scene, and with some of the family now present, there was a sterner call for all of us to come together.

We held hands and formed a circle around Brown's mother. We sang hymns and prayed as people offered hugs and condolences. Moments later the police removed the crime scene tape at the outer crime scene perimeter— the official indication that Brown's body had finally been removed. We were now permitted to walk through to Canfield Green Apartments. Then, with roses and tea lights in hand, we accompanied Brown's mom and other family members back to the scene of the shooting—the inner crime scene or rather the middle of the apartment complex, to the double lines in the middle of the street where Brown's still-visible blood brought silence and clarity to the reality of this tragedy.

INTERCUT FROM OUTER TO INNER CRIME SCENES:
GROUND ZERO AND CANFIELD APARTMENTS—SAME DAY, DUSK/NIGHT
Dusk. We are standing where Brown had lain and are memorializing the scene of his death.

Here we were—protesters and local press from both the inner and outer scenes—standing where Brown's body had lain for well over four hours on a hot August day. His body was gone, though the expressions on everyone's faces spoke to his presence. This was a surreal moment. It was indescribable, and everyone appeared deflated from seeing traces of blood still on the ground and the pain of Brown's family. His mom then took rose petals and sprinkled them over the spot. The lit tea candles were also placed there and used to spell out his name—*Mike.* As at the intersection, we formed a circle and prayed, and a couple of protesters led the group in inspirational songs. More directly, it was during this observance that the ground was somewhat consecrated, forming the later widely visited and photographed, makeshift memorial to Brown in the middle of the street.

Shortly thereafter, and almost as if officiating at a funeral, an older black man—one of many seasoned organizers in St. Louis—stepped forward and delivered a mandate that invigorated and mobilized the group. He articulated an agenda—a twofold course of action for the black community. As "I Won't Complain" (widely attributed to the Reverend Paul Jones) played in the background, the man began to speak:

> We got to be real serious on several levels, first of all in terms of the outrage. If you're truly outraged, this is just one day in a long protracted struggle to get justice, . . . and if you are serious about it [justice], then you need to organize your neighbors, you need to organize all family members. [Male voice: "Yeah!"] We need to have a motto: "No more!" [Male voice: "Yes!"] . . . And if we don't do that, then we just expressing a one-day outrage because any of us could be victims like this. . . . [Several voices: "Yeah, yes, right!"] And then the other thing we gotta do: We gotta use this as a starting point because . . . you gotta understand there's like a war going on. And so *in* fighting war, we have to get organized so that we can prevent these kinds of cries of woe that's coming from [the] outside . . . folks who work in our community [but] don't give a damn about us.

Same day. Same location. Nightfall. It is eight or nine hours since the shooting. The situation is extremely fluid.

By nightfall countless exchanges (e.g., conversations and chanting) were occurring simultaneously among individuals and groups of protesters on both sides of the street—mostly near the spot where Brown's body had lain for hours. From amid the high-spirited and somewhat rambunctious crowd, I noted that a lone police car was entering the apartment complex. It stood out particularly because in that moment it appeared that people had finally been afforded time to reflect on the day's events privately, or at least without the overt scrutiny of law enforcement. It was like taking a breather. After all, varying degrees of contentious interactions between black citizens and police had been going on for more than eight hours. However, with the arrival of this squad car, it was as if peace had been disrupted and an unspoken, temporary truce had ended. Protesters immediately surrounded the squad car with their hands up, chanting.

Unable to pass through the crowd, the officer then slowly backed the car out the same way he had driven in. Almost immediately and as if intuitively, countless police cars with sirens blaring and lights flashing raced in from the opposite direction. I remember thinking, *Oh, my God, what's happening?* It was as if someone had flipped a switch, and all hell was about to break loose. I had never seen so many police cars speed into a place so suddenly and from numerous jurisdictions. But before I could fully grasp what was happening, officers were out of their vehicles—some with rifles in hand, others with dogs—and were approaching protesters. Again, I thought to myself (as others vocalized similar sentiments): *What just happened? What is this about?* as police actions once again appeared to be unjustifiably aggressive and excessive. Their arrival only further inflamed protesters, especially as police raced straight through, and decimated, the new memorial to Brown—that is, the one we had watched his mother start with rose petals only a short time before. Some protesters just lost it.

Words could not capture *this* climate change. The atmosphere in Ferguson and throughout the St. Louis region was ripe for social redress, civil unrest, and transformation. As such, the protesters were all in, as were the police. There was lots of yelling, and in some instances police and protesters were cursing, gesturing, and seemingly goading one another. I was beyond stunned, and unbeknown to me, this volatile night would be the precursor for more of the same, with greater intensity, in the months to come.

As tensions escalated, I again observed protesters trying to reason with and protect one another, routinely pulling each other back and trying to calm each other down. However, even-tempered police did not seem to do the same with confrontational officers. Consequently, I was thinking that under the circumstances, it would take nothing more than for one person—protester or officer—to act suddenly, for this encounter to end tragically, mainly for us, the noncommissioned citizens. In the event that things went horribly awry, we (the protesters and I) would have no means of defending ourselves if the police characterized us as threatening, because they were empowered to respond accordingly. Perhaps naively, I believed the protesters and I were completely nonthreatening and defenseless, at least in comparison to the police. Yet ironically, in light of Brown's and Wilson's deadly exchange, we were still positioned for what could be another ambiguous but transformative confrontation between black citizens and police. Therefore, as others took to social media, I called and texted my family and friends to alert them to where I was and what was transpiring. Furthermore, I relied on the camaraderie of the protesters around me for relief—groups of mostly black citizens who, despite being strangers, had shown themselves able to ally with, protect, and serve one another proactively, reactively, and spontaneously.

In sum, I have depicted here my on-the-ground insights on Day One in Ferguson at key locations and the key actions taken immediately following Brown's death. A counterculture of interactions emerged among protesters as what I will refer to as a "protest community." These were mostly black citizens engaging in direct action and subject to the effects of chaos. Thus, civil unrest in Ferguson became analogous to disadvantaged black neighborhoods whose residents contend with duress daily and automatically create buffers for managing it. This situation was rife with tremendous pressure and threats amid discrimination and disorder, a combination that too often results in compromising behaviors by some protesters or neighbors and local law enforcement. During the unrest in Ferguson, as in their neighborhoods, black citizens relied on their social ties. Although these had been formed in a relatively short span of time, the citizens trusted and deferred to their impromptu familial connections. Under intense pressure, they were protective of others and then were similarly safeguarded.

In the end, the night concluded without major incident—although it was followed by absolute black citizen dissonance with law enforcement, protesters' relentless commitment to social justice, and their unfaltering preparation for direct action (protest) the next day. Only the next day (Day Two) would the world see smoke-filled streets with mostly black citizens facing tear gas and rubber bullets from police—as if in a war-torn country. In subsequent months this situation would not improve, but rather would escalate after the governor dispatched the Missouri National Guard to

Ferguson. As a result, the informal social ties of the mostly black protesters continued to be one of their many survival tactics for managing tumultuous situations.

FERGUSON *IS* ST. LOUIS: A HISTORY OF REGIONAL DIVISION

Because of the ambiguities surrounding Brown's murder and the subsequent months of relentless civil unrest, many people around the world have become somewhat acquainted with the City of Ferguson or what we St. Louisans refer to simply as "Ferguson." Ferguson has often been thought of and referred to by non–St. Louis residents as a separate, unattached city, but it is actually a small part of the broader structure of St. Louis—a predominantly black, North County St. Louis suburb. Thus, blacks' protecting and serving one another in Ferguson and throughout other parts of the St. Louis metropolitan area is significant, particularly because turmoil in Ferguson did not emerge as an anomaly or in isolation within the region.[4] In fact, protests in Ferguson erupted on the heels of other local conflicts between black citizens and police. In one such conflict, citizens, police, and elected officials were killed roughly twenty-five minutes up the highway from Ferguson; that had subsequently led to a previous intervention by the US Department of Justice.[5] Given the tenor of similar cases in the region—routine exchanges with the criminal justice system—and the socioeconomic and political disenfranchisement of disproportionate numbers of black citizens, the time was ripe for direct action. That is, Brown's premature death became the catalyst for an already simmering push for social redress. In fact, many protesters—immediately following Brown's death, in the months after the investigation, and well into the present—were not residents of Ferguson but lived in other locations throughout the St. Louis metropolitan area. However, they were, and remain, committed to mass mobilization efforts because social conditions across both St. Louis and the nation generally have remained such that they deserve examination.

Let us now turn to St. Louis, Missouri, the historic "Gateway to the West" or, as it is sometimes called, "The Lou" or "STL."

St. Louis at a Glance

St. Louis is a Mississippi River city famous for its numerous public events, celebrated citizens, and internationally known businesses and industries. It is notable for its historical significance, including being the jumping-off point for the 1803 Lewis and Clark Expedition; the place where Dred Scott filed his famous slavery case, decided by the Supreme Court in 1957; the site of the 1904 World's Fair; and the location of the sociologically infamous Pruitt-Igoe Urban Housing Projects, which were completed in 1956.[6] St. Louis has been home to legendary citizens such as Chuck Berry, Maya Angelou, Dick Gregory, T.S. Eliot, and Red Foxx, as well as renowned businesses and industries such as Anheuser-Busch, Boeing, and Edward Jones.

However, despite its grand history, in 1876 St. Louis voted to split into two sections (the urban city of St. Louis and rural, suburban St. Louis County) over disputes about taxes.[7] This became known as the Great Divorce.[8] At the time the urban population was believed to be 310,000, with 27,000 living in the rural (later suburban) areas.[9] In short, urban residents were more concentrated within a significant landmass and no longer wanted to underwrite the incongruent agenda and needs of the more rural areas. Furthermore, inner-city residents did not envision the city as advancing much beyond its existing boundaries. As a result of the vote, the City of St. Louis officially withdrew from St. Louis County in 1877, but its departure did not occur without incident.[10] There were several disputes over voter irregularities before the split, and afterward efforts were made to reunite the city with the county. Between the late 1890s and early 1900s, the city's westward expansion became more adaptable, with the introduction of boulevards and advancements in transportation.[11] As the once rural areas underwent suburbanization, whites fled St. Louis City (i.e., the urban area), taking a significant portion of the tax base to St. Louis County (i.e., the suburbs). Moreover, the tables had turned—the now-suburban population and tax revenues were increasing, in contrast to the inner-city's declining circumstances and loss of population. In an effort to mitigate the unanticipated suburban expansion, numerous attempts were made to reunify the urban and suburban areas, one of which even included developing a borough system like New York City's.[12] Nevertheless, the split held as large voter turnouts registered St. Louis County's opposition to these proposals.[13] Thus the St. Louis metropolitan area has remained divided, with each entity operating under a separate government.

Maintaining the Split with a Race and Class Rift

Today the move for St. Louis City to rejoin St. Louis County remains topical and seemingly aspirational. Under the auspices of the nonprofit organization Better Together, along with some city and county elected officials, the push to consolidate is ongoing.[14] However, reunification has yet to occur despite the disadvantages of the split for the region (e.g., billions wasted on duplicate government expenditures, internal economic competition).[15] Many of these disadvantages seem to be rooted in suburbanization, whose history hinges on deliberate segregation—that is, racial and economic separatism reinforced by geographical distinctions (e.g., distance) that safeguard white affluence from the disproportionately black and poor inner-city populations.[16] It is also for this reason that some black elected officials and residents are leary. They see reunification as potentially diluting black political advancement.[17] Together, the city and county make up the St. Louis metropolitan area. According to 2017 census data, the population estimate of St. Louis City was 308,626; St. Louis County's was 996,726.[18] As for the black-white racial divide, St. Louis City was 42.9 percent white and 47.6 percent black, whereas St. Louis County was 66.1 percent white and 24.7 percent black.[19] In addition, the median household income from 2013 to 2017 was $38,664 for St. Louis City, with 25 percent of people living in poverty, while median household income was $62,931 in St. Louis County, with 10 percent of people living in poverty.[20] Simply put, St. Louis City is significantly less densely populated and has a majority of black residents, whose median income is lower and rates of poverty are higher than—roughly double those of—St. Louis County's.[21] These disparities illustrate the race and class rift at the root of the St. Louis City and St. Louis County divide.

Furthermore, St. Louis is a city of neighborhoods, while the county, which has its own government, is divided into ninety municipalities, some of which are disincorporating; many operate their own small governments and police departments.[22] Each municipality unofficially competes with others for revenue. Ferguson is one of these. Black citizens have provided a disproportionate amount of revenue to some of these municipalities because overlapping, aggressive policing has resulted in their accruing fines, court costs, and other expenses within and across jurisdictions. That is why I have sarcastically but truthfully explained to people unfamiliar with the St. Louis region that one could easily drive five minutes down a main thoroughfare through predominantly black segments of St. Louis County and be subjected to five police stops and receive countless tickets—or worse— from five different police departments. This outcome could result from one's having passed through five different municipalities, whose economic viability often hinges on untoward municipal court practices. In another example, the Better Together website describes how a St. Louis resident who drives from the Galleria Shopping Mall to Lambert–St. Louis International Airport passes through "fifteen separate police jurisdictions during a fourteen-minute trip."[23] This motorist could be subjected to the laws of numerous jurisdictions with their own stops and fines all along that one drive. Some municipalities are so small that one resident calculated as many as thirteen could fit into his St. Louis City neighborhood.[24]

These and similar exploitative arrangements have fueled the cumulative resentment among the area's black citizens that led to civil unrest in Ferguson during and after the protests sparked by the killing of Michael Brown Jr. Furthermore, long-standing discrimination, community disorder and its effects, and black mobilization are the reasons this study captures citizens' direct actions and efforts to combat violence against blacks across communities: the Ferguson protesters, protests, and all other direct actions and residents in neighborhoods with higher crime (e.g., murder rates). From these various locations throughout the St. Louis region, black citizens' outrage gelled and sparked in response national and international efforts to preserve black life, as well as a subsequent backlash.

POST-FERGUSON CONTEXT: INFORMAL SOCIAL TIES AS BUFFERS OF COMMUNITY DISORDER

Black St. Louisans, especially the poor, had contended with disproportionate, persistent, subpar social conditions long before the death of Mike Brown Jr. If truth were told, civil unrest in Ferguson and throughout the St. Louis metropolitan area had already been on the horizon It was just a matter of time before it exploded. The region had become a "hot box" characterized by all manner of seething differential treatment of its black citizens, and Brown's killing ignited it.[25] That is why this project treats racialized treatment and denigrating social conditions as interconnected, underlying correlates of Brown's death and all that transpired afterward. More directly, this project defines, stipulates times and timelines, and simultaneously situates "Ferguson" within a cultural community context.[26] It provides macro- and microanalyses of social conditions, inequities, and resistance framed in terms of twenty-first-century "critical consciousness" and approaches to social justice.[27]

Furthermore, "Ferguson" is a template that represents a decisively racialized, sociohistorical shift whereby a sustained, oppressive interjection occurred that triangulated punitive, pre-Emancipation messages and indirect experiences triggered by the public display of a state-executed black person. "Post-Ferguson" commences with the removal of Brown's body from the scene. In other words, this project time-stamps "post-Ferguson" as beginning with the initial call to action among protesters at the inner crime scene and all ensuing forms of direct action thereafter. Thus, it has been black solidarity and a continuum of organizing characterized by the *shift* (i.e., persisting exploitation, a flashback of a pre-Emancipation, publicly displayed, executed black person: "Ferguson") and (re)igniting of efforts to preserve black life that have resulted in a particular kind of contemporary activism (dichotomous)—that is, a long-lasting, impromptu, and strategized black action that seemingly threatened, warranted, and normalized punitive enemy combatant status and state-sanctioned tactics used against black citizens.[28] More directly, "post-Ferguson" represents a multilayered cultural departure that transcended previous periodic protests against the police to provide a broad, solid template for mass mobilizing and social change. It is through this profound push for black liberation that countless populations rode the wave. They carved out space, creating a domino effect of multidirectional, twenty-first-century resistance.

Theory and Methodology

An amalgamation of pain and empowerment among black citizens is the crux of the examination for this project. It extends a platform to marginalized populations who face unyielding, front- and back-end, systemic penalizing as an added plight in the fight for social justice "post-Ferguson." Therefore, it is through those additional experiences—perceived state vigilantism and neighborhood victimization, black mobilization, and subsequent systemic retaliation—that this study is framed and examines pervasive community disorder (both physical and social) post-Ferguson. More directly, this project expands the theoretical premise of *(dis)order* to reflect black perceptions of it, or really the way black citizens (de)construct it, as a by-product of mostly racial and economic discrimination across two case study communities: the mostly black protest community that emerged from police brutality in "Ferguson" and engaged in disparate forms of subsequent direct action, and the mostly poor black citizens who, apart from civil unrest in Ferguson, routinely negotiated the often overlapping and degrading effects (e.g., dilapidation, interpersonal violence) of living in disadvantaged neighborhoods.

The Study Question(s)   This study began by seeking to understand a dichotomous situation: the efforts to preserve black life (i.e., from police violence and from interpersonal violence) and to better respond to what seemed to be increasingly routine statements suggesting that blacks needed to police themselves.[29] For example, look at how former Fox TV's Bill O' Reilly articulated this situation: "It is also long past time for African-American communities across America to begin to police themselves—criminal activity,

drug use, child abandonment, disrespect, [and] general chaos [are] all on display every single day in many places."[30]

It is partly this kind of countering rhetoric and the actions of critics with
"every single day" ideas about and references to a supposed endemic black
chaos that brought about this study by posing basic questions: "*Do* blacks
police themselves, and if so, *how?*" This question really translated into
"How do blacks protect and serve themselves?" so as not to add insult to
injury by implying that blacks alone inherently behave badly and therefore
require exceptional policing—that is, absolute and excessive self-regulation
compared with what is needed to subdue their white counterparts.
Furthermore, in this project the ideal of blacks policing themselves reso-
nated best and produced the most favorable responses when questions were
framed and articulated as "protecting and serving one another" rather than
as "policing themselves," policing disorder, or implementing informal social
control.

The Buffering Process   This study devotes attention to the role of social ties
as buffers against oppressive and distressing circumstances. More directly,
this project examines black citizens' reliance on social ties to counter the perceptions or effects (e.g., fear) of community disorder.[31] Studies suggest that it
has been in the face of hostile community relations that citizens distrust and
monitor one another and police.[32] Community disorder or perceptions of it
have been linked to alienation and have impeded protective alliances between
citizens.[33] Yet research also shows that citizens form mostly individual and
some group alliances—informal, formal, and dependent on community context—for managing disorder (both social and physical) and its effects and
implement various forms of informal social control.[34] Black citizens safeguard
themselves through a myriad of socialization processes and strategies.[35]
Despite the disorder they face, they have also been found to be motivated to
instrumentally and expressively engage or organize.[36]

Research has been limited in accounting ethnographically for black citizens' responses or organizational efforts in countering disorder or crime.
Generally, there has been significant attention given to explaining the
absence or lack of organization (disorganization) or internal social control
(disorder) across disadvantaged communities. Further, there are comparatively few ethnographic examinations that account for and explain "inter-
locking networks" of black citizens.[37] This project displays "decent and
street" interactions (conventional and unconventional)—informally negotiated communal relationships and exchanges—accounted for through the
roles of original gangsters (OGs) and gangsters (Gs), othermothers and

community othermothers, and so forth.[38] Black citizens have various lengths and forms of residencies and attachments, which sometimes advanced neighborhood participation and even community activism post-Ferguson. This study, through a rare examination, introduces a post-Ferguson framework for understanding the often unanticipated alignment of mostly black citizens as they organized to protect black lives from both police brutality and interpersonal neighborhood violence.

This study builds upon the systemic model of social organization.[39] It provides a macro- to microanalysis on the community, neighborhood, and individual levels.[40] Additionally, this project extends a reconceptualized form of disorder to include pervasive discrimination (e.g., race and class) as *social disorder*.[41] Here this term specifically includes rogue or dishonorable police behaviors and extends the typical definition, which denotes people followed by cues such as noise, littering, vandalism, and hanging out on the streets (i.e., loitering).[42] *Physical disorder* then encompasses debris, property damage (i.e., burned or boarded up buildings), and so forth at protest sites in Ferguson and throughout the St. Louis region.[43] This is in addition to the usual blight of abandoned buildings, visibly scattered trash, and similar sights in poor neighborhoods.[44] *Community* has also been extended to the mostly black protesters, activists, leaders, and organizers.[45] Furthermore, after seemingly endless months of impromptu direct actions under adverse conditions, Ferguson civil unrest itself became analogous to a neighborhood. Familiarity and comfort (i.e., emotional safety, a sense of belonging and identification, personal investment, and a common symbol system) developed within the protest community as if between neighbors or family at key Ferguson protesting locations and spread to other places.[46]

Data Collection Thus pervasive community disorder and an emerging black resistance sparked a three-year ethnographic study that hinged on direct and indirect, interactive, and often fluid exchanges with adult black citizens and countless participatory accounts, from attending years of protests against police brutality to engaging in crime prevention efforts throughout the St. Louis region.[47] This project relies on two distinct data sets, acquired extemporaneously and planned through participant observation, in-depth interviews, and focus groups while I was engaged in various forms of direct action and community events (e.g., protests against police brutality, town halls and forums, stop-the-violence marches) across the St. Louis metropolitan region. The first is Data Set One, field notes from protests and community events that consisted of off-the-cuff conversations and detailed accounts of interactions and occurrences, collected during protests and other community events in Ferguson and throughout the St. Louis region; the second is Data Set Two, field notes, in-depth interviews, and focus group comments elicited from neighborhoods with higher rates of crime, particularly aggravated assaults and homicides, across St. Louis urban and suburban communities.

Generally, I documented and closely examined clashes between black citizens and black citizens and police from three angles:(1) through my own experiences as a participant observer; (2) from perspectives learned and understood from mostly black citizens; and (3) from a combination of the previous two compared with the rhetoric of individuals who were by and large not as involved or present in direct actions.[48] The third perspective thus included the views of political pundits or others weighing in on matters mostly through the media.

This book presents a cumulation of black experiences and black mobilization efforts in the move to preserve black lives, post-Ferguson, and then uniquely enriches them by seeking to

1. extend the (dis)order framework to include race and racial discrimination;

2. challenge simplistic, stereotypical ideas about blacks as being only concerned about conflict between black citizens and police rather than disorder and criminal activity (e.g., interpersonal neighborhood violence), especially in their communities;

3. provide opportunities to examine predominantly black communities in a traditional neighborhood context and extend analyses to broader territories (e.g., protests) as occupied by protesters, activists, and organizers through various forms of direct action;

4. gauge growing suggestions about blacks distinctly needing to *police themselves,* as well as various levels of law enforcement (e.g., overlapping police jurisdictions, the National Guard);

5. provide real-time participatory accounts of a pivotal time in American history—the launch of a twenty-first-century, black-led social movement, wherein a post-Ferguson context is used to frame subsequent dialogue and actions in advancing social change;[49]

6. offer a rare comparison of black and white/dominant insights centered in black consciousness, and in turn;

7. explain how age-old dominant ideologies reemerged and propagandized responses of Ferguson civil unrest and a subsequent national/international movement; and

8. extend a platform to blacks, mostly disadvantaged, whose everyday plights and efforts to simultaneously and interchangeably buffer disorder and its effects on two fronts (with citizens and police, both urban and suburban) often go unnoticed. *When* their efforts are noticed, black citizens face dominant victim blaming, delegitimation, and overall heightened disparagement for fear of their disrupting the status quo and advancing politically, against the backdrop of a post-Ferguson America uprising.

Consequently, this project highlights the complexities of black oppression and the often inescapable denigration that blacks face when attempting to overcome them. The fact that black citizens persistently and disproportionately experience discrimination, disorder, and disadvantage is inherently institutional. Dominant ideology, practice, and rhetoric have been largely effective in distorting and maintaining perceptions of black citizens and their efforts as suspicious, threatening, and anti-American.

SUMMARY AND ORGANIZATION OF THE BOOK

This project relies on its two data sets—from the protest community and the neighborhood community—to examine *how* blacks allied to protect and serve themselves against police brutality and neighborhood interpersonal violence in post-Ferguson America. This book provides an ethnographic depiction of black citizens relying on various social ties to avert or counter community disorder and its effects—that is, the perceptions of it and its effects. I depict everyday experiences, often overburdened with disadvantage and risks, as faced, communicated, and understood by black citizens, especially those who are economically disadvantaged.

You Can't Stop the Revolution: Community Disorder and Social Ties in Post-Ferguson America highlights the complexities of black oppression and often inescapable denigration and victim blaming that blacks face when attempting to counter community disorder, post-Ferguson. Since research addressing the often ambiguous, dichotomous plight of black citizens has been limited, chapter 1 frames the interplay of community disorder or dual threats and black solidarity as a pre-Ferguson continuum, leading to a resurgence with the initial call to action and twofold agenda or *call to strategy*, post-Ferguson. Against a reflexive backdrop of my childhood experiences, this chapter affords a rare, reminiscent snapshot that depicts black citizens as customarily managing and working together in various ways to counter or buffer the effects of pervasive disparity and susceptibility to victimization. This chapter also delves further into the history of black stereotypical depictions—the ongoing (re)construction of historically racialized imagery through definitions, thoughts, articulations, and politics—associated with and leading into twenty-first-century, post-Ferguson black consciousness and the subsequent backlash. Further, chapter 1 examines the evolution of a racialized agenda, themes, and criticisms and the subjective delineation and use of race and racial politics—"black" and "blackness"—as constant catch-22s for empowering black citizens (e.g., Black Lives Matter) and, in contrast, disparaging them (e.g., "black-on-black" crime). Chapter 1 also briefly examines the role of identity politics, particularly as it relates to community and university relations (e.g., town-gown), and the politics of scholar-activism posited somewhat as a double entendre when interpreted by academics and activists.

Chapter 2 provides a reconceptualization for disorder (both physical and social), framed in a black cultural perspective, post-Ferguson. It highlights the historical and racialized (re)ordering and (re)prioritization of disorder and crime from a black perspective. This chapter also highlights the significance of social networks and alliances and the roles of social ties in advancing black citizens' engagement in community actions and efforts (i.e., through informal integration or formal participation). It examines the effects of policing as a formal social control continuum, focusing on community policing and paramilitary police units (PPUs). Similarly, it explores the various ways black citizens engage through unofficial cultural exchanges and information as a form of informal social control, compared to the formal control of law enforcement. I also review quantitative and qualitive literature on the contemporary role of social ties and social organization, devoting significant attention to black citizens and ethnography.

Chapter 3 chronicles participants who have formed individual ties and engaged in informal integration. This chapter provides insights into unaccounted for, everyday, invisible experiences and exchanges between black citizens and others, from combating fear of police retaliation to suspecting the presence of "plants" in protests. I address black citizens' "protect and serve" actions and responses as they correspond thematically to roles and tasks across communities (i.e., as marshals and through specialized support). From marshaling to offering specialized support beyond direct action, this chapter addresses black solidarity: how black citizens reciprocally align with, trust, and respect one another despite suggestions of disunity and indifference. I also address and contextualize black self-flagellation, as black citizens sometimes frustratingly combat the pressures of discrimination, all the while being critical of one another and yet simultaneously forging and maintaining social ties across communities.

Chapter 4 presents three case studies of black men who engage in various stages of neglect, hopelessness, and empowerment in search of post-Ferguson stability and advancement. I offer their narratives from childhood to adulthood, as a departure and counter to mostly posthumously acknowledging black lives as significant and as a guide to making lives matter through life or everyday experiences. The chapter captures the sometimes vulnerable reliance on the unique roles and relationships of Gs (Gangsters/younger) or OGs (Original Gangsters/older), who create a "street-savvy" neighborhood network for negotiating disparity and disorder through street credit and respect. This chapter devotes attention to "gray space"—fluctuating moments between legitimate and illegitimate behaviors—through which Gs and OGs operate and wield significant influence in curbing and/or addressing indiscretions. The chapter also reveals homelessness and incarceration as official entry points for state supervision and the significance of women-centered networks, which through culture and tradition holistically tend to the well-being of the black community as Othermothers and Community Othermothers.

Chapter 5 discusses and depicts the role of participants through formal participation and as mostly framed in crime prevention, and as *belonging* to or *benefiting from* local groups. This chapter highlights the role of formal neighborhood groups and nonprofit organizations (e.g., churches and community organizations), particularly as they provide more structured, collaborative community efforts through antiviolence campaigns and address other neighborhood issues in ward meetings, town hall meetings, and neighborhood events and programs that provide food, clothing, and so forth. I also highlight the stories and roles of crime survivors and surviving families—accounting for often unacknowledged "missing persons" in communities of color—as black citizens maneuver and mobilize through grief as a strategy for healing and improving their neighborhoods. I highlight opportunities and the groups who work to offset disorder and its effects by providing platforms for crime prevention, tackling infrastructure, and addressing local government issues and concerns, and through charity—extending neighborhood availability and accessibility of resources for addressing the myriad needs of local black citizens.

Finally, chapter 6 summarizes key findings about black social ties as counters for disorder and its effects in disadvantaged, black communities. More specifically, this chapter discusses how black citizens combat discrimination as a catalyst, and how through fictive kinship and protecting and serving in various ways across communities, individually and collectively, they find ways to navigate dilemmas and advance the race. Further, this chapter examines and contextualizes the complexities of sometimes diverging roles and agendas, along with socioeconomic and political resources that create periodic disharmony within the family (black community).

I also discuss and provide suggestions for improving disorder in communities, framed in ongoing black resistance and a twenty-first-century movement that drives political candidacies and strategies for advancing a broader political economic agenda. I recommend neighborhood representation, advantageously aligned, as collaborative partners for creating policies and practices for a changing and progressive infrastructure within the black community. This chapter promotes the need for competitive community investment through government incentives, affordable housing, accessible employment with compatible living wages, quality education and green space, and improved/extended transit systems. This is in addition to efforts to combat discrimination, the underpinning of inadequate social services and basic amenities, high crime rates, disproportionate incarceration, and police mistreatment. The chapter concludes by acknowledging research limitations and presenting ideas for extending an empirical social justice agenda, post-Ferguson.

1. Between a Rock and a Hard Place

The (Re)Construction of Blackness and Identity Politics

Imagine.

FADE IN:

INNER-CITY ST. LOUIS—COMMUNITY EVENT—DECADES BEFORE THE FERGUSON CIVIL UNREST

I remember it like it happened yesterday. I was a teenager, and it was a hot, sunny day—perfect for hanging out in "the Lou" (St. Louis, Missouri). I met up with a few friends and attended an outdoor event, where we became caught in the middle of gunplay (a shoot-out). At what had initially appeared to be a peaceful event, everyone was now running and scrambling for cover. I recall people near me motioning and yelling, "Get down, get down" as I immediately lay on the ground and *prayed* that I would be okay. So I just lay still, paralyzed with fear, waiting for the gunshots to end and for a signal that we were safe. Once the shots stopped, I heard voices saying that it was all right for us to get up off the ground. It turned out that these belonged to the police, giving orders, standing above me and in the near distance with their guns drawn. I was already disoriented, so this visual presented a catch-22, exacerbating my fears with thoughts of a possible renewed exchange between the police and the assailant(s). Despite initially thinking that the police were there to protect me, I still felt unsafe because of the threat of being caught in more cross fire. Should I not have considered this a real possibility, when police had their weapons drawn as if in anticipation? Was it safe, and how was I to get away without being injured by either side—assailants or police? I walked away from that event physically unharmed; others were not as fortunate. Innocent people were shot, and some black citizens comforted and tended to them until they were

23

examined and whisked away by paramedics. Meanwhile, others (re)assured those remaining and still visibly shaken (e.g., crying, dazed) that they were safe. From the beginning of the incident, black citizens had actively tried to protect and serve one another, yelling directives and hurriedly pushing people to the ground, then helping them back up and hugging them after it was over. This is one example of many precarious situations in which I, as a native St. Louisan, felt compromised by exchanges between fellow blacks and police.

GROWING UP IN DISORDER

Growing up in a disadvantaged, troubled inner-city St. Louis neighborhood meant living with pervasive physical and social disorder as a backdrop. In short, I grew up exposed to a broad range of compromising living conditions, ranging from abandoned buildings and vacant lots to public drunkenness and homicides. Nevertheless, I learned to make due—to improvise and navigate as best as I could with few resources and options. Doing so was part of my childhood socialization process, in which even child's play was managed around lack and deprivation. The situation was the same for other youths in my neighborhood, with whom I shared and learned to navigate a rather tumultuous environment. Vacant lots sometimes became makeshift parks in my community. Depending on the amount of grass and rubbish, they served as open play space, mostly for boys, for tumbling on worn, discarded (donated) neighborhood mattresses, among other games. This activity was synonymous with, and yet in stark contrast to, gymnastic lessons and competitions in more affluent communities. Everyone took turns performing a combination of flips and then stood back, rating each other.

Side streets (with less traffic) and sidewalks were great for racing ("track and field"); building and jumping on bike ramps; jumping rope (with 99 cent plastic clothesline); and playing two square, jacks, and with yo-yos and bolo bats. In addition, worn porches and stoops were great for congregating—for talking, listening to music, laughing, and "joning," or what some refer to as "playing the dozens." Corkball, or "cort," as we called it, was also often played in my neighborhood.[1] Young men could regularly be seen playing cort with a broom or mop stick and a tennis ball in gangways—where they established camaraderie and respect through tight spaces, time, and conversations.[2] In addition to engaging in these activities, we also made store runs for penny cookies and candy (e.g., fruit chews, Pal bubble gum), pickles, peppermint sticks, Lemon Heads, and Red Hot Riplets (chips), while a Bomb Pop (i.e., popsicle) truck played music and slowly cruised by in the distance. This was the ambience of my childhood, alternating and overlapping with neighborhood disorder. Relationships were formed and social capital was gained in these everyday creative exchanges, among both youths and adults. This was especially true for those who secured space, offered a place for interaction (e.g., lots, porches, gangways) or equipment (e.g., mattresses, jump ropes, balls), or displayed great athleticism. In short, great reputations could be earned through various forms of neighborhood reciprocity and sportsmanship.

I grew up seeing black citizens adopt informal neighborhood rules—that is, shared, impromptu community expectations with subsequent interactive interpretations that supported our protecting and serving each other in various ways. As a case in point, I remember childhood rules such as having to stay where I could be seen from a window or door while outside playing and having to come inside before the streetlights came on (i.e., before dark). Even if these were not the rules for *all* neighborhood youth, others knew them to be my family's rules for me and helped me comply. I remember neighbors who watched out for me (and others), admonished me when necessary, and later reported my actions and their consequences to my family. I also remember other favors being done by neighbors, such as those who were away for extended periods entrusting others to keep watch over their homes and apartments during their absence. Similarly, neighbors with cars gave those of us without them rides to places or lifts to bus stops; others allowed neighbors to use their phones and phone numbers for school, work, and family emergencies when their phones had been disconnected. Neighbors doled out things like sugar and butter to each other between meals and trips to the grocery store, and some also shared information regarding neighborhood occurrences, such as people moving in and out, crime, and free activities, programs, and giveaways, so that we would not miss out on alerts, resources, and opportunities.

These protect-and-serve actions were taken by black citizens despite widespread community disorder, and we did not think about or articulate them as "policing ourselves" or informal social control but rather simply as "looking out for one another." Yet these activities and others like them made all the difference by addressing the invisible, everyday limitations and frustrations of poor black citizens when social services and police did not do so in disadvantaged communities. At a minimum, "giving someone a light" (i.e., lighting her or his cigarette) or flagging down a bus for another person made one "cool or good people"—a respected ally in the community. Such acts created or reflected social ties and served as the goodwill gestures necessary for relationship building—buffering or managing disorder in the absence or lack of trusted public service and the ensuing community frustrations, all of which have been challenged post-Ferguson. White critics and others use persistent civil unrest and neighborhood violence (e.g., black-on-black crime) to leverage discriminative ideas such as that blacks inherit criminal tendencies or to imply that black unity and neighborhood organization is impossible or only temporary.[3]

Let us return to the inner crime scene just hours after Brown's death, to present more early exchanges between black citizens that garnered relatively little or even no media coverage.

Flashback.

LAP DISSOLVE TO:

CANFIELD GREEN APARTMENTS—INNER CRIME SCENE—DAY ONE, DUSK
I stand where Brown lay; he is being memorialized at the scene of his death.

Following the initial call to organize (see the introduction), the somberness of the crowd transcended into an immediate twofold strategy with directives. This was now a call to action, with goals that contextualized emotion, message, and music, becoming the premise for Ferguson and twenty-first-century direct action and grassroots efforts well before the national/international emergence of Black Lives Matter as an organization and the subsequent dominant backlash against blacks nationwide for protesting. As if officiating at a funeral, the older black male organizer continued:

> We got a lot going on in our community. They [police] are killing us, and we're [black citizens] killing ourselves. So we got a *twofold thing* to begin to stop this kind of crazy violence in our community [Male voice in the background: "Yes, sir!"]. And the only way we're going to do it is that you all have to *really* seriously get organized [Male voice in the background: "Right!"]. All this other play stuff, it should be out! We've got to get real serious because our children's lives are at stake [Female voice in the background: "Amen!"].

As we huddled together there, *this* portion of the speech was the actual mobilization plan, proposed by one of the first black organizers on the scene to the black community just hours after Brown's death. Noticeably, this twofold agenda (addressing both police brutality and interpersonal neighborhood crime) to thwart violence in the black community received little to no media coverage. The significance of the current project is that it offers a counter to routine stereotypical narratives about black solidarity and interactions—a seemingly never-ending catch-22—that always appear negatively because of dominant construction and politicization.[4]

THE POLITICS OF RACE: ESSENTIALIZING BLACKNESS AND ROMANTICIZING WHITENESS

> When white Americans essentialize blackness . . . they often do
> so in ways that maintain "whiteness" as the master trope of
> purity, supremacy, and entitlement. . . . Alternately, the trope of
> blackness that whites circulated in the past—Mammy, Sapphire,
> Jezebel, Jim Crow, Sambo, Zip Coon, pickaninny, and Stepin
> Fetchit . . . and now enlarged to include welfare queen, prosti-
> tute, rapist, drug addict, prison inmate, etc.—have historically
> insured physical violence, poverty, institutional racism, and sec-
> ond class citizenry for blacks.
>
> JOHNSON (2003, 4)

Race is conceptualized through age-old, traditional uses of oral and written language and visuals through which we continue to derive semblance. From the ancient etymology of *black* as meaning "to scorch" as a consequence of being in the sun, to biblical allegories (e.g., the story of Noah's son, Ham) of *black* as a curse, to simple descriptions such as "dark," "bad," and "nega-tive," the definition of *black* has been cumulatively extended to denote "peo-ple of African descent."[5] More directly, especially in US law, the terms *slave* and *black* became synonymous.[6] Correspondingly, *blackness* in cultural imagery has meant "Other" or "different" and because of blacks' enslave-ment has been metaphorically associated with defeat and conquest.[7]

Race has also operated as an "identity signifier" and thus has been used ambiguously to exclude or include people.[8] Consequently, *black* and *black-ness* have become testaments to racial classification and ranking. They are based on physical attributes (e.g., skin complexion, hair texture) and socio-economic and political arrangements (e.g., slavery, poverty, gerrymander-ing), resulting in persistently defaming consequences for African diasporic citizens. Furthermore, as previous research linked the origin of *blackness* to "black skin" and "dark skin" to negative physiological presumptions, black-ness became, and in many ways remains, an outward sign to many of supposedly internal inferiority—something inside that is deep and more sinister.[9] In addition to increased economic demands as a motivation for engaging in slavery, it was in this vein that African enslavement and the suggested "white man's mission" (white supremacy) became principled.[10]

As the conceptualizations of black and blackness rest in mostly white traditional intellectual thought and artistry—from discriminative lessons on black inferiority, to classical Western philosophical literature (e.g., the writings of Kant, Hume), to the exaggerated darkness of Africans aboard slave ships (e.g., in European portraits)—it is important to note that past portrayals are still poignant and influential in the current era.[11] Black and blackness are still stereotypically regarded as innately bad and through various means are romanticized as such in the minds of many people. Whether we are considering dated and false scientific vernacular or current media outlets (e.g., the Internet, television, movies, music), cultural agents continue to fuel false perceptions of what blackness means or, more directly, to present disparaging portrayals of black people.

Using prototypes or prototypical representations, media and other cultural agents routinely portray blacks as mostly engaging in unconventional roles and behaviors.[12] Such instances become encoding for "habitual ways of thinking" that encourage the negative "appraisal" of blacks.[13] This activity was evident in the repeated showing of footage of Brown's alleged strong-arm robbery.[14] That is, the replaying was a constant display that reinforced stereotypes about him and blacks in general as criminal, "overpowering," and people to be feared, justifying displays of unremitting aggression by police and others even, when confronting them.[15] As an example, police officer Darren Wilson described part of his confrontation with Brown to the grand jury thus: "The only way I can describe it is [that] I felt like a five-year-old holding onto Hulk Hogan."[16] Other descriptive, racially encoded words Wilson used when describing Brown were *it* and *demon*: "The only way I can describe it [is that] it look[ed] like a demon."[17] Based on Brown's complexion (i.e., with *black/blackness* being equated with "darkness/bad"), this now permanently fixed image of him presented him not only as "inhuman" (it) but also as a "supernaturally" darkened force akin to Satan (demon). It is through this kind of repetition that the denigrating definitions, ideologies, and portrayals of blacks have come full circle to post-Ferguson America. This usage has been a consistent trend. Dominant cultural agents have persistently projected and solidified misconceptions and implications of race—conflated with discriminatory prototypical images—that have been passed off as *real* in the minds of many. Then, in cyclical fashion, negative incidents involving populations of color have been disproportionately covered, exaggerated, and unquestioningly believed—and worse, without context.

Identity Politics and Political Alliances

Since the inception of the United States, the broader culture and its major entities have been constructed to benefit white interests. To counter this situation, minorities have formed alliances. Currently the ideal is to create political space wherein a minority's particular in-group concerns and general well-being are prioritized rather than systemically excluded and discarded. For example, there are two police unions in the city of St. Louis, the

St. Louis Police Officers Association (SLPOA) and the Ethical Society of Police (ESOP). The St. Louis Police Officers Association is predominantly white, while the Ethical Society of Police is predominantly black. ESOP was formed in 1972 as a response to "race-based discrimination within the community and [the] St. Louis Metropolitan Police Department."[18] In other words, ESOP became an alternative organization to a policing agency that disproportionately protected white interests and enabled a culture of racial bias. Consequently, it is important to note how racial identity has influenced distinct positions and actions even among the police. At the time of the Ferguson civil unrest, the SLPOA called for five St. Louis Rams players to be disciplined for standing at football games in solidarity with activists in Ferguson.[19] ESOP responded with a statement of support commending the players' action.[20] This union did this because for black citizens, identity politics is intrinsically linked to "conceptions of social justice."[21]

As this project examines social ties, we should consider the idea of blacks loving themselves and each other as a stark cultural contrast. Since racial construction posits white citizens as endearing and black citizens to be feared, "loving blackness" becomes a "political stance," so much so that when present, it leads to dominant suspicion of black citizens and racial pride among blacks as a form of political resistance.[22] This is how James Brown's 1968 song, "Say It Loud—I'm Black and I'm Proud," as well as similar slogans, hashtags, and so forth, became embodiments of identity politics and protests.[23] It is also through perspectives such as "loving blackness" as a form of political resistance that we critically assess and deliberate on the delineation of "black" and "blackness" in post-Ferguson narratives and efforts.

So Black Lives Matter, Eh? The Post-Ferguson Backlash against Black Action

> The assumptions are ludicrous. Yet you insist that African Americans only rally against gun violence when a police officer is involved. Maybe that's because you aren't paying attention.[24]
>
> GLANTON (2015)

Historically, citizens have been inundated and indoctrinated with negative ideas and depictions of blackness and its many facets, and this long-standing trend has similarly fueled adverse dominant responses to black post-Ferguson rhetoric and efforts. Furthermore, the word *blackness* and derivatives of it continue to stir "hate and fear" in the minds of many white citizens.[25] This situation has been so much the norm that it seems improbable that anyone, and more important, any people of color, would have an affinity for it. It is for this reason that bell hooks speaks to the notion of "loving blackness" as political resistance.[26] The idea that blackness could be an embraced identity or a source for positivity and camaraderie is in direct opposition to white social constructs and politics. Being black in white-constructed politics also originally meant being institutionally classified to be and understood (e.g., in law) as inherently inferior—chattel through enslavement. Slaves were to emulate the desires of their masters because their fates rested on doing so. Any perceived threat of divergence resulted in increased suspicion, regulation, and admonishment, which have persisted well beyond emancipation into current policies and practices.[27]

Moreover, cultural desirability and preference for a particular racial identity have been glamorized and idealized historically for the dominant, or white citizens. After all, previous (i.e., slave codes, black codes, Jim Crow laws) and current policies and practices (e.g., institutional discrimination, affirmative action) initiated and solidified the attraction to or preference for whiteness in the broader society. As an example, this is the reason that most children, black and white, preferred white dolls to black ones in Kenneth and Mamie Clark's doll test in the 1940s.[28] This groundbreaking evidence showed the effects of racial segregation through racial preference: children (black included) thought positively of the white dolls and negatively of the black ones and selected (or did not select) them on the basis of that perception.[29] Society's biases and responsiveness to dominant interests have resulted in differential treatment of blacks based on their "othered" status.[30] This development has meant that black citizens, directly and indirectly, have had to prioritize or consider whiteness or dominant interests even above their own—especially at times when their lives may have depended on their doing so. As another example, black citizens have had to think ambiguously about "living while black"—their tones of voice, facial expressions, and body language—in hopes of striking a delicate balance between who they are and the image of themselves that they present, as they may be feared by white citizens (e.g., white neighbors, police).[31] It is through such racial maneuvering that we recognize blackness as intrinsically linked to dominant comfort or discomfort as well as to appeasement or offense. For blacks, however, their identity and their consciousness of it—vulnerable to the dominant temperament—become operational and leveraged for safety and resistance.

Black consciousness stirs direct action—that is, movement-work among black citizens, especially to combat broad racial inequity. At its core, this "stirring" or black-led uprising exposes and counters racial preference and bias toward whiteness. Black consciousness also prioritizes black life—an action that is systemically inconceivable and therefore readily perceived by the dominant as blacks simply making trouble. Further, as the social construction of race does *not* allow for "sameness" (equality) or for all groups to be perceived equitably, but rather views them competitively through stratified populations, whereby automatic empathy for black life or humanity appears to be nonexistent. Instead, the stratification of race results in dominant pushback because black interests are institutionally excluded or considered only secondarily. In addition, any attempts by black citizens to achieve equity and equality (e.g., civil disobedience) are perceived as "disobedient" and disorderly, and therefore are met with dominant distrust, censorship, blame, and denunciation. It is through this arrangement that black-led actions and the fight for social justice fall prey to widespread ambiguity and through differential and often uninformed discourse are easily believed to be and reduced to "blacks complaining."

Black folks were taken to task for a broad array of sentiments and direct actions in Ferguson and throughout the St. Louis region. By contrast, concessions were made and the benefit of the doubt was seemingly extended to predominantly white actor(s) and system(s) that caused and engaged in discriminative treatment of black citizens. In this context, let us consider the robustness of Ferguson's (a predominantly black suburb of St. Louis) resistance and the subsequent backlash against black empowerment. Ferguson civil unrest emerged as a collective response to both the ambiguity surrounding Brown's premature death and the long-standing racial and economic discrimination at the root of systemic aggression and criminalization. During the four plus hours that Brown's body lay in the street and in the following days, reports of "black" deviant behavior started trickling out—the backlash, or rather the groundwork for defending dominant aggression while delegitimizing black protests. First, we learned of reported gunfire at the inner crime scene (where Brown's body had lain). Second, a *militarized* police presence was assigned (e.g., implying that blacks were criminal/hypercriminal), which by all accounts only exacerbated and escalated dissent at the protests. Third, as the pressure mounted to reveal the name of the killing officer and call for his arrest, footage emerged of Brown's alleged previous actions (i.e., a strong-arm robbery to obtain cigarillos), as if to *first* dehumanize and discredit Brown's life and justify his death. Fourth, an all-out, escalating campaign then ensued, one in which black protesters and activists were criticized—void of empirical examination—for apparently caring more about and addressing police brutality than about non-police-related black homicides in their communities and reacting with inaction to the latter.

It was clear that the twofold call to action for combating violence (i.e., police and neighborhood violence) by and among black citizens—recorded and framed for this project just hours after Brown's death—had been minimized or not captured. Therefore, the context for post-Ferguson action had been lost, and through a series of red herrings, black efforts were treated with mockery by both many white and some black citizens. Perhaps unknowingly or even unintentionally, some came to question black sincerity—that is, "loving blackness" or blacks caring about one another was being challenged and measured indirectly, through countering narratives and generally through debates regarding efforts to preserve black life.[32] Criticism consistently occurred along the lines of "Where is the same outcry for black neighborhood homicides?"[33] As some blacks engaged in the same scrutiny, it is important to know that they were influenced by different factors than white critics.[34] Systemic power and entitlements (of whites) or the lack thereof and oppression (of blacks) played a significant role in frustrations expressed by black citizens.[35] Furthermore, as black direct actions have always been treated as oppositional and vilified by the dominant, the easier targets and most damning of the backlash seemed to coalesce around ensuing black mobilization—the use of "Black Lives Matter" verbiage especially and the overall emergence of a twenty-first-century black power movement.[36]

While the articulation of Black Lives Matter (BLM) first emerged as a resistance hashtag following the police killing of Florida black teen Trayvon Martin, the tenacity and doggedness of mobilization efforts in Ferguson and St. Louis advanced its theme and organizing into a proclaimed international movement.[37] Although using the word *movement*, this study draws distinctions among such references.[38] Similar to the articulation and structuring of the civil rights movement, I characterize BLM as one of countless black-organized factions that fell under the auspices of the broader black effort. This study captures the twenty-first-century black movement as a collective and culmination of mostly black individuals and community and grassroots organizations and associations—birthed or revitalized post-Ferguson. That said, black lives *do* matter irrespective of organizational memberships, and that sentiment has historically been the premise for black empowerment efforts. As "black lives matter" widely resonates and may be frequently articulated or variously and thematically displayed among black citizens, it is important to note that not *all* cities have BLM chapters; not *all* black citizens—protesters, activists, or organizers—are members of this organization; and not *all* black-led direct action or mobilization efforts are linked to this organization. The lumping together of *all* black citizens in this fashion is also an endemic part of the dominant backlash.[39]

The deliberate specificity of "black lives" became a partial linchpin for seemingly well-orchestrated white scrutiny.[40] In fact, counterattacks on black direct action hinged on a continuum of appropriating *black* and *blackness* by persistently deferring to "black-on-black crime."[41] Primarily white critics ridiculed the idea of black lives *truly* mattering to black citizens and therefore depicted them as incapable of or uninterested in combating non-police neighborhood homicides or unifying with other citizens generally.[42] Former New York City mayor Rudy Giuliani was cited as calling the BLM movement "racist"—a statement that also implicates *all* black citizens and others engaging in direct action regardless of membership in the organization.[43] The theme mattered most: the uncomfortableness of pronouncing black lives specifically as being important. Many white citizens misrepresented black efforts unfavorably through countercampaigns that implied reverse discrimination and exclusion against police and white citizens, coded as "blue" and "all" (e.g., Blue Lives Matter, All Lives Matter).[44] Further, they did this while positing the "Ferguson Effect": a racialized, unsubstantiated, distorted post-Ferguson claim made by former St. Louis metropolitan police Chief Doyle Sam Dotson III that indirectly blamed increased homicide rates on black citizens' protests while framing police officers as victims.[45]

In sum, the same socioeconomic and political dynamics that worked to objectify and justify black citizens as chattel and deserving of inhumane treatment continue to be systematically perpetuated and manifested in all facets of society post-Ferguson. The systemic devaluing of black life and the concerted need to reconstruct, reassert, and denote black worth and merit are intrinsically linked to historically persistent stereotypical and typecasting effects on black life—that is, the unyielding differential treatment, victim blaming, and backlash from police and many white critics. Furthermore, the dominant construction and appropriation of the terms *black* and *blackness* have continuously proven to be a form of cultural indoctrination disadvantageous to black citizens both directly and indirectly. In response, it has become customary for blacks to empower themselves by recapturing and redefining (i.e., reappropriating) racialized verbiage and actions in an effort to provoke hope and cultural transformation. It is in this context that if we were to consider the "Ferguson Effect," it would be only as a contemporary or post-Ferguson ruse that in essence punishes blacks and strategically absolves police of preexisting and persisting differential treatment (e.g., delayed response/no response, delayed resolution/no resolution).

BETWEEN RACE AND PLACE: EDUCATION AND
TOWN-GOWN RELATIONS

> When you leave the city, you might enter into the suburbs and
> not even really know that you're in the suburbs . . . so I call it
> first tier because it's just right outside of the city line.
>
> SHELLY, community organizer

Brown's deadly encounter with police in the suburbs was an empirical testament to what I had spent years chronicling regarding the taken-for-granted assumptions about certain places and the policing of blacks in those locations.[46] More directly, Brown's death and post-Ferguson civil unrest further highlighted a stark reality about suburban residency for black citizens. The fact that blacks reside in the suburbs does *not* automatically mean that they have better living conditions and experiences than blacks living in the inner city.[47] In fact, as participant Shelly describes here, there are border suburban communities or municipalities in close proximity to the city limits that are not always distinguishable from the inner city of St. Louis. Although their governance and police jurisdictions may be different and citizens have diverse experiences with them, the sociodemographics and backdrop (e.g., segregated, run-down neighborhoods) for some blacks living in the suburbs are relatively similar to those of the inner city. Although research has revealed these similar and yet divergent experiences and attitudes toward police across locations, much more could be learned through examinations of black perceptions and responses to disorder across places.[48] This project therefore addresses disorder in general and black mobilization efforts, in particular with combating violence, irrespective of the perpetrators (i.e., police, fellow citizens) or locations.

Race and place education is important. The way we acquire, think about, and disseminate information regarding populations of color and the places they inhabit (or do not) can impede or advance social change. Similarly, it also matters *where* people go to get information—the depth and measures by which agents of socialization (e.g., schools) derive and are able to provide accurate and legitimate knowledge to and about diverse populations. This project takes all of these factors into consideration. Therefore, let us consider the complexities and perceptions of teaching-and-learning partnerships or scholar activism—empirically and reciprocally—while navigating what could feasibly become or be considered a continuum in town-gown relations.[49]

Scholarship, Activism, or Both? Academic Perceptions of Scholar Activists

> The scholar-activist . . . gets no respect in the academy. While traditional or mainstream scholars refuse to fully recognize our research-action efforts, activists criticize us for operating in the so-called ivory tower. This is a reality or predicament.
>
> HUERTA (2018)

As I embarked on this project juxtaposed between scholarship and activism, I was reminded of academic debates and assertions similar to that of self-identified Chicano scholar-activist Alvero Huerto, quoted here. His statement speaks to the plight of Mexican American scholars engaging in scholar activism or "research-action efforts."[50] Indian immigrant Ranita Ray poignantly highlights scholar-activism as a "paradox," in which she works to reconcile compromised efforts with grassroots organizing in pursuit of tenure.[51] Julia Sudbury and Margo Okazawa-Rey, the editors of *Activist Scholarship: Antiracism, Feminism, and Social Change*, refer to this partnership as a conundrum, as *activist scholarship*, which they define as "the production of knowledge and pedagogical practices through active engagement with, and in the service of, progressive social movements."[52] Sudbury and Okazawa-Rey argue for "a model of active engagement," examining pioneering research methodologies that allow for partnerships between academia and social movements, although they are conscious of power dynamics and rely on the work and experiences of mostly senior academics with tenure.[53] Huerta and Sudbury and Okazawa-Rey similarly highlight the creation of courses and programs at universities, including but not limited to social justice, ethnic, feminist, and queer studies.[54] All are considered direct correlates of community action–university alliances.[55]

It is in this context—the possibility of creating and extending broad, innovative praxes—that I have worked to chronicle some of the most volatile interactions at the onset of a black movement. Doing so has called for constant navigation of the crossroads of scholarship and activism. I have always been cognizant of (1) my own intersectional identity and experiences, along with the subsequent effects of participant observation in black-led direct action; (2) traditional academic thought that did not embrace the idea of scholars *overtly* operating or appearing as activists; and (3) the possible disapproval and shunning of some scholars by community organizers and activists for appearing disengaged, disingenuous, and exploitative when involved in or assisting with the effort.

Given these numerous considerations and complexities, I pondered critical questions during and after the conclusion of the project. For example, how was I to *adequately* account for one of the most pivotal times in history since the civil rights movement: the emergence of twenty-first-century black power direct action? Better yet, how could I *not* be drawn into the movement or activated dichotomously—personally and professionally—when my attraction to academia partly hinged on "education as a practice of freedom?"[56] Furthermore, having been baptized by the streets, so to speak (i.e., in my childhood environment), and now theoretically and methodologically trained and positioned, should I *not* be fully vested in sociohistorical processes, particularly those unfolding in my community (e.g., race, place)? What distinguishes *me* (or other academics) as a progressive social scientist and expert from random pundits or critics who peddle racialized falsehoods and propaganda about social conflict? Doesn't my actual involvement in the movement as a participant observer rather than a detached analyst make me better suited for filling in empirical gaps and pioneering contemporary pedagogy? Finally, aren't we social science catalysts for change or engaging in unadmitted activism when our often peer-reviewed projects, publications, technical reports, and presentations are interwoven with evidence-based implications (i.e., policies, practices)?

Moreover, I often had to make split-second decisions, hoping to strike a balance among the aforementioned thoughts and sentiments, some of which had been derived from "traditional or mainstream scholars'" and activists' criticisms.[57] This meant that I had to be open to spontaneous mental, emotional, and physical concessions that afforded (or did not afford) access to a movement that intrinsically affected me, directly and indirectly, irrespective of my profession. My ability to do so became workable through grounded theory ethnography or grounded ethnography.[58] Through this method, I was able to simultaneously "go deep into experience to" rightly interpret and contextualize the interactions of diverse groups across numerous settings.[59] I maneuvered systematically, accounting for processes, particularly *how* blacks buffered or responded to disorder or violence, especially across two communities (i.e., in protests and residential space). More pertinent to this discussion, my participation also made me privy to activists' perceptions of academics.

Base Coaching and "Dirty Fingernails": Activists' Perceptions of Academics

I took part in a rap session with some activists/organizers (Hakim, Kavion, and Chon) following a community meeting. This was an unplanned gathering at which our casual conversation turned serious. We talked shop about "all things black" and liberation. Then, when the subject of roles in organizing emerged, I asked what they thought about academics. After all, they knew who I was, and we were having a frank conversation, one in which we not only scrutinized the behind-the-scenes structuring of the movement but also called attention to various personalities and positions—without dropping identities—that perceivably advanced the effort or set it back. Again, it was routine for black folks to call each other out, and so, like everybody else, I was willing to stand corrected. Therefore, checking my degrees and pearls at the door, I learned from Hakim and Kavion that most "academic/intellectual scholars" were perceived as persons operating "in the middle." Since our actions were not always definitive, they thought we "could be helpin' [them]" but often did not since we were too busy "analyzin' to the point of over-analyzin'." As a follow-up to this depiction, activist Kavion further described academics as being analogous to base coaches in baseball:

> It reminds me of like stealin' bases. . . . They [academics] [are] kind of like base coaches. . . . The person analyzing, . . . he ain't gone be out, he ain't gone be safe, he ain't gone be nuthin', . . . so when he told you to break [run], he thought it was a good idea. . . . He just sittin' there watchin', . . . so when he see somebody about to be out, then he says, "Oooh, somebody send another batter up."

In other words, on the one hand Kavion thought academics or researchers were conveniently positioned. They directly and indirectly offered diverse strategies (involving interpretations and implications) that proved most consequential to activists and organizers as key players—immediately and in the future—as well as to black citizens generally. On the other hand, the activists appreciated "academics, intellectuals, and scholars with dirty fingernails." Here is how Hakim discussed this matter with me:

> *You like academics with what?*
> I like intellectuals, academics, and scholars with dirty fingernails.
> *What does that mean?*
> Meaning [that] they do something with their theories. They don't just give conjunctional analyses, but *they* actually put them into practice.
> *So what does that look like in everyday action?*
> I feel like in the Movement, Huey P. Newton died with a doctoral degree. He talked about theories of the African or black socialist, but he also made gains by walking the streets [working in the community]. . . . [He ponders.] After starting the Black Youth Education Project, I actually got to go to Oakland to see Huey P.

> Newton's house, . . . then went to the church where they [the Black Panthers] did the first program, then where they moved it [to], and [learned] why they moved it there [to the new location]. This is like amazing . . . to meet Elaine Brown! . . . And so it's hard for you [academics] to be a part of the think tank [with activists and organizers] if you gone be *above it* and ain't *never done it*. So don't bring no theory around [here about] how I'm suppose to go canvass if *you* [academics] *never* canvassed.

Hakim's comments were raw but fair. Our paths regularly crossed through direct action as well as through our associations with other community organizations. This was his usual flow, as he continued to speak sternly of roles and intellectuality. He later added:

> The consistency and intellectual work has to be done by a collective, . . . so when we [are] dreaming of freedom, [black citizens need] consistency. . . . *Somebody* has to [always be ready to] go *do* something.

As this assessment and others similar to it make clear, academics, especially qualitative researchers, have to remain reflexive and contemplative. That is, they have to stay cognizant of *their* "middle"—*where* and *how* they negotiate balance without running afoul of participating communities or offending them through arrogant and condescending detachment and inaction—all the while touting their work on marginalized experiences.

2. (Dis)order and Informal Social Ties in the United States

> 'Cause if we don't do it, who else gon' do it?
>
> FERGUSON PROTESTER

Imagine.

FADE IN:

ST. LOUIS COUNTY PROSECUTING ATTORNEY'S OFFICE—IN FRONT OF BUILDING—
DAY FOUR, MORNING

It is day four of the protests following Brown's death. Roughly fifteen or twenty minutes from Ferguson, following a press conference and a march through downtown Clayton, located in St. Louis County, direct action coalesces in front of prosecuting attorney Robert (Bob) McCulluch's office.

By now there had been four days of direct action, ranging from candlelight vigils, marches, and rallies to town hall meetings, occurring across mostly suburban and some urban St. Louis locations. This morning would be no different. As planned, citizens began and ended the morning's direct action in front of prosecuting attorney Bob McCulluch's building, where some protesters acted as spokespersons to the media or led with directions or chants during protests. Toward the end of this gathering a somewhat heated exchange took place among a few protesters. Three or four young black protesters (between the ages of twenty and thirty) took issue with Jean, an older black female protest leader (middle fifties to sixties), for attempting to correct and dial back their rhetoric. This dynamic was situational and had become a recurring theme: protesters, protest leaders, or organizers cautioning and admonishing one another about comments and behaviors. Ideally, the intent here was to curb increased police aggression and subsequent black citizens' victimization. After all, black citizen–police clashes had become even more tenuous and explosive since the day of Brown's death and the first day of protests. For days protesters had been subjected

39

to tear gas and rubber bullets as a climax to verbal exchanges and police standoffs. The escalating tactical strategies—the overt police militarization and state-sanctioned aggression—only inflamed protesters' zeal and resolve to combat the seemingly racialized practices.[1] Consequently, many protesters believed that ensuring black safety partly called for full-throated resistance against the system, or rather against institutional dominance and discrimination, although what that resistance actually looked like or meant, each time and in every gathering, was fluid and often negotiated in the heat of conflict with the police and among protesters.

Therefore, some protesters did not take kindly to actual organizing—that is, the logistics behind direct action. In fact, they perceived it to be nothing more than handing out instructions for engaging in calm, system-appeasing, passive protests. They were unfamiliar with mobilization efforts, which appeared to restrict their resistance to social injustice—that is, in real time, the strategizing part of an emerging social movement was new to and often lost on them. They wanted their voices to be heard and their presence to be felt as part of an evolving, no-holds-barred black collective. A few black protesters scrutinized the situation to determine whether this scenario actually existed and at times became critical of protest leaders and organizers. However, the fluidity of some direct actions did not always afford time for (re)explaining short- and long-term black agendas or leaders' and organizers' intentions for taking certain approaches. Hence, relationship building and trust were key, and the process for building both was still in its infancy. Furthermore, full disclosure of mobilization efforts could be compromising for protesters; therefore, protest leaders and organizers were learning to be no more transparent than law enforcement was in revealing its strategies. This approach was especially important because they suspected that police and other "countering" actors (i.e., plants and informants) had been embedded within the protests.

Consequently, post-Ferguson direct actions could be characterized as both spontaneous and deliberate. They embodied the different sentiments and responses of the protesters, alternately impulsive, intentional, and contemplative. In many instances, protesters complemented one another—all benefiting the movement by contributing to its diversity. However, at other times their divergent thoughts and ideas created distractions and heightened preexisting anxieties. Thus, while protesters were pushing for black solidarity, there occasionally were incidents of conflict among black protesters, protest leaders, and organizers—the side effects of a broader, more inclusive form of disorder (e.g., poverty, segregation, biased policing). Due to protesters' different vantage points—their roles and experiences (or lack thereof) in collective action—those involved were sometimes acting solely on their emotions and therefore were unable to grasp the specific protest objectives necessary for longevity in the movement. Misunderstandings arose, but they were a manageable component of the emerging, primarily black protest community.

As the morning's direct action (a press conference, march, and protest rally) was ending, Jean had begun rounding up protesters and encouraging them to leave the scene. This was one of the early examples of a practice that later would become common among protest leaders and organizers; that is, someone would signal an end to a direct action at a particular location and then push all protesters to leave together. As with soldiers in battle, the idea was to not abandon or leave fellow comrades (i.e., protesters or freedom fighters) behind by themselves once a mission had been accomplished. Their civil disobedience alone was enough cause for them to anticipate retribution, and the protesters feared that being left behind alone or with only a few others would make them even more vulnerable to police contention and aggression.

Furthermore, with a somewhat rough-and-ready schedule planned for the day, direct actions were only ending at this location. There were other actions (e.g., a press conference by the Brown family attorneys and Al Sharpton/the National Action Network, rallies) lined up for the day across St. Louis. Breaks between events gave protesters planning to attend more direct actions some downtime or at least travel time to the next location.

Jean addressed what she believed to be some protesters' continued provocations. Using a megaphone, she had repeatedly tried to get them to leave and had been unsuccessful when she countered the few who were still yelling and not leaving by ad-libbing a song—"I don't wanna go to jail, I don't wanna go to jail, I don't wanna go to jail"—in front of police. This action did not sit well with the few young protesters, sparking a disagreement. Refusing to be silent and attempting to make a point, Dalton, a young black male protester, said this during the exchange that followed:

DALTON: Do we *all* have to die . . . for somebody to get it through their skull? Do we *all* have to die? [Looks at Jean.] Is that what you want? . . . When you say "be quiet and go home," [does that mean] somebody else gotta go to jail for no reason, gotta get killed for no reason, gotta . . . [Jean cuts him off.].

JEAN: It's time for us to go home. . . . We [other protesters] not going to jail because of y'all mouths! Don't nobody have no bond money!

When some of the young black protesters heard this response, they were even more irritated. After all, they were seemingly committed to both the cause (i.e., protesting social injustice) and the action (i.e., resistance), with possible arrest being the least of their worries. Reread the statement in which Dalton spoke of them all dying, "somebody else" going to jail, and future encounters. His focus was clear. They were passionately protesting for their own protection, which they perceived to be a matter of life and death. They were also proactively trying to ensure the future safety of others. Therefore, they took Jean's comments as minimizing their efforts and empowering aggressive police tactics. From their perspective, she was singing and making arguably counterintuitive statements in front of law enforcement. Furthermore, her actions were perceivably embarrassing to Dalton and his group, who believed she was making them look fearful or weak, all the while potentially incentivizing the police to make arrests. Subsequently, as if to reassert strength and courage, Deana, a young black female protester, interjected her response by motioning with her hand as if to shoo Jean off and then saying to her, "We don't need [have to] to go to jail. . . . [Go] find something else to preach about." What Deana really meant was for Jean to mind her own business.

This exchange was not the first time that Jean had initiated a charged dialogue about protesting that involved the younger populations. Though arguably misplaced from Dalton's and Deana's perspectives, Jean's attempts seemed to be related to negotiating direct action in ways that minimized police aggression for *all* protesters. She apparently approached these black citizen–police exchanges as if they were solely contingent upon certain protesting behaviors, when in fact civil disobedience in and of itself is reason enough to generate negative police responses. Furthermore, some of the more modest protesters or black citizens generally had been subjected to the worst of the police actions before Brown's death and during the subsequent protests, so differential policing obviously occurred irrespective of black citizens' actions.[2] Therefore, taking into account trends in everyday policing, the ways in which officers might become suspicious, and the death that ignited these protests initially, extralegal factors such as race (i.e., populations of color) and age (i.e., youth, young adults) may further exacerbate conflicts.[3] This situation is especially the case when such factors are tied to the tenacity of the younger populations.[4] In any case, just the night before— on day three of civil unrest, at a National Association for the Advancement of Colored People (NAACP) town hall meeting—Jean had ardently expressed her apprehension about younger protesters being left alone to face tear gas and rubber bullets in the absence of older black leaders and organizers.

Flashback.

LAP DISSOLVE TO:
August 11, 2014. It is dusk, and an NAACP town hall meeting is being held at a church in Normandy, the suburb where Mike Brown Jr. graduated from high school. It is day three of the civil unrest and the night before the exchange between Jean and Dalton.

Former national NAACP president Cornell William Brooks, along with St. Louis chapter presidents, hosted a town hall meeting to address events and actions directly related to Brown's death and civil unrest in the region. More broadly, this meeting was intended to begin a dialogue regarding the perceived widespread social injustices and discrimination throughout the St. Louis region and beyond. This town hall meeting was occurring on night three of the civil unrest, after some protesters had already experienced two nights of seemingly unrestrained police aggression. Therefore, some citizens were already enraged when they came to this meeting, especially after having been directly and indirectly subjected to armored tanks, semiautomatic weapons being pointed at them, police dogs, tear gas, rubber bullets, increased arrests, and so forth. These actions were all perceived to be increasingly overt, brazen, state-sanctioned attacks by the police—even worse than the previous abuses that perceivably had led to Brown's death and triggered the protests. This rapid escalation of events, or rather the mostly black citizens' exposure and now vulnerability to militarized police tactics, had been traumatizing for them. Therefore, expectations for responses from the local black leadership had intensified as black citizens sought expeditious intervention and justice.

As black citizens packed the small church and a significant overflow crowd stood outside, they sought answers and a tangible plan for moving forward, particularly under militarized circumstances and, by all appearances, in the face of what was beginning to look like civil war in the St. Louis region. As an example of the mood on the streets before this meeting, here is how one protester communicated their frustration, while still hoping for justice:

> We just tired of asking, we tired of talking, . . . we want to let them [the dominant] know where we coming from. We fed up!

Similarly, another protester, while participating in a direct action, expressed the need for timely "action" rather than "discussion" while looking and hoping for some form of intervention in the absence of justice:

Something needs to be done, but it needs to be done *before* this goes to trial . . . *if* it [the police murder of Brown] makes it to trial.

In other words, "We need to do something fast"—organize and strategize—was the general sentiment prior to this meeting and was a strong shared feeling among those seated in the audience. Determining what that "something" would be called for more contemplation, and this town hall meeting, in many minds, seemed to be the right place and time for it.

With the church jam-packed with local community organizers, emotionally overwrought citizens, and press, the evening's discussions began with prayer, followed by introductions of the speakers and panelists. Notably, the dignitaries (mostly men) were seated in the front, passing the microphone among themselves (see figure 4). They provided general assessments of or responses to problems in the black community—what they thought should or could work to move the ball forward toward justice. Frustration and hurt about perceived injustices were evident and expressed by all parties in various ways. This reaction was even more obvious during the question-and-answer segment. During this time Jean, infuriated, expressed her thoughts to the panel. She confronted them (and actually the entire venue) for apparently leaving or allowing the young people across town (i.e., in Ferguson) to protest and face the police by themselves while the panel pontificated at this town hall meeting.

In addition to being at the St. Louis County prosecutor's office, Jean had apparently also been at ground zero during the previous nights and was irritated by what she believed to be at best negligence on the part of those who self-identified as the more experienced black community leaders and organizers. In her mind, they had been absent from the trenches in this instance. To her, this absence was particularly important because she saw part of their role as protecting the black teens and young adults who were mobilizing in that moment, in this immediate situation, without those leaders—who for all intents and purposes were doing nothing but talking at the town hall meeting. As she scolded them, she vehemently voiced her thoughts about what they should be doing instead and why, where, and with whom they should be doing it. It seemed as if she had shown up at the meeting in search of reinforcement. When that outcome did not seem likely, she offered strategies or proposed actions of her own, the kind that she believed would garner support and protection for young protesters.

By the end of the meeting, many issues had been discussed, ranging from unaccredited black schools to inner-city violence among black citizens. However, there was still no definitive plan or a tangible directive for how to

FIGURE 4.   Day three, town hall meeting called by the NAACP. This meeting was held at a church in Normandy, one day after the first use of tear gas and rubber bullets on protesters in Ferguson. Normandy is another small suburban community like Ferguson. Brown had graduated from the Normandy school district weeks earlier. Protesters left this town hall meeting and returned to ground zero to face another night of tear gas and rubber bullets. Photo by author.

proceed in the coming days of hostile police militarization and interpersonal neighborhood violence. Nevertheless, as if getting ready to report for an additional work shift, some protesters (including me) were mentally gearing up for more nighttime direct action—for what were sure to be more black citizen–police clashes back in Ferguson.

LAP DISSOLVE BACK TO:
Day four, at the site of the protests in front of the St. Louis County prosecuting attorney's office.

Unbeknownst to the young adults at this protest, Jean felt a sense of responsibility to be present and attentive to their well-being, especially during direct actions. After all, just the night before she had admonished others for not doing so. In some sense, she appeared to be "community othermothering" in the movement—"doing gender" or mothering at the center of direct action by being conventionally attentive or, arguably, nurturing younger protesters—despite receiving backlash in atypical circumstances (e.g., the heat of civil unrest and an uprising).[5] Fellow black citizens attending to one another in this way is an extension of their everyday engagement, whereby black women especially provide care to individuals living in or passing through their neighborhoods under sometimes desperate circumstances. They have persistently done this regardless of whether they are involved in civil unrest. Nevertheless, by doing this Jean presented herself as a "mother knowing best," an action that translated to Dalton and his crew as an insult to their adulthood. This is one example of how disorder (i.e., police brutality and broad, systemic discrimination)—as blacks identify it—leads to hit-and-miss communication or clashes between black citizens in their communities (e.g., the protest community, neighborhoods). This dynamic is especially true in the heat of a crisis (e.g., poor education, unemployment, segregation), in which the status quo leaves blacks so discouraged and desperately seeking change that they unknowingly or sacrificially turn on one another.

However, as this exchange continued to unfold in front of the police and possibly within the range of the media, other protesters made several attempts to tone down the disagreement. In fact, J'Quan, another young black male protester, spoke up and said to Dalton, who by now was the most agitated in the group, "Ay, just ignore it [the exchange with Jean] so it don't look like we out here arguing." J'Quan realized the significance of the optics and was proactively trying to mitigate them. In essence, some black protesters were *policing* their appearance—trying to regulate and protect themselves from conveying stereotypical depictions of themselves as divided and lacking self-control. As Jean walked away, Dalton reiterated his position to the few remaining protesters. He concluded the dispute by saying:

> It's just that at the end of the day, we talkin' about real issues here. . . . I got family members and friends who have died from these Bitches right here [loudly addressing and pointing to police]. I got a cousin that's *not* gon' have her father due to the police, and you [Jean] wanna tell me to chill out. Somebody else just lost their son in the middle of the street [Mike Brown Jr.]. [Yelling:] THAT'S killing. THAT IS KILLING! And you wanna come over here and put *more* energy into telling *me* to stop than investing your energy into destroying the Establishment? Something is wrong with that! You need to literally rethink that! Because I haven't hurt nobody. I never murdered nobody.

"LITERALLY RETHINKING THAT": A RECONCEPTUALIZATION OF (DIS)ORDER

It is important to note that black protest leaders and organizers emerge under varying circumstances, with different access to resources and supportive overhead. They often find themselves disagreeing as they tackle a broad range of seemingly impossible issues that call for immediate solutions, all of which depend for their effectiveness and success on tangible support well beyond what is expected and sometimes provided by black citizens or protesters in place of direct action. Furthermore, not all black leaders or organizers are in the same places at the same times all the time, sharing detailed, strategic information about "all things black" as if they were a monolithic group and movement. Although black advancement continues to be their ultimate shared mission, they envision and take different approaches to confronting pertinent issues within the black community. Take, for instance, Jean's situation. She clearly embraced the idea of serving and protecting one another, particularly younger protesters. She thought it was the responsibility of older leaders and the elders of the black community to lead the way. Leaders may agree with her position about the need to provide an example of service for youth and young adults, but some may also take exception to Jean's claim that they have not been attentive to the progression of the movement overall. Since protesting is not the entirety of black mobilization efforts, these leaders may regard themselves as leading through other forms of resistance. In fact, some leaders have grown critical of the idea of protesting and are pushing back against it so as not to have protests be identified as the only form of the black effort. At the NAACP town hall meeting, one leader on the panel alluded to blacks as "professional protesters." In doing so, he was not implying that they were paid actors, but rather indicating that protests had become "automatic"—a historically well-practiced go-to or strong suit for black America—while he perceived other areas of response as lacking similar involvement. It is important to take notice of the notion of "professional protesting," used as a counter-response by some white critics to mock and delegitimize protests and other forms of direct action. By using this term they imply and emphasize the idea of "paid" protesters in order to portray all or most protesters as disingenuously working to disrupt peace rather than serving in protest actions based on their moral convictions. This particular typecasting has more to do with the dominant's angst regarding resistance and is used to disparagingly encourage scrutiny of all protesters. In the present case, one black female protester explained, "I'm out here to represent [the race]," while other black protesters said they were there "to support [it]" or "to stand for justice." These sentiments seemed to be the overall attitude of the participating black citizens irrespective of disagreements and different approaches.

Dalton was one of countless black citizens making the case for rethinking behaviors. He was commenting on how the perceived actions of blacks (e.g., his statements in protests), whether or not they are criminal acts, often take precedence over the "KILLING" and widespread systemic injustices committed by white or dominant populations. Such instances only muddy the water and become distractions from the real issues. For Dalton, it was unreasonable to focus on his retrospective statements, even if the criticism came from another black person. His sentiments afford one of many opportunities for examining and understanding how black responses to turmoil (i.e., disorder) easily become red herrings or distractions from the long-standing role(s) and culpability of the dominant. He pointedly blamed "the Establishment"—the institutionalization of discrimination—for initiating and advancing all-encompassing conflict (e.g., police brutality). More important, he called attention to it as the rightful target for scrutiny—that is, the source of power and control by which the biased police killing of black people became tenable and justifiable.

There is much to gain from a deeper examination of disorder from the perspective of mostly disadvantaged black citizens—those historically and disproportionately characterized as prototypes of, perpetrators of, and unfortunate dwellers within that disorder. This study highlights (dis)order—disorder and order—as culturally relative and sequential across diverse populations. It broadens the tent for thinking about "prescribed" behavioral norms (order) and violations of them (disorder) post-Ferguson.[6]

Through post-Ferguson mobilization efforts, "order" and "disorder," as black citizens perceived them, were turned right side up and, extraordinarily, became the target. Dalton's referring to and redefining the police killing as the problem (the cause) rather than his comments (the effect) is an example of black citizens' comparably realigning and reprioritizing disruptive dominant actions. "The Establishment" or "the system" (i.e., the dominant power, the government, and the criminal justice system) emerges, directly and indirectly, as a central theme. Look at how the primarily black protesters spoke about this matter through protest chants:

> Unite,
> Resist,
> Send those killer cops to jail,
> The whole damn system is guilty as hell. . . .
> (I say) The whole damn system is guilty as hell.

Moreover, (dis)order is reconceptualized in this study as dependent on historical context and as integral to the social construction and (re)appropriation of blackness in the United States.[7] In a black, post-Ferguson context, I define *(dis)order* as historically structured, differential conditions that through institutional means, directly and indirectly, persistently impede or disrupt black advancement. These conditions manifest socially and physically, noncriminally or criminally, and "engender . . . fight or flight" responses from black citizens.[8] It is the "fight" portion that becomes most evident and becomes a focus for analysis through post-Ferguson black direct action and mobilization efforts. Furthermore, it is through direct action that (dis)order as innately "systemic" and characteristic of dominant construction materialized as the premise for the movement.
Fast-forward.

LAP DISSOLVE TO:
Nightfall. I am standing across the street from the Ferguson fire and police departments. It is the night the indictment decision is announced.

Roughly three months after the NAACP meeting, prosecuting attorney McCulluch's office—across town in Clayton—issued the decision not to indict former police officer Darren Wilson (who killed Brown Jr.), which sent shock waves throughout the St. Louis region and the country. Here I look at how some protesters in Ferguson voiced their sentiments in impromptu conversations upon learning of the decision. They spoke openly about police killings, double standards, and unchecked authority as evidence of a rigged "system" (e.g., the police and the prosecutor) and about its actors as conveyors of disorder and disruption. Harmen, a black male protester, said contemptuously:

> Basically what they [the system] are telling people is that it is okay to kill somebody as long as you have [a] police officer's uniform on. . . . If I have to shoot a person six times, that's excessive. . . . Like if I feel threatened for my life, . . . all I need is [to fire off] about two, maybe three shots, so anything more than that is excessive.

Shortly thereafter, Bryah, a black female protester standing nearby, chimed in: "It was expected. . . . I knew they weren't going to indict him." As she was talking, LaKeitha and Jaleesa, two other black female protesters, also reacted:

LAKEITHA: It's just a decision . . . between whether they [prosecutor and other officials] [were] going to file charges. He's a cop. He's immune. Cops are immune.

BRYAH: Which is why Bob McCulluch didn't charge him [Darren Wilson] in the first place.

Suddenly Jaleesa spotted police somewhat covertly positioned on the rooftops of the Ferguson Police and Fire Departments. As if catching them and blowing their cover, here is how she sarcastically responded while pointing up at them:

JALEESA: Oh, they popped their heads up. Oh yeah, . . . [Yelling and waving] HEEEEEY, SNIPER [police]!

BRYAH: [Pointing] It's a sniper over there too; he's right on top!

LAKEITHA: [Speaking as if talking to the officers:] Right! So just shoot [fire down on] us so we don't know where the hell the bullets came from!

Their comments evolved from their frustration over the decision not to indict to assuming a lack of accountability by Wilson or the police and a general yet persistent devaluing of black life. Their low expectations and general indifference toward the "system" were such that their depiction of the police as "snipers"—who were covertly positioned and waiting for an extemporaneous signal to rain down a hail of bullets on them—appeared plausible. These were poignant comments and reactions shared among members of a group of protesters as we stood across the street from the Ferguson police department and fire station. It is especially important to keep in mind the context and full implications of all that had just transpired. These were the initial moments—sideline conversations following the no-indictment announcement—as reality sank in, with some members of Brown's family at the scene. It was now official, after weeks of relentless direct action and primarily black citizens being subjected to a continuation of excessive state aggression, that it had been decided—as if with the snap of a finger—that Darren Wilson was not going to be held legally accountable or punished for the murder of Mike Brown Jr.

The primarily black protesters milled around the scene, seemingly trying to adapt their thoughts and actions to the announcement. Groups of protesters were still scattered about the street and on sidewalks, spanning numerous blocks, when I began to hear police announcements. Having witnessed routine clashes with the police since Brown's death, I had come to recognize audible and inaudible police announcements as one of many indications that the tide was turning—meaning that police announcements amid civil unrest often occurred as black citizen–police exchanges were escalating to the point of tear gas and other aggressive tactics being used, whether or not the citizens realized this was happening. Before I could fully cover my nose and mouth with my scarf, I saw sparks in the sky a bit farther down the street. Tear gas had been released, sending me and others running north on South Florissant Road, roughly fifteen minutes after I talked with Harmen, Bryah, LaKeitha, and Jaleesa. My initial fears were realized. I had the same feeling that I had experienced on night one, only hours after Brown's death—that this night was going to be especially bad. By some people's accounts, it was like reliving the initial alerts about Brown's death. The decision not to indict Wilson had apparently landed on many like a barrage of gut punches, not to mention the unfathomable blow to the Brown family. As I ran, I could hear the windows of a beauty supply store that I passed being smashed—the sounds and actions baked into a perceived systemic betrayal and civil unrest. I sensed that this night was just beginning. It was inconceivable that the weight of the decision and all that it represented would result in black citizens nodding acceptingly, offering no resistance. We were located on the "white side" of Ferguson at that point, but later that same night the world would watch as countless businesses burned on the "black side"—the part of town where Brown had died and where some blacks, pre- and post-Ferguson, lived, and which disproportionately faced a continuum of very racialized socioeconomic and political injustices.

FADE OUT

For days images of burning buildings and police cars dominated the news. Although the destruction was sad and certainly not condoned by the protest community, the outcry against and criticism of those who had started the fires seemed to indicate that some valued property more than black lives. The fact that some of the lost businesses were black owned was unfortunate as well. However, property ownership does not negate black owners' susceptibility to broad racialized treatment, since entrepreneurship does not grant reprieves for blackness. This situation also does not mean that blacks aim to destroy themselves and their communities. Such a charge acts as another stereotypical conjecture, presumably used to turn a critical lens on blacks and shame them into silence and inaction. This explanation appears especially valid since the arsonist(s), whether white or black, still remain at large today. More important, for many blacks civil unrest and direct action took precedence over the destruction of property, as the movement prioritized and safeguarded black lives.

The real underlying problem was the profiteering of the criminal justice system, which especially solidified revenue through the disproportionate criminalization of poor black citizens—as disclosed in a US Department of Justice (DOJ) investigation in 2015.[9] Ferguson's local government essentially operated as a local version of a prison–industrial complex. Black citizens had long been unfairly targeted and penalized through racialized policing as a lucrative funding source for the local government. Although this conclusion may not have been the understanding of some business owners, especially black owners, it was through the same political economy that they were all linked. They were partnered with, were vested in, and benefited variably from, even if indirectly, exploitation by the local government, which by all accounts first burned poor black citizens through exhaustive harassment, fines, and incarceration that left them reeling from these unalterable life experiences.[10]

Let us now turn to (dis)order—that is, to how black citizens make sense of (dis)order sequentially and through social ties and move to police or buffer its effects in their communities.

WHEN (DIS)ORDER IS OUT OF ORDER: A BLACK CULTURAL PERSPECTIVE

> To throw tear gas . . . and to shoot those [bullets, thinking that]
> . . . those [are] rubber bullets. . . . Those are not police officers;
> that's military. . . . You don't bring tanks and shoot at us [mostly
> black protesters] when we're trying to peacefully protest!
>
> SYLVIA, black female protester

The historic discrimination against or differential treatment of black citizens has generally not counted as disorder. Its long-standing effects—

community or neighborhood social and physical signs or reminders of chaos—have mostly been treated as if they were pathological to blackness and potentially threatening to the dominant. Historical threads and trends of oppression have been routinely overlooked and conflated—neglecting the sequential ebb and flow of discriminative actions and consequences across time, beginning with slavery. This result has occurred because at the root of (dis)order, there are semblances of white supremacy and protection of dominant structuring that correlate well with a particular order: the prioritization and preservation of economic and racial stratification along with white comfort. The move to recast black citizens as enemies of the state despite their "peacefully protesting" speaks to this inverted arrangement—the often unacknowledged and unaddressed transposing of dominant disruption and threat—and then to the ensuing tenor or understood *(re)ordering* of dominant disruption and threat within the broader culture. The protester Sylvia reported other reversed threats and subsequent unrestricted, unchecked state abuses:

> An older lady was recording on her iPad, [and] [police] ended up arresting her and slamming her into the police car! They stomped on her iPad and threw it away! [Yes, all] because she was documenting [protests and police exchanges]!

Although there is no substantive way to confirm this account, it became a vicarious experience—one that was easily conceded and shared as being more true than not due to an established history of unknown, hidden, or ignored everyday black citizen–police exchanges involving intimidation. That said, not all officers behaved in this way, although the mostly black protesters were aware of and impacted by the ones who did, who by their behavior appeared committed to and enamored of the possibility of using force on fellow US citizens. It was as if they had returned home from military duty on foreign soil to receive full military honors because they had done so.

Police brutality, when acknowledged, is discrimination that is generally passed off as one of many institutional "imperfections" or isolated behaviors within a more widely improving system. In contrast, interpersonal neighborhood violence among black citizens is deemed pathological and is disparagingly portrayed and articulated as if blacks are inherently criminal and irredeemable. The dominant construction of blackness takes precedence, justifying the widespread differential treatment of black citizens as principled. The result is (dis)order out of order, as a matter of practice. It benefits the status quo from two angles: one, the (dis)ordering of historical agenda and accounts, and two, the (dis)ordering of behaviors that follow thereafter. Let us now take a closer look at history—why and how pervasive turmoil first manifested for black citizens in this nation.

(Dis)Ordering History and Violations

The economic and political stability of the new nation hinged on racial distinctions: the superficially rigid delineation and categorization of people. It leveraged an order (or disorder) whereby the dominant could broadly and comfortably advance their superiority. Thus, power and control were solidified through the imposition of a disparaged black identity and enslavement, an "othering" process whereby blackness came to be understood as a fixed, rigid arrangement subjugated by whiteness.[11] Enslaved Africans' grasp of white domination—what it meant and how it materialized in their everyday existence—made them ever so cognizant of their new US black group membership and a shared way of life (i.e., culture) governed by it. Therefore, it is important to note that black responses as a community—whether perceived as good, bad, or indifferent—should be realized as recourses in response to trauma that, due to an ongoing history of racially atrocious events (e.g., enslavement), left an "indelible" mark on the black identity.[12] This is an identity whose very evolution "often defies categorization" and has been in lockstep with confronting systemic abuse and oppression.[13]

It has been through culture—as a process and product of past-to-present interactions—that the indoctrination and protection of dominant interests became widely imperative and normative.[14] It was a civic duty to think and act in accordance with prioritizing dominant comfort; policing slaves is one of countless examples.[15] Although there were slave patrols, all white citizens were obligated to ensure compliance from slaves or freedmen.[16] That dictum was consistent with systemic arrangements: a hierarchical categorization with social control integrally incorporated to safeguard it. After Emancipation, white mobs and riotous behavior became overt instances in which the dominant initiated more disorderly behavior—extremely threatening and disruptive—even engaging in displacing actions toward blacks. In many cases, these actions were murderous rampages (e.g., lynch mobs, massacres), recurrent incidents and events that occurred indiscriminately across the nation (e.g., the 1917 East St. Louis race riot, the 1921 Tulsa riots), often leaving populations of color, particularly blacks, even more targeted, fleeing to safer locations, or dead.[17]

However, these events (race riots, race wars, lynch mobs) appear to have been almost lost in historical accounts. White critics especially do not acknowledge them as historically reprehensible acts provoked and inflicted by *their* community. Previous white improprieties or violations often go unacknowledged or have been minimized through seeming lapses in history.

Next let us consider contemporary community or neighborhood (dis) organization, with (dis)order as its evidence and concurrent with and following from historical discrimination.[18]

Social (Dis)organization and (Dis)order Theories   Social disorganization refers to "the inability of a community structure to realize the common values of its residents and maintain effective controls."[19] This social structure theory highlights community breakdown or dysfunction—centered on ecological characteristics such as economic strain, racial/ethnic heterogeneity, and mobility/instability—and a community's inability to regulate itself.[20] These three factors also have direct and indirect correlations with social disorder, and disorder has some association with crime.[21] Disorganization also focuses heavily on weak social ties.[22] Disorganization has been empirically measured through the presence or absence of social networks (e.g., friendship ties, organizational participation) and relied upon for explaining crime and delinquency.[23] Disorder, on the other hand, focuses on weak social controls and is measured based on the perceptions of residents or community members.[24] It is thought to be the social (e.g., public drunkenness, noise) and physical (e.g., trash, vandalism) evidence of community or neighborhood disorganization.[25] Disorder has been found to affect residents' ability to develop bonds among themselves, thus negatively affecting social cohesion and their ability to mitigate or combat the disorder.[26]

Disorder or perceptions of it have also been found to have a curvilinear effect on participation.[27] In other words, not all residents or community members have been found to be detached and unresponsive in places that appear to be characterized by disorder and crime. Some residents have been found to be more trusting of one another in more racially/ethnically homogenous places.[28] In addition, neither high nor low but rather moderate concern about disorder and crime has been found to have encouraged the participation of residents.[29] In any case, the current project maintains that informal social ties make a difference. Previous studies have found that some residents connect and respond to community issues despite the presence of disorder and crime or perceptions of them.[30]

This study builds upon the systemic model of social organization. It describes "instances in which individual or collective problem-solving goes up" across mostly poor homogenous populations and places despite the occurrence of disorganization and disorder and their effects. I examine *when* (post-Ferguson) and *how* (through social ties) black citizens actually organize "toward common ends."[31] I study instances in which we see an interchange among social ties, organizing, and informal social control among black citizens in the heat of historic disruption (e.g., civil unrest) post-Ferguson. For example, here is how Karah, a middle-aged black female protest leader, rallied black citizens:

> *Where* you gon' live? *How* you gon' live? *How much* you got to live off of? Come on people, let's pull together because when we [blacks] tearin' up our [black] communities, you goin' against us [ourselves]. . . . Let's do it the right way. . . . They [whites/the dominant] got all these high-profile attorneys that's trained to kill us on paper. . . . Come on now, . . . work with us [black leaders/organizers] so we can work with you. Let's do it the right way; let's do it!

Post-Ferguson organizing was holistic. It addressed a broad range of community issues pertinent to black life, emerging from but not solely limited to police brutality. Consistent with Karah's message—the perceptions and mobilization efforts of black citizens post-Ferguson—this study addresses (1) black citizens as active engagers at risk of various forms of victimization, even "on paper" (institutional), and (2) the historical structuring or arranging of society as it is a disproportionately constant (versus citizens' responses) and underlying social force and a source for discriminatingly disrupting black life (e.g., through residential segregation and disproportionate criminalization).

This project devotes significant attention to history and the social construction of economic and racial hierarchy. Disorganization literature has generally not provided this depth of historically racialized analysis ethnographically. It generally articulates structural disruption in communities of color quantitatively and to some degree as emerging and evolving social conditions isolated from and independent of the onset of U.S. history. However, these arrangements are not happenstance; rather, they are the top-down-first, hierarchical cause and effects purposefully constructed and maintained in the best interests of the dominant. It is in this vein that I examine double standards in distinguishing or conflating disorder and criminal activity.

(Dis)order and Distinctions with Double Standards In Disorder and Decline: Crime and the Spiral Decay in American Neighborhoods, theorist Wesley Skogan describes disorder as being culturally relative and as a violation of "widely shared values" that is unable to capture nuanced

behaviors.[32] Although most people regardless of social demographics agree on what is considered crime (e.g., theft, murder) by their society, the same is not true about the concept of disorder. Crime is disorder, but not all disorder is crime. Crime is legislated, and disorder is "uncodified"—the point at which "violations" result in a plethora of subjective behavioral expectations, often to the detriment of black populations.[33] In short, this condition is the legacy of enslavement and racialized policing, whereby slave codes, black codes, and Jim Crow laws, which normalized everyday behavioral expectations for blacks, differed from expectations for whites. Contemporary policies and practices still reflect this trend, and this situation is the reason for black female protester Genesha's distrust of and demand for answers from the police (i.e., the system) regarding Brown's shooting.[34] She stated:

> Honestly, what they did to that man [Mike Brown Jr.], . . . kill[ing] him in cold blood like that, . . . that's what got me out here [in protest]. . . . These police ain't shit. . . . They lie and lie. I can't [take no more]. . . . We need some answers.

Since at that time no reasonable answers had been given for Brown's killing, Genesha believed the police had been "liars" in the past and expected them to continue to be so in the future—that is, presumably ready to provide stereotypically inverted narratives of events as a cover for their own criminal behavior.

Similarly, Cody, a black male protester, said:

> I think the system is unjust to a certain demographic. . . . I don't think that's right. . . . If we all do the same . . . as every other American citizen, why do the rules seem *not* to support us [black citizens] . . . [when] all we ask for is peace and safety?!? It's not right.

Cody is clearly calling out the double standards regarding rules and violations. He highlights contradictions with respect to peace and safety for the black community. Likewise, Lolita, another black female protester, called attention to perceived inconsistencies that she attributed to peace and justice:

> I want all of my brothers and sisters to just have peace . . . and justice because there will be no peace until there is justice. . . . Why would they give that cop pay and release [no jail]? If it was a black man [who murdered someone], they would have locked him up cause there's no justice, there's no peace.

Cody's and Lolita's comments provide an opportunity to think about *how*, in cases in which citizens, irrespective of race, seem to share the same values (e.g., protecting life), the results are starkly different for blacks. In addition, this inconsistency among participants speaks to fairness and justice, or the lack thereof, as a catalyst for (dis)ordering and conflating distinctions in the best interests of the system. It is for this reason that chants such as "No justice, no peace, no racist-ass police" are commonly bellowed across protest scenes. Justice and peace appear to be moving targets that more often than not seem unattainable for black citizens.

INFORMAL SOCIAL TIES: INCORPORATING A SYSTEM OF PEACE

> I would really like for us to incorporate a system of *peace* officers instead of *police* officers. . . . All we [blacks] want is to be able to live and for our family and for our kids to not live in fear [of] the people that are paid *by us* . . . to *protect us* [but who] use those *same* methods to *incarcerate us* and make billions.
>
> DEXTER, black male protester

Predominantly black places—where black citizens live or situate themselves (e.g., in neighborhoods, at protests)—continue to be over- and underpoliced when compared with their white counterparts' living situations and primarily white locations.[35] Therefore, just as poor black communities especially are more likely to face aggressive policing, black citizens are more likely to be subjected to increased suspicion and heightened encounters with police. They contend with direct and indirect racialized contacts (which are vicarious, involuntary, or voluntary) irrespective of criminality.[36] More specifically, black citizens are more likely to experience proactive policing, as their more affluent white counterparts encounter the police both reactively and voluntarily—typically when they call for them.[37] Black citizens are apparently more often subjected to incarceration than to police protection. As previously communicated by Dexter, these encounters even occur at the expense of black taxpayers.

Rifts persist within black citizen–police relations, often in addition to subpar social services, leaving citizens disadvantaged and sometimes responding desperately to their situations. These are broad structural problems. They result in domino effects that are not easily resolved locally or among some black citizens or residents. Therefore we should think about the relationship between community disorder and black citizens' responses, as follows: (1) blacks' policing themselves has more to do with *managing* and *navigating* perceptions of disorder, crime, and their effects in their communities, and (2) blacks' policing disorder, crime, and their effects interactively is mostly understood and agreed upon when articulated as "protecting and serving" one another in their community. Taking these points together, black citizens are found to be relying on informal social ties post-Ferguson to combat perceptions of disorder and crime and their effects. It is through this informal cadre of trusted persons or alliances that black citizens acquire instrumental, emotional, and informational support for collective action, often in addition to or in lieu of family members' support, to compensate with goods and services through a series of interpersonal exchanges.[38]

"YOU, Be Peaceful!": When They Treat Us Like ISIS

> YA'LL [police] learn how to be peaceful! Don't keep telling us
> about being peaceful; YOU be peaceful.... I'm thinking about
> [my] brothers and sisters in the streets, ... and if we can't get it
> [peace or justice], shut it down! [He chants, then returns to
> speaking:] We want the world to know that ya'll are treating us
> like ISIS, and you [the press] wanna put a mic in front of my
> mouth and ask us how we feel? How [in] the hell you think
> we feel?
>
> PEARSON, black male organizer, one-year anniversary vigil for Brown

Local law enforcement agencies (i.e., formal social control) have traditionally been tasked with addressing community or neighborhood disorder (e.g., vagrancy, drunkenness). This arrangement seemed reasonable, as police were largely responsible for maintaining and preserving order. However, policing disorder among black communities has historically proved to be different or racialized. In segregated black spaces, policing is often followed by regulating and scrutinizing black citizens excessively and then increasing such efforts when blacks are found in or within close proximity to predominantly white places.[39] Negative attitudes toward the police (ATP) and contentious responses therefore remain a constant. More specific to this study, it is for these reasons—racialized police treatment and black citizens' subsequent experiences with the police—that such encounters are factored in as disorder in black communities. Furthermore, since police were already facing scrutiny in black communities before Ferguson, it is ironic that they emerged in a worse light post-Ferguson. Police indiscretions that were witnessed and experienced by black citizens during the Ferguson civil unrest generally included police presence from overlapping jurisdictions, spontaneous policing by these forces in contradiction of one another during protests, overt escalation of conflicts through provocative police actions and as part of a militarized police (MP) continuum, and the coining of the term Ferguson Effect as a backlash against black mobilization efforts and justification for police ineptitude.[40]

It was therefore under some of the greatest duress of civil unrest for black citizens and during the commemoration of the one-year anniversary of Brown's death that the aforementioned community organizer, Pearson, called out the hypocrisy of the police and others generally in demanding peace *from* black citizens. Pearson recast the Establishment and police especially as the ultimate disturbers or provocateurs and addressed the brazenness with which blacks were perceivably being treated: as if they were enemy combatants comparable to ISIS. In short, Pearson (re)ordered disorder and backlash from the black perspective. Along with the protester Dexter, he recast blacks as advocates of peace who were unwilling to forego it, irrespective of discrimination. Similarly, I discuss the effects of racialized policing as leaving blacks feeling no different than they would feel when facing crime in black communities.[41] "Respect and human decency for people of color are compromised by officers through everyday interactions. Efforts to decrease crime and victimization, particularly in vulnerable communities, become indistinguishable when the trade-off is police aggression arbitrarily applied."[42] Moreover, "shut it down," part of the protest chant in Pearson's comments, speaks to black citizens' shutting down "business as usual" for the dominant.[43] This action turns the tables by denying everyday comforts to them. Since blacks disproportionately contend with the consequences of a broad range of criminal and noncriminal institutional decisions and conditions, ranging from derelict buildings to differential policing—seemingly with no sense of concern about black lives or the quality of them—black direct action returns the favor. As one citizen plainly put it at a Ferguson City Council meeting, "You will not rest until we can."[44] The idea is to afford whites the same level of everyday discomfort or uncertainty that blacks experience by participating in noncriminal disruptions such as blocking highways and closing shopping malls.

As things now stand, formal policing alone cannot be successful in black communities. In order for that to happen, policing would have to become what it has historically been for white communities—that is, resident driven (e.g., involving unsuspecting, voluntary experiences)—extending full protection and the benefit of the doubt to black citizens. Furthermore, most black citizens who live in high disorder and crime areas are law abiding, so protecting and serving them calls for transforming the broader culture and police subculture.

Formal Social Control: Community Policing Compromised

Community policing had in part become the contemporary policing answer for tackling disorder and even crime, particularly in black places.[45] Its success significantly depended on neighborhood volunteers: black citizens willing to plan and organize efforts with the police through various agreed-upon programs and initiatives (e.g., a neighborhood watch).[46] Interestingly, the tenets of community policing to some degree counter stereotypical depictions of black citizens as being uninterested in preserving their communities. This situation contains numerous contradictions. As a case in point, why would community policing be offered as an option for reform—predicated upon black citizens' involvement—if blacks supposedly do not care about their communities and are generally not willing to do anything to offset disorder and crime? Furthermore, what are the actual possibilities for true community policing or for the policing of black communities post-Ferguson on the heels of previous research showing that some poor blacks hold unfavorable views of the program, and now, in addition to police militarization and ISIS-like treatment of blacks, tear gas, bean-bag systems, and rubber bullets are used?[47] How about the suggestions of the Ferguson Effect?[48] This is a "blame-the-victim" campaign against black citizens post-Ferguson. Such community policing suggestions appear disingenuous. History shows the police as both overpolicing and underpolicing in black communities.[49] Their disengagement (e.g., delayed responses, no responses) did not begin with Ferguson.[50] More important, while there is no comprehensive empirical evidence for a Ferguson Effect, there is a wealth of data that demonstrates the existence of discriminatory, disconnected policing long before Brown's death.[51]

The state continuously reveals the ever-evolving extent to which it is willing to go in policing communities of color. These efforts result in both direct and vicarious experiences for black citizens particularly and are the reason that community policing has been starkly contradicted by the use of police paramilitary units (PPUs) in the twenty-first century.[52] Although there have been some instances throughout St. Louis in which the police have collaborated with local citizens and organizations generally to launch various programs and initiatives, PPU interactions now exist in the background of both pre- and post-Ferguson black citizen–police interactions. Black citizens have been disproportionately exposed to direct and indirect private or mass combat-like standoffs in private homes and in entire communities.[53] This has especially been the case in the suburbs, where there are "black" and "white" sides of town and where race, place, and policing convey an interactive effect through increased group and racial threats.[54]

There are several notable aspects of the role of community policing and the normalization of PPUs post-Ferguson. While some research on community policing contrarily suggests a decrease in disorder (i.e., in the perception of it) and some favorable attitudes toward community policing among citizens and police, it remains subjectively dependent on neighborhood context.[55] The twenty-first-century use of PPUs as community policing's extension is contradictory, racialized, and normalized at the higher end of the militarized police (MP) continuum.[56] Despite initial suggestions about using PPUs for hostage situations, terrorism, and other similar crises, research has shown a 1,400 percent increase in their deployment and has shown their use is directly correlated with the war on drugs.[57] That is, the proposed total crackdown on drugs in actuality translated into the mass targeting and incarceration of poor black citizens.[58] PPUs have become commonplace, from no-knock drug raids to policing of hot spots.[59] Some of these tactics have been seriously botched, resulting in questionable citizen deaths, but they are nevertheless a part of the MP continuum and presumably a complement to community policing.[60] Let us now turn to how police officials link PPUs and community policing.

Researchers Peter B. Kraska and Victor E. Kappeler, in "Militarizing American Police: The Rise and Normalization of Paramilitary Units," documented "a self-proclaimed community police chief" as stating: "It's going to come to the point that the only people [who] are going to be able to deal with these problems are highly trained tactical teams with proper equipment to go into a neighborhood and clear the neighborhood and hold it[,] allowing community policing and problem[-]oriented policing officers to come in and start turning the neighborhood around."[61] This viewpoint sees the policing of disorder and crime (and citizens)—even if not fully enacted in all places—as *beginning* with an escalation in force (e.g., not tolerating "broken windows") and *increasing* to the point of full militarized police saturation and neighborhood occupation.[62] Only then would the community and problem-oriented aspects of policing be introduced to neighborhoods.[63] This approach would essentially mean putting entire black communities under siege—implementing policy and practices perceivably in direct contrast to peace and order, as often projected onto black citizens.

Black citizen–police partnerships come "at a price," as study participant Diane, age fifty-two, put it, as she underwent a cost-benefit analysis of police interactions that made her vulnerable to overlapping victimizations prior to Ferguson and even more so post-Ferguson. Black citizens, especially the poor, face "damned if they do, and damned if they don't" decisions in their everyday lives. They risk neighborhood interpersonal backlash for appearing to collaborate with the police against a *few*, since twenty-first-century policing post-Ferguson especially appears to criminalize *all* citizens of color indiscriminately. The post-Ferguson period futuristically reflects the normalization of treating black citizens as if they were enemy combatants and of the use of PPUs—a continuum of passive- to super-aggressive police tactics. In response, black citizens rely on social ties for organizing—buffering disorder and its effects (e.g., discrimination) and implementing informal social control in their communities.

Informal Social Control: Black Social Ties and Community Participation

> We all collectively called each other and said we gon' come out [to the protest] . . . . 'Cause if we don't do it, who else gon' do it? . . . We gotta stand [up] for each other. . . . That's the reason I come out here. I've been out here like two or three times this week just to show support. . . . Injustice is what it is, . . . and things like this is gon' push us [blacks] toward the right direction to get *that* justice.
>
> SABIEN, black male protester

Social ties are established among members of a community. As evidenced by Sabien and his friends, there are social bonds that hinge on common beliefs and shared values.[64] The fact that social ties are invariably part of an informal social network and often are used to explain the presence or absence of informal social control in communities of color is significant in this project. The diversity, size, and strength of social ties are integral to dealing with community and neighborhood conditions. They tend to be familial, and identifiable; for example, black citizens directly or indirectly refer to one another as "play" family members ("play" brother, "play" cousin).[65] The primarily black Ferguson protest community does this, often referring to one another as "family" or "fam," as there is an informal understanding that members are looking out for each other. It is through these connections and everyday exchanges that black citizens are empowered enough to organize—to respond or buffer themselves—against systemic discrimination and its effects (e.g., victimization) despite stereotypical, pathological narratives advanced by many white critics and the broader dominant culture.[66] Here is how a black female protester, Janet, recalled impromptu organizing in protests:

> I heard those young [Ferguson] activists sayin', "We got this [managing protests and protesters]. . . . *YA'LL* [police] disperse! We don't need the military and all that. . . . *WE'LL* handle it. *WE'LL* de-escalate it [the conflict]. . . . We got it!" They did a good job too. . . . They knew how [to do it]. . . . I was happy to see that . . . they picked their pants up, . . . held their chests up.

Her comments speak to the efforts of the mostly black activists and protesters—particularly young black men—who took to monitoring direct actions as a counter action to the militarized police tactics. By recycling the police directives, "YA'LL disperse" turned the lens on the police as the heavy-handed peace disturbers and recast young black men as capable leaders—who proudly "picked their pants up" and "held their chests up" to curtail state mistreatment of their community. This is one of countless instances in which we see a resurgence of black empowerment and mobilizing that becomes a direct counter to the pervasive denigration of black social organization. Moreover, these actions are not limited to protests; they also occur outside of direct action and through everyday neighborhood exchanges in places where social services or public amenities are often subpar and there is limited news coverage compared with that given to crime stories.

Contemporary research makes the case for social organization among black citizens, even those economically disadvantaged.[67] Quantitative and qualitative studies at the ecological and individual levels, through the application of diverse social organization perspectives (i.e., on urban poverty, systemic issues, and social needs), have found that black citizens are variously engaged with community organizations or participation depending on a number of factors.[68] These include (1) *community or neighborhood characteristics* (e.g., racial/ethnic heterogeneity, residential stability/instability, stable low/middle income), (2) *types of relationships*—informal (e.g., kinship ties, friendships, and neighboring) and formal (e.g., group solidarity, collective efficacy), (3) *types of participation*—informal (e.g., individual integration, problem solving, or neighboring) and formal (membership in organizations), and (4) *motivations for participation* (i.e., instrumental, expressive).[69]

Quantitative Research   Recent studies have found citizens forming social ties and participating in efforts to counter or buffer disorder in their communities. This trend has occurred despite fear and assumptions of distrust, as illustrated in a study by theorists Ross and Jang, who, through a quantitative sampling of 2,482 phone interviews, found that social ties and participation correlated with perceptions of neighborhood disorder. Those perceiving their neighborhoods as having high levels of disorder were thought to possibly have low levels of informal (i.e., individual/informal integration) and formal (i.e., group/organization membership) social ties, and vice versa. However, Ross and Jang found that social ties worked as buffers against the effects of disorder—fear and mistrust—through mostly individual, informal integration and less formal participation in groups or organizations.[70] In this sense, social ties did not eliminate disorder but rather reduced its effects. Further, my study resembles Ross and Jang's in that it too examines the buffering effects of social ties on disorder—albeit ethnographically. It also finds that black citizens primarily participate individually through informal integration and reciprocity and participate less often formally in groups (see table 1 in chapter 3).

Similarly, Ralph B. Taylor examined the impact of social ties, providing insight into citizens' attachments to place(s) and responses across neighborhoods.[71] Relying on survey data from 1,622 phone interviews—a mixed field/phone approach for completing surveys—Taylor asked about neighborhood conditions and reviewed the variety of citizens' responses to them across sixty-six randomly sampled Baltimore neighborhoods. Consistent with the systemic model of attachment and the neighborhood use model, Taylor used Furstenberg's (1996) citizen-based classification and individual-level responses (i.e., avoidance/accommodation, mobilization/resistance) and found neighborhood stability and class to be the greatest predictors of citizens' attachment to and involvement with their neighborhoods. In addition, as questions have persisted regarding the roles of ethnic homogeneity and community versus neighborhood-level examinations, my project considers and accounts for multilevel, macro-to-micro, racially homogenous analyses through community, neighborhood, and individual ethnographic responses, as diversely affecting and in many instances varyingly increasing attachments, alliances, and participation in unlikely places post-Ferguson.[72]

Pamela Wilcox Rountree and Barbara D. Warner also relied on the systemic model to explain the effectiveness of social ties in fighting crime.[73] Since research had been limited in measuring the value of social ties across social groups—race, class, gender, or age—or had produced mixed findings similar to my project mostly regarding race, Rountree and Warner examined the efficacy of social ties through a gendered context.[74] Using aggregate-level data from one hundred Seattle census tracts, they highlighted the interactive effects of female-headed households at the community level and "female ties within a systemic model of community crime control" and found the following: (1) the link between female social ties and social control is conditional and contingent upon neighborhood context, (2) female social ties have a significant statistical effect on violent crime control compared to men, and (3) female social ties having a deterrent effect depending on the proportion of female-headed households in the neighborhood and then are most effective where there are few of them.

Theorist Melvin Oliver, on the other hand, reframed the community question by asking how urban industrialization had affected the structuring of black social ties. He conducted his study by employing a network analytic technique and three proposed community arguments (i.e., community lost, community saved, and community liberated).[75] Oliver examined black organizational patterns across three contrasting black neighborhoods in Los Angeles using 352 phone and computer-assisted interviews (CATI) and found that the urban black community was *not* disorganized and pathological.[76] Like this study's results, he found blacks connecting and developing kinship ties based on "community saved" and "community liberated" perspectives. Oliver's study also showed fictive kin and friendships through reciprocity—often reciprocal favors as found in this study and in Ross and Jang's work—a common vehicle for organizing or arranging resources and services.[77] This is found especially among poor blacks.

Ethnographic Research   There has been limited ethnographic work done to examine black communities or neighborhoods that are organized around social ties. However, Mary Pattillo's article "Sweet Mothers and Gangbangers: Managing Crime in a Black Middle Class Neighborhood" focused ethnographic attention on neighborhood organization.[78] Relying on participant observations and twenty-eight taped, in-depth interviews, she uniquely situated her analysis in Groveland, a black middle-class Chicago neighborhood. Using the systemic model of social organization theory, she examined neighborhood responses with residential stability as a benefit for establishing social ties or an intertwined network. This network was a blend of noncriminal and criminal residents, whom she found were preventing the complete eradication of disorder and crime in the neighborhood due to their own indiscretions but who were instrumental in containing and managing them. In short, Pattillo discovered that crime or gang leaders had the same values and interests in maintaining some semblance of order in their neighborhoods that noncriminal residents did. She also discovered that for various reasons crime and gang leaders found neighborhood alliances necessary and beneficial. Like Oliver, Pattillo advanced the idea of organization in the black community— that residents do organize to address disorder—but the ways in which they do so deserve more examination.

Similarly, Elijah Anderson's *Code of the Street* set a precedent for my project though its depiction of black life by ethnographically capturing a particular kind of organizing—culturally coded in black neighborhoods as "decent" or "street," with the "decent" conforming to conventional norms or "orderly" living. The "street" citizens, on the other hand, generally act contrarily.[79] They act out of survival. For them, this sometimes means acting in ways that reflect or circumvent their social conditions (e.g., deprivation, isolation, distrust of police). Anderson's work is also significant in that it called attention to the informal social control that exists amid disorder through black citizens' use of street codes.[80] He highlighted unofficial, informal neighborhood rules that make "interpersonal violence" or the threat of it and other forms of disorder manageable in the community.[81]

Other theorists have also highlighted similar socialization and organizational processes that serve as buffers or strategies for action. Examples are Ann Swindler's unofficial street-level toolkits; Mary Pattillo-McCoy's cultural toolkits of the church—"prayer, call and response interaction" for organizing; E. L. E. Bell and S. M. Nkomo's "armoring" as a counter to racism; Rod Brunson's and Ronald Weitzer's use of cultural codes to explain black citizens' interactions when "negotiating" contentious police climates; and Waverly Duck's reliance on kinship ties and codes for explaining street life in the context of drug dealing.[82] It is through these learned, unofficial resources and methods that black citizens navigate their everyday interactions.

Furthermore, Anderson's work provided a trailblazing framework for explaining neighborhood nuances that hinge on "respect"—which by and large was a serious determinant for black alliance and community participation in this project. In addition, Nikki Jones's *The Chosen Ones: Black Men and the Politics of Redemption* ethnographically extended the significance of neighborhood respectability by examining the seemingly impossible plight of black men as they attempt to "make good" on improving their lives. Jones depicted an interplay of masculinity, accountability, and transformation in which black men move from past indiscretions and reputations in the streets to nobility in their community. This study is extraordinary and timely in that Jones called attention to men as "residents-turned-activists," as they work to make a difference through new redemptive identities.[83]

Jones uniquely directed attention to redemption as a transitional process for black men through antiviolence organizing. More directly, as Jones highlighted redemptive space and the complexity for achieving it among black men, she furthered social organization through the politics of crime fighting. Finally, Jones addressed the meaning of *community* by focusing attention on a series of networks and roles ranging from "gatekeepers" to buffers and bridges—all the while depicting black men's ability to redeem themselves and participate in community change despite past and ongoing social constraints.[84]

CONCLUSION

Just to see . . . to see this [Brown's death and civil unrest] as part of history, . . . I feel like this is, you know, bringing out our community together . . . trying to make things right!

PORTIA, a black female protester

There is evidence of black citizens participating in and organizing their communities and neighborhoods through various alliances. This project ethnographically examines *how* black citizens protect and serve one another—implementing informal social control through social ties and a socialized cultural etiquette—amid macro and micro levels of engagement that act as counters or buffers to disorder, crime, and their effects. This study highlights the ambiguousness of black life and continuously evolving everyday, unofficial exchanges that structure the black community. It presents insight into a more holistic strategy of black efforts to preserve black lives during and following civil unrest and captures that strategy as a springboard for black mobilization, direct action, and renewed forms of resistance.

This study also extends disorder and social ties literature by offering a racial/cultural reconceptualization of disorder through a black cultural perspective and as afforded and introduced through post-Ferguson context. Since blackness and black citizens defy dominant categorization and are not monolithic, especially in the creation and wake of a twenty-first-century empowered movement, this study lends itself to broader explanations for mixed results through the systemic model of social organization. It addresses a myriad of relationships, alliances, attachments, and participation among mostly poor homogenous black populations as they are able and willing to engage despite age-old constructed narratives.

Since research has been limited in ethnographically examining motivating factors in simultaneously combating the overlapping victimizations of blacks (i.e., by police brutality and interpersonal neighborhood violence), through a post-Ferguson context this study extends and reframes such experiences broadly as discrimination and, more specifically, as the abuse and devaluation of black people in provoking favorable community responses (informal integration and formal participation) and engagement. The interactive effects of black victimization, social ties and mobilization, and police continuums have not been a significant part of contemporary disorder or the race, place, and policing frameworks—part of the reason that this project centers the evolution of black action post-Ferguson. The theoretical tenets have to be more inclusive and reframed in ways that call attention to racial/cultural history and perspectives as part of contemporary occurrences and examinations. Individual, informal integration is addressed in the following chapter, as it was the more likely response (i.e., in the form of reciprocity) and form of participation among black citizens compared to formal organizations post-Ferguson.

3. "A Change *Gotta* Come": Informal Integration

Flashback.

LAP DISSOLVE TO:

WEST FLORISSANT BOULEVARD—ACROSS THE STREET AND JUST EAST OF THE
BURNED DOWN QUIKTRIP—DAY TEN OF PROTESTING, AFTERNOON
*August 18, 2014. It is afternoon, and having just arrived, I am walking
down West Florissant Boulevard toward the protesters.*

As I was walking down West Florissant Boulevard toward the protest, I was
met by a black female protester who cautioned me on her way out. This
dynamic had become common—that is, protesters informing one another
about things transpiring at scenes of protests, especially if someone
appeared to be just arriving. Inversely, if opportunity permitted, newly
arriving protesters would ask those who appeared to have been there for a
while about the state of things "on the ground." These short, impromptu
exchanges occurred in a manner similar to police briefings and likely more
fluidly. Protesters were shifting in and out of protest zones regularly. As
this particular protester approached, she told me to be careful and watch
myself "'cause they [police] down there [on the street] trippin'." I stopped
her and asked what was going on and what she meant by her comment; I
wanted clarity. More specifically, I was interested in the actions of the police
or the degree of aggression that I might encounter. After days of unending
protests, I had witnessed some of the worst of black citizen–police interactions—short of shootings in real time—and was frequently assessing my
own vulnerabilities. Furthermore, I felt more threatened by police than I
did by protesters, even though some of their behaviors could also be com-

promising. As a general rule of thumb, I was always trying to gauge and assess direct action before entering into it, as were others.

The black female protester responded, "You have to keep moving and stay on the sidewalk"—the police were threatening to arrest people who were standing still or in the street. As for protesters in the street, I understood that the police would consider their congregating a safety issue; someone could be hit by a car. However, I was quite taken aback by the notion that no one could be "just standing still" anywhere. This was a direct action, so such a directive was inherently impossible to comply with by virtue of the nature of civil disobedience, not to mention that at any given time there had been and could be hundreds to thousands of protesters around. This situation meant that many people, with varying physical abilities, would be constantly trying to move (or not move) within a small area. Logistically, this condition seemed to be ensnaring and became more of a cause for citizen concern. It increased the vulnerability of protesters and legitimized more spontaneous arrests of anyone present, regardless their actions. I could see and hear the distress of this protester as she was leaving, and I was also somewhat alarmed. My privileged space in academia did not make me exempt from possible police aggression. So I asked again about the "standing still" part, and essentially what she said was that a "five-second rule" had recently been imposed that appeared to have been extemporaneously created. If we appeared to be not moving for more than five seconds—which is how we processed the order—we risked being arrested. I thanked the woman and uneasily but determinedly continued walking toward the protest. I was especially interested in verifying what she had just shared with me.

As I moved closer to and into the group of protesters, they were fervently shouting and repeatedly reminding one another to "stay together and keep moving . . . just keep moving." All the while, they were complaining about feeling bullied, trapped, and even afraid. They believed that the police were sneakily violating their rights through the application of improper restrictions and could freely and unjustifiably arrest them. The police were also blatantly instructing protesters to keep moving, a command that only provoked them. They had been nonviolent yet were still being accosted, so some of them stopped to talk with CNN's Don Lemon about the situation. Since the press was often nearby and reporting live, this seemed to be an opportune time for citizens to express their concerns to the world, since police aggression was often hidden or below the radar. The situation then began to escalate, with the police ordering everyone, including Lemon, to move and pushing them.[1]

I purposefully cleared the crowd and stood off to the side of the CNN camera crew in order to avoid being captured in the live newsfeed. I often avoided media in this way, except in instances when I perceived that being near them would be a safe position—a buffer against fear and arrest.[2] The media presence sometimes minimized the mistreatment of citizens, since some police appeared to be more conscious of their behavior in front of a live camera. For me, being arrested would mean time away from direct action, causing me to miss documenting critical turns of events in the heat of real-time protests.

Suddenly a couple of protest leaders intercepted, directed, and led protesters away to a pseudo-safe meeting place. There, protesters coalesced and rested (e.g., by standing still or sitting down) in an empty parking lot behind a local business. This place became somewhat of a temporary staging ground where protesters privately and freely vented their personal feelings. Here is how some of them, in almost overlapping statements, discussed fear:

ETHAN: I'm not afraid of 'em [police].
HAILEY: I live in the City of Ferguson and I'm scared . . . [She is interrupted.]
TIANA: [Well,] I AM scared [too] 'cause I don't wanna go to jail.
ETHAN: [Speaking as if he is able to protect her:] You ain't going to jail!
HAILEY: If it wasn't for my kids [thinking aloud] . . . [and] my family, [I would not be out here], . . . but I'll just stay here and support this battle . . . 'cause a change *gotta* come. . . . [Yelling:] This [is about] EVERYBODY. . . . [This is about] respecting everybody!
TIANA: [In the background, yelling:] "I don't wanna go to jail 'cause I got rights out here. . . . I got rights!"

This exchange spoke to the nervousness of some black protesters. Their fears were real, as police encounters were escalating from rules to threats that seemed to be routinely changing. Similar conversations continued as protesters and protest leaders encouraged and conferred with one another about how to proceed. After decompressing together, they returned to the main street (i.e., West Florissant Road). There they continued with refreshed perspectives and directives as if approaching a next shift.

FADE OUT

This chapter examines how black citizens came to perceive disorder (e.g., discrimination, police brutality, black violence) and endure its effects (e.g., fear, mistrust) across communities. More directly, it aims to show the conundrum facing and sentiments of black citizens in real-time conflict. It is in the heat of the moment that we witness people grappling with admitted fear and seeking redress for it. This chapter affords an opportunity to account for social issues and ensuing environmental cues that perceivably challenge black citizens' safety. It is through recounting protest exchanges and other seemingly compromising interactions that this chapter reveals how black citizens engage in informal community integration. They form alliances or social ties wherein chatting, visiting, and reciprocity become crucial means of safeguarding themselves. Furthermore, it is in the aforementioned context that we can think critically about how black citizens navigate perceived disorder and its effects in other locations. As is the case at protest sites, it is in mostly disadvantaged neighborhoods that black citizens are sometimes first compromised and then move to assess and determine the degree to which and circumstances in which they trust, respect, and help each other interactively. In addition, it is in protests and places where mostly disadvantaged black citizens reside that we learn of black citizens becoming anxious and yet still sacrificially engaging to protect and serve one another, out of a sense of obligation.

FIVE SECONDS TO FEAR AND MISTRUST

What was most noticeable on that day about the five-second rule was the comfort with which protesters openly communicated their feelings. Many had not appeared to know one another prior to the civil unrest and uprising. Protesters were becoming familiar with one another—recognizing each other and growing accustomed to how each "moved and grooved" under duress. This often meant learning how each positioned himself or herself in relation to others and personally connected with others during downtimes (e.g., when there were no immediate threats of police standoffs), as well as in fiery confrontations (e.g., during impromptu police standoffs). This was also the case with protest leaders and organizers. Familiarity, solidarity, and empowerment increased among protesters, almost as if they had been derived from each incident that had occurred (e.g., a police clash) and seemed to lead to more commitment to and participation in the movement. Relationships were formed through communication and reciprocity, particularly among those who had become constant participants in direct action. By spending unending days and nights with the same people, protesters coalesced as a community. Their shared plight of historic injustices, along with the imposition of the new "five-second rule"—at least for that day—affirmed this cohesion. The state apparently knew no bounds in its aggression toward black citizens, especially those protesting. It also exacerbated black citizens' fear and mistrust of state authority and law enforcement and contradicted police and state suggestions about resolution and improvement.

The climate had increasingly worsened with each day, until protesters could not keep up with what they could or could not do to express public dissent without being punished (e.g., arrested). The five-second rule was one example of this situation. Concern about being arrested—or the threat of it—was a recurring theme, especially during protests. The use of pepper spray and arrests were mostly daytime threats; tear gas and rubber bullets were additional threats more commonly used at night. Diverging from the exchanges with Jean, the protest leader who had sung about "not wanting to go to jail" in front of the police (see chapter 2), the five-second rule confessions were occurring away from law enforcement. They were privately disclosed among allies (i.e., protesters and protest leaders), then taken account of by fellow protesters and addressed as strengths rather than as weaknesses. In this context, protesters who expressed fear but nevertheless did not leave appeared courageous. Their resolve to stay spoke volumes, as there was an unspoken understanding among protesters that everyone had personal obligations (e.g., child care, employment) that sometimes determined their latitude—that is, how long they could be present and the extent to which they could engage—in the movement.

Since the degree to which protesters could be involved in possible police clashes and endure subsequent sanctions differed, many protests were intentionally peaceful. Although aggrieved and angered by what they believed were injustices, the protesters primarily wanted to be present and stand in solidarity for social change with other black citizens. Their in-group status (e.g., race) and common experiences led to empowerment and ownership of a new movement. This development posed "political danger" (e.g., increased resistance and collective action) to the state, as "the people [had] never felt closer" to or "more threatened . . . by legal violence exercised without moderation or restraint."[3] Black citizens collectively wanted to express their First Amendment rights—at least as they knew and understood them and could do so within the constraints of civil disobedience. However, as many protesters set out to engage lawfully in protests, they faced seemingly unrestricted state discretionary power and tactics and subsequent entrapment. There was a persistent sense that the game was rigged—a feeling that provoked and catalyzed the primarily black direct action and increased the protesters' ongoing sense of distrust and fear of the system and of the police generally. The implementation of the five-second rule, along with other impromptu directives stated as law, involved them in inadvertent exposure to possible criminalization, even when they were perceivably acting prudently. *Any* resistance to state social control appeared intolerable to the police, and their apparent practice of making up rules on a dime seemed to confirm the protesters' fears.

Protests became constant up close and personal reminders of how black life was devalued when it butted up against dominant expectations and state aggression. The protests were occurring under compromising circumstances, with physical and social cues reminiscent of insurmountable state power, control, blame, and backlash as a response to black resistance. The police's show of force alone was overwhelming, as their efforts to maintain order or ensure absolute compliance made the mostly black peaceful protesters subject to extemporaneous expectations from law enforcement and subsequently to all forms of police aggression. Thus, there was a continual need to be mindful of influxes of protesters, as some were more radical or took more risks than others did. The "no-limit soldiers" at times acted in total defiance of the police and all state actions (e.g., yelling things at police, staring them down), especially when they sensed that more clashes were looming. With each escalating event, protesters were further angered; their resolve to dig in deeper and commit to the movement was solidified.

At the other end of the spectrum, there were "plants" or provocateurs embedded within the protests. These people deliberately attempted to pass themselves off as peaceful, when in actuality they were involved in the protests to ensure that hostile exchanges with the police occurred. Since the police had revealed themselves as manufacturing reasons (e.g., the five-second rule) to react violently against protesters, it seemingly did not take much for antagonists to goad them (e.g., by throwing bottles and rocks at them). These provocateurs purposely played into the hands of the police by acting as adversaries who instigated encounters and then inconspicuously withdrew or hid themselves within peaceful groups of people. These actions resulted in mostly peaceful black protesters being accosted by the police. These incidents were perceivably instigated primarily by white citizens acting as provocateurs—although black citizens were not exempt from playing such roles—who disguised themselves as allies and were sometimes not even from the St. Louis region. Protesters also suspected that some provocateurs were undercover law enforcement agents. Therefore, some members of the protest community learned to clear (i.e., watch and assess) protest sites and crowds in a manner similar to law enforcement's practices. The idea was to pay particularly close attention to individuals who were not readily recognized or who otherwise seemed to not belong in the environment. The need for such scrutiny reflected protesters' (including my) growing distrust and suspicion of others.

I was especially cognizant of protesters' concerns because they were similar to my own, and I made a point of being "in the know"—genuinely forging ties—identifying, connecting, and engaging within the protest community whenever and wherever possible. This engagement was inevitable because I was regularly present in direct action, at town halls, and at other locations, and as a St. Louisan and local professional, I was already familiar with people in various locations. My frequent involvement in these activities, along with my visible preexisting commitment to social justice throughout the region, was significant. All of these factors increased my credit (credibility) in the streets, as did the word of those who knew and vouched for me as "family."

Nevertheless, I sometimes still felt challenged, as I could always sense mistrust of me in the environment despite my insider status (i.e., my blackness and being a native St. Louisan). This awareness sometimes made me feel uncomfortable while examining and methodically documenting direct actions. I was constantly negotiating my behaviors and also engaging in protect-and-serve actions. Regardless of my academic platform, I wanted to emulate care and safety rather than fear; therefore, I always greeted people and engaged in friendly small talk.[4] During downtimes we talked about matters ranging from being tired and hungry to losing weight from running to avoid pepper spray, tear gas, and police force. The interaction was about lightening a heavy situation—confronting perceived injustices and broad threats to the black community. Protesters would sometimes overexert themselves, which warranted wellness checks such as "Are you okay?" or "Would you like some water?" or "Do you need to sit down for a second?" Willingness to help to ensure the well-being and safety of fellow protesters went a long way toward establishing and maintaining respect and camaraderie. I can also recall times when even in passing we would tell one another to "be careful" and "stay safe," especially when the atmosphere was fluid. People were conscious of their need to account for evolving actions and interactions, from police to protesters, and a concerted effort was made to do so, as situations could change drastically on a dime.

Plants and informants remained a concern. The mostly black protesters mistrusted unfamiliar, unvouched-for, noninteracting people and were concerned that they might be embedded within with protests; this was in addition to their concerns about police aggression and the provocateurs who instigated "state-sanctioned violence" at the expense of protesters. These provocateurs provoked narratives that increased the risks for the protest community and undermined the black effort, which inevitably became talking points and rationales for committing violent acts against black citizens; these narratives in many cases did not match real-time, actual accounts of actions on the ground. This situation demonstrates the significance of ethnographical documentation.

Protesters were aware of inaccurate, disparaging reports about them; they too followed the news. Consequently, members of the press—especially those at certain networks—increasingly found themselves being admonished by protesters. On the other hand, the media presence provided cover, safe space, and confirmation of protesters' accounts in some instances, such as CNN reporter Don Lemon's reporting on the "five-second-rule day." He captured in a live feed the inconsistent and excessive mistreatment of protesters by the police as he and protesters were being incited and unnecessarily pushed.[5]

Nevertheless, there were reporters, commentators, and contributors who appeared to act in a negative manner and who without fail depicted blacks in the worst light, stereotypically as hardened and deviant actors, irrespective of the particular direct action being covered. Consequently, those media outlets found themselves strategically shut out by some organizers. They were publicly rebuked, warned, and at times shooed away by black citizens. Negative media coverage often resulted in some protesters shouting directives for the media to get cameras "out of people's faces"; ordering the media to stand back, stand down, and not film or record at all; purposely shutting cameras out of direct view of actions; and establishing human barricades to distance the media so that they could not hear protesters' plans. The dissemination of protest information became a commodity, and a person *had* to be considered family to receive any. This tactic was particularly notable during sensitive moments such as prayer or emotional exchanges in which survivors of violence or families of victims were experiencing breakdowns (e.g., crying, venting). Those moments were reserved for "family only" (i.e., biological and fictive kin among protesters) to "love on them" (comfort them) and protect their right to respond privately by being outwardly transparent, vulnerable, and emotional, but only within the group.

Years later one of the most visible incidents of protesters clashing with media followed the 2017 acquittal of former police officer Jason Stockley for the murder of Anthony Smith. Due to a perceived pattern of disparaging accounts about the black community (e.g., about crime and black citizen–police conflict), networks and reporters such as KTVI Fox 2 News's Dan Gray became targets for admonishment.[6] This network had been perceived by some as reporting negatively about the black community. As a result, they were shut out by the community. Nevertheless, protesters balanced and countered one another's actions and even provided some measure of protection for the media during protests. Some black protesters routinely intercepted heated exchanges as an informal check and balance on one another's behaviors. The fear was that someone might go too far in the heat of the moment, which would only result in negative reprisals and propaganda criminalizing the black effort.

"Who Are You Here With?"

Imagine.

LAP DISSOLVE TO:

WEST FLORISSANT BOULEVARD—ONE-YEAR ANNIVERSARY WEEKEND MARKING BROWN'S DEATH—NIGHT.
August 10, 2015. It is almost midnight, and after a full day of direct action, protests continue. This is the main protest location for the night.

It had been a day of provocations, one that had begun with civil disobedience training followed up by direct action at the Thomas F. Eagleton US Courthouse in downtown St. Louis and the shutdown of Interstate 70. Protests were ongoing in St. Louis despite the decline in national and international media coverage. There had been countless police encounters and arrests spanning St. Louis City and County. By nightfall we were back on West Florissant Boulevard (at ground zero) in Ferguson for more direct action.

The police were out in full riot gear as usual and staged on one side of the street, with protesters on the opposite side. Periodically, the police would march up and down the street; protesters would do the same, sometimes chanting to drumbeats. This was the calm period, with opposing lines for police and protesters, each congregating on their respective side of the street but keeping a watchful eye on the other. Then suddenly one side would do something provocative, as if to break up the monotony. The tension would increase, making it easier for snatch-and-grab arrests to occur. This tactic was common but was infrequently employed. The police would zero in on individual protesters, swiftly dash into a group, snatch the targeted people out of the crowd—sending other protesters scattering—and arrest them. It was during these types of exchanges that protesters sometimes chanted:

Back up, back up
We want FREE-DOM, FREE-DOM!
All these killer ass cops,
We don't need 'em, need 'em!

Snatch-and-grabs seemed to happen more to known protesters or those easily identified with the movement rather than to those who were more moderate or unknown within the protest community. After several bouts of such exchanges (e.g., standoffs, snatch-and-grabs), both sides would eventually retreat to their original positions on the street.

It was during one of these moments of retreat that I noticed a lone white male idly standing on the protesters' side of the street. A group of young black protesters was calling him out as working with the police and threatening him. Oddly, he appeared unfazed by these charges and ignored the threats. Those who were observing seemed more alarmed and concerned about his safety. I had been talking with a black female protester when she decided to ask this white male protester questions. We felt relatively safe around the group that was hurling threats at him. Our position in the protest was clear, as was theirs compared with his. We understood the young folks' concerns and audacity. They were posted next to a car, with music blasting, talking and keeping watch—protecting protesters' territory as if "on the block" (i.e., a neighborhood block)—and the optics presented an uneasy scene. This visual of what seemed to be a detached, lone white man, late at night and comfortably in the dark on what was essentially "the black side" of the street, was disconcerting. There were other white citizens out protesting too, but they were involved, recognized, or vouched for by the protest community. This man displayed no behaviors indicating that he was an ally, appearing oblivious to the codes of protesting (the particular kind of etiquette for direct action). He was a spectator who was not interacting. His demeanor was odd, and no one could be sure why he was there.

As threats directed toward him continued, the black female protester with whom I had been talking made small talk with him and asked questions such as, "Where are you from? Who are you out here with? Do you hear those threats? Are you not afraid?" He answered that he was a student at a local university and that he had come out by himself to support the protest. He also said that he had heard the threats but was not afraid. We were taken aback by this response because the threats were so intense and graphic that even we, as accepted members of the protest community, were alarmed. How could he, as an outsider and target, *not* be disturbed by them? Why would someone want to be among an intimate black protest group, knowing that he was not trusted and was regarded as possibly being with the police? His response led to more questions, as he now appeared to have come from a university across town by himself at midnight to show support rather than come with others during the day. I stood there with the woman as she asked more questions: "So you drove *all the way* over here at *this* time of the night *by* yourself to protest? Do you want to leave? Where did you park? Would you like us to walk you to your car?"

By now the message was clear: he should leave to quell the confusion. In fact, the female protester had explicitly encouraged him to do so, and I had agreed with her. We were afraid for him directly and for ourselves indirectly should something happen. I thought that if he were indeed with the police and had been planted on the protesters' side of the street, he was being watched by law enforcement. That scenario might explain his confidence and lack of concern for his safety. The police visibly filmed and took pictures at every protest, and this night's event was no different. It was likely that they too were constantly "clearing" (watching) the area. Therefore, any sign of distress from or danger to him—this mysterious white man—could have triggered danger for the young protesters and for us as well. We just wanted to change the dynamics, and he was not buying in, a response that was even stranger. In short, he seemed nice, approachable, and apparently nonthreatening during our conversation, although his full presentation—his body language, what he said coupled with what he did not say, and so much more about him—felt menacing. We then decided to walk away, since protest environments are constantly evolving; staying in one place for long periods is not always advisable. In the end, he thanked us but still acted suspiciously and did not appear compelled to leave. The female protester then left; she was a health-care worker and said she needed to rest for work later that morning. I stayed longer, but by all indications, nothing seemed to come of the threats—at least not while I was present.

This was also the same night, later turning to morning, on which several white men dressed in plain clothes, some camouflage, and Kevlar vests, and visibly armed with rifles walked straight through the protest site in Ferguson. This visual was jaw dropping. With countless black protesters watching in dismay from across the street, these men, better known as the "Oath Keepers," first moved about freely on the other side with the police. Black protesters were beyond livid as they watched them casually engage with and move about the riot team, with no combative responses from police in what seemed to be an ordinary occurrence. These were brazen contradictions and displays demonstrating just how devalued black lives seemed to be when unarmed blacks were compared with armed white citizens. These armed white citizens appeared acceptable and orderly to the police, in stark contrast to the previously pepper sprayed, tear-gassed, rubber-bulleted, arrested, and otherwise mistreated black citizens, who by all accounts feared death due to discriminative treatment. More specifically, this action was witnessed by blacks, who faced police aggression or the threat of it simply for being present—in many instances not for any expressed words or actions, but simply for participating in protests against police brutality. Black attendance alone apparently warranted state vengeance. Several years later a few protesters—known and accepted members of the protest family—similarly appeared visibly armed during direct action.[7] This maneuver was a form of resistance and a very stark, public pushback that extended the imagery for black citizens and protesters generally, who also had a "right to bear arms," and was a provocation to white comfort.

Protests and, more broadly, mobilization efforts that involve black citizens and police are especially risky for black citizens. As a result of day-to-day uncertainties, physical and social indications are constantly evolving in the environment that expose the vulnerabilities of mostly disadvantaged black citizens. They stir historically racial/cultural sensibilities, prompting informal alliances and sometimes unlikely arrangements and diverse responses— all solvents for distrust and fear in the face of oppression. This type of reaction also occurs in disadvantaged black neighborhoods. In places where some live, poor black citizens may find themselves knowingly or unknowingly facing spur-of-the-moment incidents and having to manage them through informal, pseudo-safe means. Even when dangers or threats do not materialize, black citizens are still cognizant of their susceptibility to risks. Let us now turn to neighborhood dynamics in which daily mental and emotional assessments and concessions emulate and transcend protests as counters to disorder (discrimination) and its effects (e.g., fear, dual victimization).

"Damned If You Do, Damned If You Don't": Neighborhood Vulnerabilities

From suburban to urban locations, some black citizens, particularly those economically disadvantaged, have faced similar plights (e.g., broad historical discrimination, the threat of police and black violence). The police, neighbors, and others residing in or passing through their communities reportedly did things that routinely compromised their safety. This situation was the case irrespective of black citizens' participation in protests. In other words, some participants lived in disadvantaged neighborhoods, participated in protests, and shared similar vulnerabilities at home and in direct action, while other black citizens did not attend protests but also faced mistrust and threats

TABLE 1. Documented Participant Exchanges

Mode of Contacts/Exchanges	Number (N = 125)
In protests/direct action—Impromptu conversations/ exchanges	75
Out of protests/direct action—Individual, in-depth interviews	41
Out of protests/direct action—Focus groups:*	9
Focus Group 1, urban = 4	
Focus Group 2, suburban = 5	

* Seven of the nine focus group participants had previously lived in both locations, urban and suburban.

TABLE 2. Participants' Perceptions

	Out of Protests/ Direct Action— Individual, In- Depth Interviews (N = 41)	Out of Protests/ Direct Action— Focus Groups (N = 9: Urban = 4; Suburban = 5)
Believed *most* black citizens in their community/neighborhood were willing to engage in or already engaged in action(s) to "protect and serve" themselves and others against disorder and/or victimization.*	41/41 = 100%	9/9 = 100%
Believed that police brutality and interpersonal neighborhood violence were equally important and alarming.	41/41 = 100%	9/9 = 100%

Believed *most* black citizens in their community/neighborhood thought police brutality and interpersonal neighborhood violence were equally important and alarming:
    Yes = 29**
    Somewhat = 6
    No = 6
	29/41 = 70%	9/9= 100%***

* Participants' responses reflect "protect and serve" questions versus "self-policing" or "policing themselves."

** The "yes, somewhat, and no" participant responses are from individual, in-depth interviews only.

*** Due to group discussions and fluctuating perceptions, focus group numbers reflect a group consensus.

from similar risks in their neighborhoods. Those who did not participate in in-depth interviews but who shared their thoughts and ideas about safety and justice with me while involved in protests often expanded on their comments about police brutality to address interpersonal neighborhood violence. Often there was a general progression to this subject in conversations when discussing the (de)valuing of black lives.

Through in-depth interviews and focus groups, participants offered their thoughts about St. Louis, their neighborhoods, safety, police, and neighborhood violence as well as their views of Ferguson civil unrest and black mobilization efforts generally (see tables 1 and 2).[8] Some discussions that I was able to record during direct actions also noted that change needed to happen for blacks in both areas (e.g., regarding both police brutality and interpersonal neighborhood violence). This response was also common among focus group participants. They specifically discussed the need for social change regarding police conflict and neighborhood violence. In all documented responses—impromptu exchanges during direct action, and in-depth interviews and focus groups out of direct action—pertaining to threats of police and neighborhood violence, these joint concerns emerged on at least one occasion and tended to revolve around issues of black unity and solidarity.

For example, Focus Group 1 was conducted in St. Louis City with four participants: three urban residents (Bria, age thirty-seven; Angel, age twenty-two, and Laila, age twenty-one) and one recent county/suburban resident (Fajah, age twenty-eight).[9] Their discussions captured a broad range of issues that were all directly and indirectly linked to their perceptions of St. Louis (e.g., what they liked and disliked) and community disorder—especially violence—and criticized institutional decisions that left some black citizens particularly disadvantaged. Here is what they said:

FAJAH: It's about what they [are] feeding to our community. They're just feeding us death. . . . They're killing us.
Who is they?
FAJAH: The white [people] . . . they systematically keep oppressing us.
BRIA: Honestly, I understand what you [are] sayin'. . . . .[It's like] you damned if you do, damned if you don't. But at some point, we as black people have to take responsibility for our own stuff [too], you know?
FAJAH: We do.
So how do we do that?
FAJAH: By holding people, holding our politicians accountable. If we don't want three dead [homicides], . . . three freaking gas stations, or

three liquor stores, we shouldn't have three liquor stores. . . . They
could put laws in place [saying that there] can only be a liquor
store within [certain] miles of . . . other[s]. You think these white
people got [that]? They ain't inundated with crime, are they?
What they got? When you drive up to Bisby, what do they got
out there?[10] [The group goes quiet.]
[To the group:] *So what do you think?*

BRIA: [So] I'm not trying to be like [difficult]. . . . I grew up in the city
[expressing connectedness]. [But] I was following Hollands Place
[white affluent suburb], and they wanted to put a porn shop in
Hollands Place. . . . Them white folks was out there [protesting,
saying,] "No!!!"

FAJAH: Yeah, they was like that.

BRIA: That's why I said, at a certain point, *we* [blacks] have to take
responsibility too.

FAJAH: But at the same time, they [whites] ain't got a bunch of liquor
stores, and people ain't feeding drugs into their community.

Since there is no monolithic black thought or voice, focus group discussions provide opportunities to learn of similar as well as diverse black
perspectives. There were points on which participants agreed and disagreed,
but overall, they all spoke about wanting what is best—racial unity,
collective action, and institutional equity and equality—for the black community. This common desire was the reason that they referred to white
affluent areas for comparisons; conditions in those neighborhoods differ
overtly from those in their own. In the absence of numerous liquor stores
and porn shops, the more affluent white communities (the suburbs named
here) are less susceptible to disorder and its effects in their neighborhoods.
The translation is that white citizens—especially affluent ones—are less
compromised in their everyday lives by disorder and crime, which sometimes produce environmentally endemic consequences for poor black communities. Furthermore, it is through the cultural reconceptualization of
disorder that Bria's rebuttal—"But . . . people ain't feeding drugs into their
community"—lends itself to the reordering of disruption. Drugs and
alcohol are examples of easily accessible vices that in the face of systemic
discrimination and institutional neglect only work to solidify preexisting
disarray in disadvantaged black neighborhoods. In short, it may be that the
more vulnerable members of black communities—children, drug addicts,
alcoholics, the mentally ill, and the "unhoused" especially—are so affected
by and exhausted from fighting systemic oppression and despondency,

desperately, unconventionally, and sometimes illegitimately that they lack the wherewithal to do so politically.[11]

These conversations speak to power that, specific to this project, means the ability (or lack thereof) to leverage broad cultural (dis)ordering in ways that inevitably secure socioeconomic and political advantage (or disadvantage) across race and place. Continuing the discussion, focus participants drew institutional correlations with and gave prioritization to the power and detachment of decision makers regarding black community dynamics:

FAJAH: For [a] perfect example, . . . [take] the stadium, the Rams' stadium, right? People was trying to get that. . . . "Oh, we need to build a new stadium." . . . They collected about a billion dollars, . . . a billion dollars to build a stadium??? . . . You need to be focused on why these cops shooting people [angrily]!!! We done raised a billion dollars to build a stadium, but you can't raise a billion dollars to invest in these communities???

LAILA: That's 'cause they're so concerned about tourists, when tourists . . . they don't even want to come here because of what's going on.

The participants were very passionate when speaking about the money raised for the stadium. Their grievance spoke to disorder—perceivably misplaced priorities—and the little regard for black life and the quality thereof (e.g., cops shooting people, not investing in "these" communities).

Focus group conversations provided pseudo-neighborhood interactions. They organically played out as if they were conversations among actual neighbors in real time. Focus groups are the closest interactive arrangement for gauging group neighborhood dynamics other than speaking with formal neighborhood organizations and associations (i.e., engaging in formal participation), which is often a more official setting. Formal participation provides analysis of official and more structured neighborhood efforts and is examined in chapter 5.

The focus group participants' comments in this study reflect the urban and suburban neighborhood experiences of individuals who at different times have resided in both places.[12] Sometimes participants were able to provide comparative and holistic perceptions of both locations as residents. Following is part of the dialogue from Focus Group 2 (suburban, five participants), made up of four black females and one black male: Bess, age fifty-eight; Spree, age forty-nine; Eden, age thirty-three; Kay, age sixty-two; and Benton, age twenty-four. When asked what they liked and disliked about

St. Louis generally, Spree linked black unity, Brown's death, and civil unrest to homicides and social change:

> I like sometimes how we can all come together like as one when it's a tragedy, . . . not even so much when it's a tragedy or disaster or anything, period. We can all pull together, you know what I'm saying, and not have prejudice.
> *When you say "we," do you mean everybody in St. Louis or . . . ?*
> I'm saying our race is what I mean.
> *So blacks?*
> Yes. 'Cause it's like hard for us. . . . So like [in] 2014, I saw a change, but it also has been a lot of killing. But since Mike Brown [death and civil unrest], I have seen a lot of unity, basically. . . . As far as more "togetherness," . . . it [Brown's death and civil unrest] brought about a little more change. . . . It's bringing more out [opportunities for dialogue] for more people to wanna talk and come together about all [of] the killing and stuff. . . . Now they [black citizens] [are] coming out [attending events] more.

When Spree thought of St. Louis, she was reminded of homicides, which by the end of the year that Brown died had increased more than 30 percent.[13] This was with the highest homicide count since 2008 and part of the reason for the suggestion of the Ferguson Effect, despite the highest spikes having occurred before Brown's death and Ferguson civil unrest.[14] Consequently, she mostly framed black solidarity, or "coming together like as one," through that lens. More specifically, her impressions of her neighborhood similarly spoke to more "unity" and "togetherness" following Brown's death. She recognized concerns about violence from police and other black citizens. However, her general theme was one of improvement—that is, "a little more change" that she now associates with the Ferguson uprising. As other participants weighed in, they likewise discussed community conditions, fiscal decisions, and the need for additional improvements in the region. Here is how they spoke of change:

BESS: See this is the thing about St. Louis. [It] seems like at the top they don't have any money for this; they don't have any money for that. But [as] soon as the crime arise[s] [Brown's murder], and it's a big announced crime [high profile], here come the funds.

SPREE: Right!

EDEN: That's what I'm saying!

BESS: Here come the funds, no matter what, because they [the dominant] gone give us [blacks] the funds [now] . . . 'cause they want us [blacks] to calm down and be quiet [stop protesting].

Similar to participants' responses in Focus Group 1, Beth called out the supposed lack of funding in St. Louis—at least when it comes to funding or addressing subpar conditions for the poor or people of color. There seems to never be money for addressing disparity, and yet there is plenty of money contingent upon the subjective interests of the dominant. She tied "newfound" money to the widespread prominence of Brown's death and the ensuing civil unrest and sarcastically reported its sudden use in the community as nothing more than an attempt by the powerful to placate black resistance. The discussion continued:

> *So you feel like that's when money turns up for black folks?*
> BESS: [Yes, for] any community where the high profile crime started.
>   And it's *gotta* be high profile. It cannot be low profile because
>   [then] it's not worldwide; everybody's not looking at it.
> SPREE: And everybody's not participating.
> BESS: But see, Mike Brown was so big that they [elites, the powerful]
>   gave the money for the Starbucks, they got a brand-new
>   community center over there [Ferguson], . . . but if it never
>   would've been a *high-profile* crime, the QuikTrip would still
>   be there.

Bess was referring to the QuikTrip store, which was burned during the first days of civil unrest. It is now the location and home of a recently constructed Urban League Community Empowerment Center. She indirectly offered a correlation between successively higher profile events (e.g., Brown's death and the civil unrest) that had garnered national and international attention, since she believed that they were the only reason for the sudden economic development. To be clear, no one condoned the destruction of property, but they all agreed about what they believed to have been monetary concessions quickly made post-Ferguson that resulted in two construction projects (i.e., Starbucks and the Urban League Community Empowerment Center).

Nevertheless, as the conversation continued, matters of distrust, crime, and neighborhood safety emerged in different ways apart from discussion of the protests. The participants recalled incidents when they had felt compromised in their neighborhoods. They reported times when they felt trapped between a few black neighbors and police, which for several participants centered on reporting crime. They all admitted to having reported crime to the police on occasion—despite stereotypical characterizations and assumptions centered on "snitching"—an action that counts as neighborhood participation and engagement for this project. Here is how they, especially Kay, responded when asked *if they had reported* or *would report crime*:

EVERYBODY: Yeah, sure.

SPREE: Several times.

KAY: I have [reported crime] several times. I called them [the police] three times. . . . I saw this [action,] and I told them, and they got to the point [when] every time something happened, they would come [and] call my [phone] number. They [even] call[ed] me by my nickname. [She imitates the police:] "Hey, Ms. So-and-So-and-So-and-So, we know you were out there [outside]. . . . We know you saw it!" . . . I'm like, "Wow!"

They started calling you directly?

KAY: They called me DI-REC-TLY . . . [She deliberately pronounces the syllables as others chuckle in the background, shaking their heads].

How did you feel about the police calling you?

KAY: I was OUT-DONE . . . .

It has long been documented that black citizens are compromised by the police when reporting crime in their communities.[15] They risk being outed in their neighborhoods (e.g., via name-dropping or police visits); therefore, they are often not motivated to report crime. Kay's situation was no different; in fact it was even worse because she apparently took a chance when calling the police, who subsequently repeatedly called her back regarding other crimes. This outcome is harassment; it is an unwelcomed, recurring imposition by law enforcement, one that left Kay "OUT-DONE."[16] Furthermore, it is one example of many of how black citizens can easily find themselves facing victimization by the police as well as simultaneously by some black citizens. The fact that the police have reportedly called Kay by her nickname is even more disconcerting. It posits their interactions as indications that they have a personal relationship with her.

Other participants also communicated their feelings of having been compromised. Spree commented, "You see and you don't see," and on another occasion stated, "Don't ask my daughter shit." Police had tried to question Spree's teenage daughter following a neighborhood incident while Spree was away from home working. In these instances, Spree reframed silence as refusing to "be preyed on for a story" by law enforcement (e.g., being haphazardly mistreated or harassed).[17] Regardless of others' opinions in the neighborhood, her decisions whether or not to report crime reflected her freedom to choose—a situation that makes for a contested variation of power and resistance, especially in the face of disorder and crime.[18] These were not blanket statements for disengaging but rather situational decisions filled with nuance. Spree may not have reported *all* situations to the police, but she admitted to having reported some and personally intervening in others—ones in which she thought her connections and efforts would produce better results. For example, Spree reported being used to hearing and seeing neighborhood fights and sometimes, after briefly assessing things, offering help or attempting to stop them. Angel, age twenty-two, from Focus Group 1 reported doing the same thing—intervening in situations in the community. Here is how she described what she did while witnessing an altercation:

ANGEL: I didn't want to get caught up in it to a certain extent, . . . [but] like, this dude was beating his girlfriend, and you could call the police, but then his reaction [would] probably [be] to say something to me or even charge at me, so like what I'm supposed to do? Am I supposed to, you know, like stay out of it?

Were you afraid that he would say something to you because you were calling?

ANGEL: Yeah.

So in that instance, you [just] didn't?

ANGEL: As far as like trying to stop it, yes. But calling the police? No.

So what did you do to try to stop it?

ANGEL: Got in between them. I don't, I don't mind getting hit by somebody 'cause I'll fight [back].

Did you know them?

ANGEL: I knew them, but I didn't "know them, know them." [They were familiar but not known intimately.]

This is situational reporting. Angel was familiar with those involved and for a number of reasons (e.g., fear of their being criminalized) thought that it might be less complicated for everyone if she tried to handle the situation instead of calling the police. Angel was "on papers" (i.e., on probation) at that time, but she wanted to help. She personally intervened in order to not make things worse, including for herself.

These are examples of how black citizens engage in reciprocity—extending good faith in exchange for peaceful resolutions—as a compromise and an informal alternative to law enforcement.[19] That said, silence (e.g., not calling the police) in disorderly or crime-infested communities does not necessarily equate to black citizens' "doing nothing" or passively sitting by and simply "not wanting" to protect and serve their neighborhoods. These are circumstantial decisions, which that through social and cultural construction can range from denoting distress and disagreement to "being silent" (empowered) or "*being* silenced" (lacking power), two often interchangeably used and yet contrasting situations.[20]

Similar negotiations often occur in protests when protesters step in between to "put their bodies on the line." Their actual bodies or physical beings *become* the ultimate resistance—an embodied counter to possible police aggression. Although all protesters accrue risks in direct action, there are some who purposely situate themselves to take the brunt of them. For instance, "front-liners"—the first line, first seen, first physically contacted resisters or protesters—bear greater risks than others do in a head-on clash with the riot team. Their bodies provide immediate cover for other protesters by dealing with pepper spray, tear gas, arrest, or other consequences first—and their sacrifices (or willingness to be sacrificed) are noted within the protest community. In turn, trust, respect, and safety increase for them among "the family," extending opportunities for others to brave state aggression and engage similarly. These negotiations are constants irrespective of the context, as I have physically intervened in some fairly intense protester-protester arguments. Although social, those interventions felt natural because I was already standing nearby and was generally familiar with someone or several people in the group, at least in those instances. They were typically teens or young adults, whose emotions ran high in a chaotic environment, as they sometimes rambunctiously engaged in direct action in pursuit of social change. I understood these situations as stress. These spats were often quickly rectified through short, forced separations—with others and me stepping in between them and sometimes physically pulling them to opposite sides, one by one, to talk them down and allow them to decompress through "sideline" conversations. As happens in sports, they respectfully regrouped and got back into the game as if nothing had happened; these were incidents and interventions that occurred due to fluid and volatile circumstances.

In sum, there are no absolutes for daily neighborhood interactions. Every day is different, and citizens are constantly assessing, negotiating, and making concessions contingent upon evolving (or not evolving) situations. Let us now turn to individual, informal integration—chatting, visiting, and reciprocity—as it becomes the means through which citizens establish relationships and safety across neighborhoods.[21] In in-depth interviews (forty-one) and focus groups (nine), all fifty participants admitted to engaging in individual, informal neighborhood alliances and integration out of protests as counters to disorder (see table 3 in the next section).[22]

INFORMAL INTEGRATION: CHATTING, VISITING, AND RECIPROCITY

> I gotta speak to where I come from, the black community. . . .
> There are some people that are great, gracious, and kind. . . .
> They don't get as much publicity as those who seem to find
> themselves on the wrong side (of the law), but there are some
> great [black] people within this city, and I wish they could get
> put out there [be widely acknowledged]. . . . St. Louis is basically
> a place caught up into a time capsule, and it's time to crack it
> open.
>
> DORINE, age fifty-eight

Research has found that neighbors are more likely to connect individually and informally through informal integration.[23] *Informal integration* involves social ties that reflect causal neighbor-to-neighbor engagement and the extent to which neighbors visit and talk with one another.[24] These informal connections and alliances also speak to whether neighbors help one another out by "lending things, watching each other's houses, giving each other a ride," and performing similar actions.[25] Reflecting Dorine's sentiments, this study highlights black citizens and instances in which they individually ally and connect with other neighbors in ways that protect and serve each other and counter disorder and its effects in their neighborhood. In this project, all individual, in-depth interview and focus group participants were found to have individually connected with their neighbors and engaged in informal integration outside of protests (see table 3).

These participants were also found to be more likely to engage in informal integration than in formal group participation or organizations.[26] They did so through chatting, visiting, and reciprocity.[27] All participants, apart from protests, alluded to or spoke directly to various forms of reciprocity, which included varying degrees of chatting or visiting and a network of reciprocal favors. They reported knowing of or experiencing situations in which someone needed help or assistance, and various degrees of familiarity provided enough connection and mutual opportunity to provide it. Ernestine (age sixty), for example, reported:

TABLE 3. Participants' Community and Neighborhood Involvement*

Types of Participation	Out of Protests/Direct Action—Individual, In-Depth Interviews (N = 41)	Out of Protests/Direct Action—Focus Groups (N = 9: Urban = 4; Suburban = 5)
Participants were frequently involved in and committed to their community/neighborhood through individual, informal integration.	41/41 = 100%	9/9 = 100%
Participants were frequently involved in and committed to their community/neighborhood through group organizations, formal participation:	18/41 = 44%	1/9 = 11%***
18–34 years of age = 2/41**		
35–50 years of age = 6/41		
51+ years of age = 10/41		

*Involvement ranges from greeting others, associated with individual informal integration, to volunteering and donating, individually or through group, formal participation or serving on neighborhood watch, to planning local programs or events as group, formal participation. In addition, volunteering and donating "individually" speaks to participants who acted on their own. Example: a participant acting alone, cooking at home, and passing out food plates and bottled water from her front yard or the sidewalk in front of her residence.

**The age brackets reflect participants from individual, in-depth interviews only.

***Since responses did not involve fluctuating perceptions, this number reflects direct answers from individual focus group participants.

> I got sick one time and I was unable to get to the hospital, and my neighbor was, like, do you need me to take you? . . . and I was, like yeah, because I was unable to drive.

It is highly likely that any of Ernestine's neighbors would have assisted her when she was sick. Many were probably familiar with and connected to her, since she reported that she cooked and passed out food and water in the neighborhood, and handed out free T-shirts to younger children and job applications to those unemployed and formerly incarcerated. These gestures were often performed at her own expense, except for the distribution of T-shirts, which had been donated to her. Here is how she managed the donation:

I just gave the T-shirts out to the little kids [or] the people that I know got kids in my neighborhood, that use drugs, and [whose] kids be dirty [and neglected because of it].

The following discussion presents exchanges similar to those recounted by Ernestine. It describes instances in which in-depth interview participants reported protecting and serving one another or reciprocating in ways that seemed consistent with roles or tasks associated with direct action. Consistent with the various tasks or roles I witnessed in direct action, I discuss participants' reciprocal roles and efforts in two ways: as *marshals* and as *specialized support*. *Marshals* afforded reciprocity through advancing or "connecting" actions—those that initiate or sustain relationships—by greeting, informing, watching, or alerting one another throughout the neighborhood. *Specialized support*, on the other hand, assisted in focused ways by aiding neighbors who required more critical or targeted help in the neighborhood (e.g., drug addicts, the unhoused). This study found that both roles occurred simultaneously and overlapped and were interchangeable among all members of a community.

Neighborhood Marshals

Please don't do *that*. . . . We don't do *that* out *here*! . . . [When you are] going to the bus stop, . . . [you] eat'n a bag of chips [and] throw yo bag on the ground. . . . *WE* don't do that!

JAZZ, age forty

That is how Jazz recalled a conversation she had with some kids in her neighborhood. She explained having to "do something" about their throwing trash on the ground. She had first talked with the kids and then with their parent(s), and she explained her decision to do so: "It's not always in *what* you say but [in] *how* you say *what* you say." Communication was key in her situation. She described how, as if she were a neighborhood marshal, she sometimes rounded kids up to have them help her pick up trash on their street.

To be consistent with my descriptions of occurrences in direct action, I have labeled individual neighbors' efforts to correspond to similar roles or tasks in protests. In this section, *protest marshals* are watchers and connectors; they watch, greet, inform, instruct, warn, and so forth with the overall flow of direct action. These tasks are similar to actions performed across neighborhoods. While all protesters may do these things at various times—individually and informally or collectively and formally—all in-depth interview and focus group participants in this project indirectly, directly, and diversely reported engaging in similar efforts. Ava, age twenty-six, outlined actions for addressing suspicious activity:

Just notify [someone] if you see anything going wrong at your neighbor's house. Just be like, "Hey, I saw something suspicious going on;
I just wanted to let you know." . . . In case they didn't know. . . . Even if
they did [know,] . . . just be a good steward.

Ava was speaking about protecting her neighbors' properties from possible
break-ins or home invasions. Like someone watching and notifying protesters, protest leaders, or organizers, she encouraged people to notify
neighbors of activity around their homes. She also recognized that they
might already be aware of the activity, but she still encouraged giving
notice as if they were not. She expected reciprocity from her neighbors, as
she felt safer knowing that *they* would also alert *her*.

Jay, age twenty-nine, reported keeping watch and having to address
unsupervised children in his neighborhood. Here is how he described reach-
ing out to their parents:

I come around [and] tell them their kids [are] running all around the
corner and everything like that and they got to keep an eye on them. . . .
That's about all I can do. . . . They [are] just letting their kids run
around, so it's like [the mother then says], "Thank you; I'm gonna keep
my eye on them more,". . . something like that. . . . [It's] happened
about four or five times within the last three years that the kids be
running around and the parents don't know where they at . . . so
I usually want to talk to the parent first. . . . [He continues, thinking
out loud:] I've seen four-, five-, [even] three-year-olds running around
the corner, yeah, with no supervision. For real!

This information was especially important to share because children are the
more vulnerable members of the community. Jay described repeatedly
spotting kids and alerting their parents as they were racing around the
neighborhood unsupervised. The fact that Jay was aware of where the children lived instead of only knowing the location where he found them running speaks to his familiarity (i.e., being familiar enough with parents to
alert them) and ties with the neighborhood. He also reported picking up
trash, which was sometimes the way that he spotted the kids and knew
their residences, since he routinely walked around the community. He
knew that the children were too far away from home to be visible to their
parents, so he intervened as a matter of protection. Jay was concerned that
something bad (e.g., being hit by a car or kidnapped) could happen to them
and repeatedly stepped in to help.

Kelsey, age thirty-three, reported checking on the elderly. Senior citizens
are also vulnerable residents. Here is how she described checking on an
elderly neighbor living next door to her:

There's an old lady staying next to me. . . . I go check on her sometimes. She just stays in the house . . . by herself. . . . She don't be sitting outside [or anything] for real. I don't see her [at all]. So I just go over there and make sure she's all right. . . . And [I] just be like [knocking], "Hey, this such and such [Kelsey]. I was just seeing if you [are] all right. That's all." She be like, "Oh, hey, baby [laughter]. . . . She's like, "How are the babies [your children] doing?" I'm like, "They [are] all right!" . . . I'm like, "You need anything?" She like, "Uh un," and I then just go back home, . . . [but] every two days [I check on her again] . . . 'cause she's old. . . . Like if somebody be blowing [their car horn] outside, [or] whatever, she's probably go[ing] to church. I'm like, okay, I see them [her ride]. But then like if I don't see her none Sunday evening or none Monday, then Monday night I'm going over there. . . . Before I put the kids to bed, I'm gonna check on her.

Kelsey has established a great connection with her elderly neighbor, who lives alone and appears to have no family. They are both equally excited to hear from one another. It is as if Kelsey is caring for her grandmother. She takes the relationship personally, albeit through fictive kinship. Her concern is then reciprocated, in that her elderly neighbor expresses care and concern for her children since Kelsey is a single parent. She works a lot, and when she is home, she is sometimes frightened when she hears gunshots in what she believes is a drug-infested community. These interactions make a difference—establishing camaraderie and visuals of neighborly exchanges as signals to others watching—and decrease the likelihood of victimization.[28] This awareness of a connection between these residents also provides great generational lessons for Kelsey's children.[29] They too have been taught to be listeners and watchers for others and for their "neighborhood grandmother." Kelsey and her elderly neighbor's relationship is not burdensome but rather is a "willing" arrangement. Kelsey is the woman's pseudo-caregiver, noninvasively keeping track of her, extending comfort, and acting as a safe contact in the event that she needs something.

Joyce, age forty, watches and "speak[s] to all neighbors." She stated:

I pretty much stay to myself unless I really have to come out and look around or something, but I speak to all my neighbors.

Joyce establishes familiarity and a friendly line of contact by simply greeting her neighbors. She participates in brief pleasantries that go a long way in communities often filled with disorder and hopelessness. She does this despite her initial statement that she stays "to herself"—a prefatory assertion that someone may take negatively and literally without having the additional information. In another instance, Joyce described her neighbors as looking out for her and even provided an example:

> They look out for you. One day I was taking a bed apart and I was making a lot of noise, and my neighbor next door came out and was like, "Aw, I just wanted to see who was back here making all of that noise." When he found it was me, he was like, "Aw, as long as you [are] okay."

Negative assertions or criticisms preceded numerous discussions on black interaction and life generally. Like Joyce, other participants negatively and contradictorily reported that they kept "to themselves" (e.g., Bess, in Focus Group 2), among other things. Then they later admitted that they engaged in a variety of reciprocal exchanges or pleasant encounters with the black community and some neighbors. As another example, Trina, age twenty-seven, responded indifferently when asked about relationships and interactions in her neighborhood:

> Nobody really wants to help each other anymore. . . . If I look at stories from different places or from people from different states and everything, . . . people [who say things] like "Oh, when So-and-So's family [member] died, I took potluck over there," . . . you just don't see that where I come from; it's really sad.
> *There's "no one" from your neighborhood who does things for others?*
> Well, my mom, she does things . . . but no. If she makes dinner, she'll take a plate over there to a neighbor's house, if there's some left over, . . . she'll feed the [neighbor] kids. . . . She put that [helping out] in me too, but . . . you just don't see that from neighbor to neighbor. . . . They'll [neighbor kids] come to the house. . . . If we [are] feeding our kids and [if] that child [a neighbor] is sit'n right there [too,] . . . of course [we will feed them too]. . . . It just doesn't sit well with you watchin' a kid look at you eat. . . . [She says as if talking to child:] "Come on and eat!" But I [still] say [there is] disunity because there's not very many people like that.

Notice how Trina initially offered a negative generalization about her neighbors—"no one" wanting to help "anymore" as compared with neighbors' actions in other places. But then she later acknowledged that her mother—a resident in the neighborhood—fed neighbors and neighborhood children. She admitted that her mother took food to neighbors' homes and had some of their children over to hers, all the while still maintaining that she (Trina) was definitely the only helpful one or one of few and suggesting there was "disunity" in the community.

Sometimes black citizens inadvertently speak of themselves through the imposition of "double-consciousness."[30] From hair texture (i.e., good hair or bad hair) to skin complexion (i.e., too dark or too light), some judge themselves and their communities "through the eyes of others" as they fight for respectability.[31] Respectability in this sense means "policing behaviors in your community" or neighborhood so as not to attract unwelcomed white attention.[32] This self-flagellation or self-criticism is then articulated in a manner similar to the criticisms of white critics.[33] Some blacks negatively typecast the entire race even while working to advance it. They sometimes do this unknowingly due to shared dominant socialization and the expectation that they should conform to white middle-class norms.[34] It is then through shame and aggravation that unintended debasement among blacks can occur. Mason, age fifty-three, stated:

> I get frustrated sometimes with things that go on. . . . The younger generations don't have respect for the elder people; they don't have respect for themselves.

Mason added, "*We* just don't reach out to each other anymore. . . . We fear each other," but the truth is that *some* black citizens *do not* reach out while others *do*—as is situationally evident in this project. As for fearing one another, Mason spoke to internalized racism, a structural and "limited sense of self that can undermine people of color's belief" and understanding in their everyday life and full humanity.[35] Iris, age fifty-nine, said this situation exists "'cause it's *no* togetherness *no more*," but the truth is that there may be *some* dissension in *some* instances and *some* unity in *other* situations.

For more context, I followed up with Trina regarding neighborhood perceptions, and here is what she added:

> They say it's the millennials that's gon' change everything, you know. We all have a desire to like, see change. . . . The only problem is the lack of finance or the lack of opportunity to put forth those visions. . . . I want to see progress, I want to see growth, [and] . . . I want the children to have a chance. . . . I know that a lot of things that we deal with right now in our community, you can trace [them] all the way back to people's childhood[s].

Trina eventually came full circle. She transitioned from a place of irritation to one of hope and thoughtfulness regarding members of her community. She provided perspective on why they had not been able to advance. She said that their lack of progress has been due to limited institutional support (i.e., due to lack of finances, lack of opportunities, and neglect). Mason and

Iris later responded similarly after additional questioning. Despite their obvious irritation and exhaustion concerning the overall plight of blacks in their neighborhoods, they found good in their hope and love for their community and labeled most problems as systemically discriminative. Mason especially maintained that if the system were different, the community would be different too, stating, "They [the dominant] make their own rules, [and] they change the rules that [are] already on the table" to create the often no-win dilemma faced by blacks in America.

In sum, neighborhood interactions are fluid and occur in various circumstances similar to involvement in direct action. Citizen bonding and reciprocity do not occur among *all* black residents or citizens at *all* times in the *same* way in *every* neighborhood. They also do not occur for *all* white neighborhoods, or more broadly, across *all* racial/ethnic communities. Such assertions create false premises and drive more narratives of indifference about disadvantaged black neighborhoods or blacks in general. As these narratives become more widespread generalizations, they are politically repurposed without sociohistorical perspective or context.

When entering protest sites, one can sometimes encounter someone distinctly (or subtly) acting as a marshal. That person might greet newcomers (e.g., as Joyce greets her neighbors)—invariably welcoming and directing them when necessary as part of the direct action. The marshal may also be found doing a number of other things, from watching the scene to informing and providing general directions or assistance as needed. These actions are consistent with those of the aforementioned black citizens who reported watching, informing, and offering assistance to protect property, children, the elderly, and others in their neighborhood. In general, marshals assume duties that manage the crowd. *Specialized support*, on the other hand, does the same but addresses exceptional issues (e.g., jail support, medical help). In the next section, black citizens describe providing thought and directed care for managing the unhoused, mentally ill, drug addicts, prostitutes, and others in their neighborhoods.

Specialized Support

There's a lot of people scared. . . . I'm not. I've seen the wors[t].

AEISHA

In direct action, there were protesters who had been trained or were experienced enough to directly assist with specific complications as they arose among protesters. To name a few, jail support was provided to those arrested, and medics or others operating as such assisted those who had

been tear-gassed or pepper sprayed or who were suffering from other medical difficulties while involved in protests. An informal understanding and
expectation existed within the protest community that one should stop and
provide aid to those experiencing immediate harm or duress resulting from
extenuating circumstances. Participants reported helping members of their
neighborhoods who were on the streets and also suffering from some of the
"worst" conditions. These included, but were not limited to, drug addiction,
unhousing, prostitution, and mental illness. Although these members'
needs were somewhat different from those of the protest participants—but
nevertheless were some of the persisting, underlying reasons and conditions that prompted the mostly black outcry and uprising in the region—
some participants reported assisting neighbors who required special attention. In many instances, they tailored the help these neighbors received to
their unique circumstances.

Patsy, age fifty-four, provided specialized support to someone sitting
across the street from her home:

> It's this one lady. . . . I'm talkin' about every time I saw this lady, she
> was musty. Her hair had never been combed, and she had dirty
> clothes on. It was cold outside one day, and I was sittin' on the front
> [porch,]and she had this little sweater on. It was *really* cold and I have
> been blessed to [have been] given nice things, and I took off my leather
> coat and I gave it to her, and then I went into the house. I got a pair
> of my boots; I got a comb and a brush, a bar of soap, and the biggest
> clothes that I could find and [gave them] to her, and I said, "Have a
> God-blessed day!" When I'd given [them] to her, she said, "Fuck
> you, bitch!"
>
> *Did she take them?*
>
> She took [them], but *that* was just that. . . . That's what my whole
> mission was—for her to take [them] no matter what. I believe this:
> I'm not accountable for how people treat me. I'm accountable for how
> *I* treat people. So long as she took [them], what she did with [them I
> don't know,] but I'd given [them to her].

Based on Patsy's account, it is probable that this lady was suffering from
mental illness and perhaps was even "unhoused." It has been estimated that
African American citizens are as much as 20 percent more likely to face
mental health problems than the general population, with only one in three
receiving treatment.[36] In addition, homelessness and exposure to violence
increase the risk of mental illness among African Americans.[37] African
Americans also represent 40 percent of the unhoused population despite
representing only 13 percent of the overall population.[38] They also disproportionately contend with lack of insurance and underinsurance, cultural

incompetence, distrust, and misdiagnoses—all effects compounded by or correlated with poverty and disorder generally.[39]

Patsy is familiar with this woman; she sees her neighbor all of the time. She is an indelible presence in the neighborhood and a reminder to Patsy of her own previous struggles. Patsy explained:

> Yes, I lived the life of drugs; I lived a life of homelessness. . . . I lived the life of all that, so I've learned [a lot over the] years.

It is easy for Patsy to have patience and compassion for her neighbor despite having been called a bitch. She spoke with me about the years of addiction that had left her reeling in the streets doing all sorts of unbelievable things. It is through her own experience of crisis that she is now able to give space to this alliance and reciprocated connection. It is also in this context that this project similarly examines informal ties and social control, particularly during a time conducive to black empowerment. Some black citizens are uniquely inviting neighbors back into the fold irrespective of their circumstances, rather than excluding them. This project found participants extending redemption to some of the most obviously troubled citizens as a testament to *how* all black lives should matter.[40] They embrace these neighbors nonjudgmentally—being only concerned about their condition and general well-being. In the face of disproportionate police brutality and the interpersonal neighborhood victimization of blacks, there are black citizens extending protection and service as a counter to institutional negligence.

Michelle, age forty-three, is another participant who reported having extended specialized care in her neighborhood. Here is what she said about those who find themselves living diverse, "disordered" lives:

> Drug addicts, drug dealers . . . [There is] a lot of prostitution . . . and drug dealing in this area, and people are afraid to go up and try to help [them]. And I'm one of the neighbors that's *not* afraid to come up and say, "Hey, we got this class today; would you like to come to this class? And if they say no, [then] they [just] say no! But I like that it's [a local community center] open like that, that I could bring them here and they can do an art class, and [I can] bring them here to eat. . . . They [just] have to be willing to take the class. . . . We got free GED classes and all that.

Michelle regularly visits a community center in her neighborhood. She takes advantage of its programs and has garnered favor with the employees. She is known, trusted, and respected for her neighborhood involvement. This response is the reason that she takes it upon herself—apart from the efforts of the community center—to invite prostitutes and drug addicts to come to classes.[41] The classes are diverse, plentiful, and free, and even if these individuals are not interested in them, she has strategically introduced herself to them as a safe friend in the community. She then moves to target their immediate needs. Her hope is that they will eventually become comfortable and receptive to help. She continued:

> At all times of [the] damn night . . . [and] walking past drug addicts [and] prostitutes all day, . . . [T]hey [residents] were talking about them on the news, saying that they're tired of seeing them. . . . Of course, we don't want to see that bad behavior in front of our children, day and night. . . . But if they are willing to listen to someone like me say, "Hey, would you like to go take you a shower? The center doesn't care. . . . Take you a shower, get something to eat, let me see where you are educationally, . . . how can 'I' help you?" That's my work [her calling], and I do it free . . . [only] if they allow me, . . . [but] I'm not gon' put myself in a dangerous situation. I have to kinda assess the person. Sometimes I'm walking around the neighborhood and I'm thinking, "Well, maybe *this* person may allow me talk to them today or [give me] a little bit at a time." I'll get a chance to talk to them. Then they'll feel comfortable enough later on for me to say, "Come on, let me tell you where the center is . . . where you can clean up or [how] the pantry opens at a certain time." . . . I *literally* have to observe 'em. . . . Like the other night, I was getting ready to take the trash out, [but] I couldn't take the trash out because there [were] two—a lady and a man—squatted down in between the dumpsters . . . to shoot up [inject drugs]. I always look out before I go out, . . . and it wasn't dark yet, so I didn't expect to see that, but [then] I couldn't go out. . . . I [had] to observe the situation. . . . The other guy was leanin' up against the other one [dumpster] lookin' around like he could rob somebody. . . . He was [really] watching out to make sure that nobody could see them.

These are surreal visuals in Michelle's neighborhood. She is a single parent with concerns for neighborhood children and her own, yet she works to create trust with local prostitutes and drug addicts. Here is how she rationalized her actions:

> Some people say, "Just arrest them!" [But] how are you helping them if you are arresting them? . . . THEY NEED HELP! It goes back to the way I was raised. . . . You can't avoid them, and it doesn't take anything to smile [at them]. It doesn't take anything to say hello to someone that's down. They wasn't always like that.

Michelle humanizes addicts and prostitutes. She pushes back on arrests for not providing actual help—a common position taken by people advocating for substance abuse treatment and improving social conditions. Studies show that incarceration of drug addicts is costly and ineffective when compared with the costs and results of treatment or rehabilitation.[42] Incarceration acts as a temporary fix that fails to address the underlying causes of addiction, neglecting treatment for it as an illness.[43] Addicts are then released back into the neighborhood, still susceptible to committing crime, creating a vicious, unresolved cycle often reciprocally connected to mental illness and compounded by criminalization.[44] It is for these reasons that Michelle shows compassion. These are complex human rights issues and health crises that call for nuanced perspectives and solutions. They are often "unavoidable," just as some residents cannot afford to move. Greeting these individuals and offering them locations for taking showers, eating, and obtaining other necessities negotiates opportunities, creating pathways for trust that may be enough for some to receive additional assistance (e.g., drug treatment).

Respect

Having relationships or being familiar with compromised neighbors—prostitutes, drug addicts, the unhoused, the mentally ill, and others—can go a long way. Like Michelle, Aeisha, age thirty-one, extends kind gestures and goodwill in exchange for neighborhood safety. She described her neighborhood and explained negotiating behaviors:

> It's a family-oriented neighborhood, but they [neighbors] have grandchildren and children [who are] into that lifestyle [drugs], and that's what keeps the stuff going . . . 'cause I have seen a lot of stuff to where some *real* bad things [were] getting ready to happen, but the young fellas seen me . . . and went the other way and didn't do it.
> *Why do you think that made a difference? When they saw you?*
> 'Cause they looked at me, and they seen that I smiled at 'em and wasn't scared.

As in protests, fearlessness or the appearance of it becomes operational and translates to coded behavior. These are informal, selfless, and trusted sentiments that lead to street credit, neighborhood respect, and informal social control among residents. Aeisha's description also speaks to Pattillo's findings that suggest disorder and its effects are negotiated but not eradicated due to the ongoing criminal actions of some residents.[45] Like Michelle, Aiesha sees "not being afraid" as a negotiable neighborhood commodity. She repeatedly referred to it as an advantage:

> It's a lot of people scared to stand up, [but] I'm not. I've seen the wors[t,] and if nobody stands up or does anything, it's [crime that is] gon' keep on happening. I'm not scared of nothing. I'm God fearing.

It also helps that Aeisha's family are known in the community. Their history and her own behavior curry favor for her in the neighborhood. She explained her interactions with the "unhoused" and local drug addicts:

> Sometimes I go spend my money buying care-packages, or I put money in care packages and go around and give it to 'em [drug addicts]. That might feed their dope high for the day, but at least that'll be one day they ain't out here trying to rob and steal. . . . [I'll buy a] toothbrush, like a sandwich, or probably [put in there] fifteen or twenty dollars. . . . It's a lot of 'em that know me. . . . They trust me. . . . They know I'm not gone harm 'em[.] Imma help 'em out, . . . so they respect me.

Respect is earned and negotiated and can be reciprocated diversely as a survival strategy. Aiesha attempts to manage people's behaviors through familiarity, respect, and care packages. She knows that when she adds money, the addicts could potentially go buy more drugs (and perhaps overdose). She rationalizes her decision by believing that her efforts maximize safety and minimize criminality. They decrease the chances that these addicts might steal or rob someone. They also reduce the chances that the addicts could be hurt *by someone* or inflict hurt *on someone* in a botched attempt to steal. Remember, Aiesha is familiar with them and has some sense of things that they may do. She concluded by mentioning their respect for her—trusting that they will make good with her help, given in the hope that they will oblige and not do things that endanger themselves or others.

Concessions are routinely made in countering disorder and its effects. They become informal, impromptu exchanges between neighbors for negotiating space, garnered by respect. Here is how Ms. Carol Ann, sixty-nine, described her response when she found a group of young men from her neighborhood sitting in front of her home:

> One evenin' when I came home, I don't know where I had been, but they were sittin' on my steps. So when I walked up, [they said,] "Oh, ma'am, . . . we so sorry, but it was too noisy, . . . so we came over here so we could talk and just have a little peace. . . . It's a li'l rowdy over there." I said, "Oh, that's ok. It's fine . . . just [as] long as you sitting here in peace, and you're not doing anything." I said, "You know what, I love you, and Jesus loves you, and it's gon' be all right." And they said, "Thank you, ma'am. Thank you."

Ms. Carol Ann had previously described living in a drug-infested neighborhood. She suspects that these young men are involved in drugs. Yet she makes a point to demonstrate care and concern for their well-being. They do the same, as if they were her grandchildren. The young men are seemingly careful with Ms. Carol Ann. Here is how she described their relationship:

> I talk to the young men. . . . I basically speak to them from a spiritual point of view. . . . They listen. . . . But how much is gettin' to 'em, I don't know. They show a lot of respect for me. . . . Every morning when I come out [of] my door, [they say,] "How you doin', ma'am? Ma'am, you doin' okay?" [She answers:] "I'm doin' great!" These are young men with the saggy pants and all of that.

The young men never miss an opportunity to greet and check on Ms. Carol Ann. Despite their perceived lifestyles, they have seemingly established a boundary, one that they do not cross. It is informally managed out of respect and specific to interactions with her. They recognize Ms. Carol Ann's genuineness and appear to draw much needed peace and calm from her and her property. This response has resulted because she is spiritual and nonjudgmental, and she extends love to them as if they were family. She offers hope through spiritual conversations, which in turn become likely counters and balances amid dicey and distrustful everyday hustling. They flex etiquette for Ms. Carol Ann, their neighborhood grandmother.

CONCLUSION

Consistent with Ross and Jang's study, this project found black citizens establishing and entering into alliances.[46] They forge diverse ties within and outside of direct action. Through participant observation and exchanges at protests, along with in-depth interviews and focus groups, participants were mostly found to be countering disorder individually and through informal integration.[47] Familiarity, reciprocity, and respect were interchangeably exchanged in varying degrees at the crux of navigating destitute circumstances. More directly, black citizens were found to be selflessly adjusting and making concessions—from frontline protesting to managing interactions with prostitutes and drug addicts—in the best interests of both communities and their members (i.e., black protesters or black neighbors). For a myriad of reasons, these efforts often proved to be challenging. Black efforts (or the perceived lack thereof) faced the usual and expected criticism from many whites and even in some instances from blacks who out of frustration engaged without context or perspective.

In sum, black people still bond despite disorder and crime. They often do so by creatively connecting and empowering other black citizens broadly, across neighborhoods and communities. However, because of the weight of and exhaustion from dealing with relentless discrimination, victimization, and "double-consciousness," the small and yet significant details of black effort often go unrecognized. This chapter has highlighted individual blacks fighting in the trenches—working to serve and to protect one another from overlapping victimizations. The next chapter provides neighborhood case studies that help in understanding how some black citizens managed to survive and who they were.

4. Making Black Lives Matter

When black lives are under attack, what do we do?
(Stand up, fight back!)

PROTEST CHANT

Three years of ethnographic examination on community disorder and its effects afforded me invaluable opportunities for chronicling black lives wholly shaped by widespread institutional neglect and injustice. As I learned from participants in Ferguson civil unrest and at countless town hall meetings, anti-gun summits, and nonviolent marches, black citizens disproportionately face some of the most denigrating everyday experiences, which leave them desperately clinging to life, not knowing whether they will make it out alive. Through mostly informal street networks and neighborhood socialization processes, participants in this project managed to deal with extremely destitute circumstances. Their interviews were all encompassing, providing insightful and yet painstaking narratives that spanned childhood to adulthood.

This chapter opens by chronicling the lives of three young black males (Tevin, Khareem, and Ted) who have spent much of their lives fighting to survive by any means possible. Their stories reflect the everyday nuisances and denigrating effects of systemic deprivation. They are examples of how black lives come to be marred disproportionately and generationally, sometimes facing cycles of pervasive isolation and neglect. It is in these seemingly inescapable social conditions that they are often forced to make desperate and impulsive, risky decisions.

Tevin's, Khareem's, and Ted's stories symbolize countless unaddressed black lives that, for a lack of better words, hang in the balance. They have managed to survive and now lend themselves to combating hopelessness and despair back at home in their neighborhoods and in other locations. Through timely alliances and snippets of empowerment, they continuously work to transform their own lives amid post-Ferguson civil unrest and unnerving interpersonal neighborhood violence. Their accounts show how some black citizens navigate life with one foot in an inner echo chamber of desperation—one citizen referred to it as "the underground"—and the other foot in the broader community, vying for change. They represent the minority of the minority—those citizens who have needed specialized support (e.g., for drug addiction, housing) in their communities, as discussed in chapter 3. They reflect the few in neighborhoods who easily "get caught up" and after constant institutional negligence become the images strategically used to stereotype the majority of black residents who navigate their world legitimately. Further, they are the reason that "making black lives matter" *should* matter as an everyday practice and experience for all black citizens.[1] Despite being in seemingly impossible plights that reduce them to invisible statistics and trends, they provide relatable interactions and respected connections in their neighborhoods and beyond. Once having lived life on a sliding continuum between social progression and regression, they are testaments to progress—examples of ongoing change through increased black consciousness.

"I GREW OUT OF IT"

Meet Tevin, age twenty-two.

> Yeah . . . I was a part of the problem, but then I grew out of it.
> It's always a time that you grow out of it and I grew out of it once
> I had my daughter. . . . I saw that I had another life to raise. . . . But
> I tell all my homeboys. . . when I do go down there in the hood: "Get
> a job!" I try to make my lil' homeboys [be] something that I wasn't . . .
> [He speaks as if talking to them:] "Just get a job or just get off the
> streets . . . ain't nothing out here but graves!" It ain't no more jail
> [just death]. . . . I don't consider prison no more, cause in prison you
> die too!

Tevin has had to "grow out of" many things, overcoming numerous overlapping challenges. His story depicts a young life riddled with drugs, violence, and death. He recounted pivotal moments in his upbringing, ranging from his mostly feeling "raised by the streets" (reared) to later facing his own commitment(s) to parenting. Tevin's journey to change began with several consecutive, short prison terms. After his release the journey extended to the eventual birth of his baby and the realization that he *had* to change *for her*. For context, let us now turn to Tevin's childhood to learn of his beginning: how the unfortunate breakdown of interactions with his parents left him dependent on the streets.

Tevin's Childhood and Plight

> I didn't really start going bad until I turned [He ponders.] 12, 13.
> [That's] when I start really seeing the older generation getting'
> a lot of money . . . and that's when I really just started thinking
> about, I need to get money too!

Tevin often spoke of his mother as a single parent. He reported that she was sick, unable to work or care for him as he grew older. He said that he did not know his biological father, and his stepfather was detached and uncaring. Here is how he remembered a representative exchange with the man:

> One time me and him got into it. [Then he said:] "I'm not yo *real* daddy, so I don't have to care about you." . . . Once you tell me that, then oh, okay. [He speaks as if talking to the stepfather:] "*Now*, I don't have to listen to you . . . *now* I'm gone treat you like you just a nobody. You ain't nothing to me!"

It was in this vein that Tevin poignantly told me, "The streets was my daddy!" This situation compounded rejection for him; he did not have his biological father and now discarded his stepfather. With a sick mother, his persistent insecurities about her life, and his refusal to depend on a state check, he decidedly needed a backup plan for "making it" (surviving). The fight to live began here, without the wherewithal to construct a safe, intelligible plan consistent with broad cultural expectations of him. A child living in an isolated, blighted neighborhood, here is how he legitimized his decision(s):

> I had to make it some type of way out here in life for myself. I couldn't depend on my momma. . . . [M]y mentality was, "What if my momma leave [die] today or tomorrow?" Then what I'm gon' do? I can't be worried about her [government] check. . . . I can't do nothing [work]! I can't worry about a [social security] check that they [might] give me for her dying. I don't want it.

This is a lot for a child to contend with: the worry of having no family and how to live or fend for himself. It is in these kinds of ambiguous circumstances that some poor black citizens are enticed by and introduced to illegitimate opportunities, which seemingly become reasonable means to an end in critical moments. They can easily bring about long-lasting entrapment in locations characterized by rampant desolation and desperation. Vulnerable situations like this are exacerbated by persisting detachment; absence of tangible resources; and noncriminal, unobtrusive intervention and assistance. As a twelve- or thirteen-year-old unable to legitimately work, Tevin internalized and framed economic opportunities in his community:

> *You started seeing the older generation getting money, meaning what?*
> Meaning that . . . I started seeing them, like, they were just gettin' a lot
> of money. Like, they could buy anything they wanted and everything
> [they wanted]. Like, they didn't have to ask [nobody for nothing].
> *[Do] you mean getting money in the streets [illegitimately]?*
> Right. . . . Like, I just saw them and that's what made me start
> actually [thinking and] wanting to get money with them.

In this way the connection between "Gs" (young neighborhood gangsters) and "OGs" (older, original gangsters) is begun, through the creation and extension of criminal subcultures (e.g., gangs, organized crime) across disadvantaged communities.[2] They develop fictive kin relationships, in which some older men who alternate between legal and illegal actions assume roles as pseudo fathers, uncles, brothers, and so forth to younger ones. This becomes a network of reciprocity, filled with illegitimate opportunities in response to strain and in the absence or lack of socially acceptable means.[3] Through direct and indirect socialization processes, OGs "put them Gs up on game." They teach them about "street" life—in which they learn or attempt to master survival codes—and how to earn money and "street" respect of their own.[4] OGs become a symbolic representation of success amid impoverishment by acquiring money, status, and the semblance of power in disadvantaged neighborhoods.[5] They can help out a few residents like Tevin by providing resource(s) and connections where resources for basic needs are lacking.

Young Tevin's visuals of men "gettin' a lot of money" can be likened to children admiring and aspiring after role models. These men are tangible examples of what is possible—success, even if illegitimately obtained—for youths and others whose only frame of reference centers on how well people "appear" to be doing in poor environments. At one point, Tevin said, "So far as we gettin' money, like, that's all we knew" when reminiscing about hustling in his neighborhood.[6] He said this as if he and his friends had never learned anything different or even thought to consider actual employment as a real option. Drug dealing provided immediate solutions and was a lucrative means to an end that did not call for an application or hiring/selection process away from the block, where they would earn significantly less. In any case, employment is subjectively (un)attainable in isolated communities, as it is contingent upon job openings, employability (e.g., age, skills), and accessibility (e.g., location, transportation), and the pay is subsequently delayed (e.g., waiting on the first check) or limited .

It is important to note that not *all* older black men in poor black communities introduce the young to or engage in crime. There are black men who unquestionably help out in their neighborhoods legitimately. They provide a broad range of services in the community, from "working on cars" (i.e., doing auto repair) to lawn care, and assistance with a variety of emerging issues. In addition, not *all* black citizens, even the poor, commit crime. Further, not all G-OG interactions and exchanges involve illegitimate or criminal socialization. Sometimes alliances between Gs and OGs can simply be about garnering and negotiating respect, space, and protection within black neighborhoods.

Illegitimate lifestyles and street exchanges "get old once you grow up," as Tevin put it. He came to this realization after countless run-ins with the police, charges, and convictions. He described the ambience of his neighborhood before he entered prison:

> *What do you mean, "it gets old?"*
> Like standing out there [on the block] being noticed . . .
> *Noticed by who?*
> Noticed by the police . . . just being out there in your neighborhood
> . . . like we sitting outside 50 to 60 people . . . females and dudes. . . .
> So we, we not doing nothing. I mean we doing something, . . . but we
> really not . . . cause we're just standing out there having a good time
> with each other.

"Doing something" and "not doing nothing" are coded statements. Taken together, they are contradictory assertions that speak to Tevin's awareness of disorder, its subjectivity, and his move to reprioritize it. Following is the reason for reconceptualizing disorder in this study. It is probable that Tevin and others were smoking weed (marijuana) in addition to hanging out. He knows that it is illegal to do so but perceives and talks about it as unimportant in the grand scheme of things. This is especially so because they are "peacefully" hanging out. This common scenario—the back-and-forth suspicions, egos, and negotiation of behaviors among Tevin, his friends, and the police—had become exhausting for him. All things considered, why would and how could smoking weed or the size of the group be something to get up in arms about in light of the fact that Tevin and his friends are living in a food desert?[7] How could their community be infiltrated by drugs but lack access to quality housing, decent schools, and grocery stores, just to name a few resources? This is how "doing something" (e.g., smoking weed) becomes "not doing nothing" (i.e., something less important). These are structural issues that reflect institutionally contradictory decisions and conditions that Tevin and his friends contend with daily. From countless vacant lots to closed schools and dilapidated buildings, nothing seems to move the dominant or broader culture with any sense of urgency about *their* neighborhood, except for suspicion of crime and criminalization. It is only then that the state and its actors (e.g., police, social services) attend to them, assessing their race, age, group size, music, location, and violations as if they are suitable candidates for interpersonal neighborhood violence or incarceration.

Tevin's example reveals other gray area(s), including the unacknowledged calm—peaceful interactions among young black men especially—and an unnerving knowledge that it could end abruptly due to actions involving each other or the police. This is important, given the propensity for violence and preponderance of media coverage on it. However, neighborhood disagreements and gunplay (shootouts) do not occur every day in all disadvantaged neighborhoods, all the time. Black citizens bond and amiably interact, sometimes by "sitting outside" or "standing out," passing time with one another, despite disorder or the possibility for imminent tension looming in the backdrop. This has similarly been the case in direct action, in-between black citizen–police clashes. Sometimes the mostly black protesters are talking, laughing, and eating together, with music and dancing to escape stress, connect, and refresh from persisting duress. They and others do this while fully aware that anyone or anything could suddenly trigger a standoff with the riot team. This is also the case with contentious police encounters in neighborhoods. Still, moments like these affirm camaraderie and humaneness among black citizens, despite structural and environmental contradictions. This is so even though they realize that they cannot always account for all behaviors, all the time for one another or the police, particularly as a constantly sliding continuum and interplay of heated exchanges are anticipated in hostile environments. Yet blacks are holistically typecast as relentlessly violent and subsequently criticized for being peaceful, as if they were incapable of it and it is contradictory to the dominant construction and the appropriation of black/blackness.

Prison, Then the Baby

> Soon as I turned 17 that's what happened. . . . [M]y first case was a bad case . . . [A]t the time, I was being a follower, . . . [but] once you laying down in the cell by yourself and you just looking at walls . . . you don't see nothin' . . . nothin'. . . . [Y]ou don't see no windows . . . you don't see nothin'. If you look out of your cell, you don't see nothin'. . . . You just see cell, like you see metal. . . . [Y]ou just sit back and think and just shed tears 'cause you like, how did I get myself in[to] this predicament? [Now] you just gotta live through it.

This was Tevin's first time being incarcerated, and he regrettably served several short consecutive sentences. He had survived being shot, as well as numerous police encounters, and yet found himself alone with tearful thoughts and no one to call. Here is how he described feeling abandoned:

> When you *not* locked up [incarcerated], you can call everybody and everybody pick up. . . . [W]hen you locked up, you don't have nobody. Everybody turn on you. . . . [T]hey don't *have* to talk to you if they don't want to.

Tevin's journey to change began incrementally through time spent and conversations with other inmates, especially a lifer. Tevin reported what this inmate said to him:

> He talked to me face-to-face [and said], "I could break your neck right now and not get no charge. . . . I can kill you right now and not get no charge. What I got to lose? But I'm telling you to get up outta here cause I wanna see you change. . . . I wanna see you in five years on my TV talking about you did something to progress our neighborhood."

Tevin took the man's words to heart, although when he was released he was still battling an all-too-familiar way of doing things. It was not until he learned that his girlfriend was pregnant that he finally made the break from the streets. He got a job; here is how he excitedly described his baby and new employment:

> I shut it down [stopped selling drugs]. . . . I saw what I was having. It was a baby inside of her [girlfriend]. She didn't do it by herself. . . . I'd get off of work, go straight home, . . . jump in the shower, get out, we lay down, watch a movie. . . . I'm rubbing her stomach the whole time. . . . Even when she fall asleep and wake back up, I'm still rubbing her stomach, just to let the baby know, like "You got a daddy and a father." I'm both. I'm gone be there. I'm never gone leave my baby.

While it had been the fear of his mother dying that initially sent Tevin into a downward spiral, it was expecting his first child that motivated him to make positive changes.

"I JUST WOKE UP"

Meet Khareem, age twenty-six.

> [Y]ou come to the city and it looks like a war zone. . . . [W]e tryin' to bring the black people together to develop a positive neighborhood. But it's very hard to do when you live in those [war zone] conditions . . . just to even give another black person hope. . . . [T]hey're traumatized. . . .

[Y]ou can tell that there's no hope there, . . . and I used to be that same way: . . . real pessimistic, . . . but it's like one mornin' I just woke up and was just tired. . . . [T]he night before that . . . I had [been] praying. . . . I was just so fed up.

The "Unhoused"

It is no wonder that Khareem had been praying the night before "his "awakening." His family faced relentless hardship for years, and prayer provided solace. They were homeless or without housing, more recently referred to as "unhoused."[8] As mentioned in chapter 3, this term is used by community organizers and advocates instead of "homeless" or "homelessness" to avoid stigmatizing and ostracizing sizable populations. The unhoused are members of many communities, who actually "live" rather just "sleep" in neighborhoods. This was the case with Khareem's family. While he did not specifically report them living on the street, he recounted years of living with other people and in shelters before moving into a home of their own:

[A]fter being evicted out of our home, out of our previous home, . . . we were homeless for like a year or two, you know and we were stayin' with relatives as long as we could. . . . [W]e would eventually get kicked out . . . after the managers of the buildings realized that us relatives were stayin' there. . . . [Then] we were movin' from place to place. . . . [T]hings were hard and we finally found a home.

The home that Khareem and his family finally found was still problematic because it was condemned. Here is his grim depiction of it:

[T]he house was abandoned, . . . so we bought it from the previous owner. . . . [T]here was a lot of work to be done. . . . [T]he grass hadn't been cut in two years, . . . holes in the wall, which, you know, was really hard to manage cause we bought the house, . . . which means we had to fix up on it ourselves and none of us knew anything about that type of work. . . . [W]e just did what we could. . . . [It] was really hard livin' there. . . . [I]t was very difficult, . . . but we made the best of the times. . . . [W]e didn't have any resources in the house. . . . [We had] electricity . . . [but] that was it. We didn't have gas, we didn't have heat, we didn't have water. . . . [W]e barely had a stove, . . . [and] that [the stove] eventually stopped workin'. . . . [W]e bought these big cookers and we had to constantly just use our neighbor's water hose to fill up buckets and buy bottled water. . . . We lived there for nine years.
In that condition?
Yes.
So you went nine years at that address with only electricity?
Pretty much. . . . [W]e *did* have water on for years but we weren't payin' and once the water company found out, . . . they cut it off.[9]

Khareem's living conditions and all that they entailed help us to understand how he came to be "pessimistic" and ultimately "fed up" with life. Through his narrative we learn of overlapping, long-standing consequences from years of inadequate housing. Like Tevin, a series of disruptive childhood experiences ultimately resulted in Khareem's hopelessness. His account allows us to see his reliance on family, as well as neighbors, to buffer some of the effects of social destitution and desperation. Relatives and neighbors provided his family with basic needs ranging from housing to water. By looking at these alliances and years of improvising, I meticulously examined and highlighted the toll that unhousing took on Khareem especially.

Despite having had a rather tumultuous childhood, Khareem characterized his mother's efforts to raise him and his siblings as doing "best as she could." She was a single parent with a middle school education, who reportedly had never been employed. Generally, Khareem provided limited information about her. He was respectful and protective of her. When asked for context—how they first came to be without housing—he did not appear readily or comfortably prepared to implicate her as playing a tangible role in all that had happened. It was as if Khareem was trying to be sure not to directly blame or disparage her. I also wanted to be careful not to do that, and consequently I allowed him to lead by portraying her as he saw fit to do.

The family were finally housed, at least apart from living with other people.[10] Their homeownership had dire consequences for Khareem and his family. After being "kicked out" of numerous places, Khareem placed great value on "having a place of their own." He prioritized stability—the fact that they no longer had to keep moving around—over the condemned status of their new home. This logic led to rationalizing the deplorable conditions of the property (e.g., holes in the walls, no utilities) and compromising the well-being of the family.

Social Services

> I remember bein' told that we had to straighten up the house
> really quick because, you know, child services was comin' to the
> home to inspect the house, which [cleaning up] was impossible,
> 'cause the house was messed up [obviously unlivable]. We had
> holes in the walls. . . . [It was] just real desolate in the inside of
> the home. It was just a mess.

Khareem characterized his neighborhood as a "war zone," and he recalled and described the inside of his home as unsafe; its condition resulted in numerous encounters with child services. Here is how Khareem remembered such encounters:

> At one point, Family Child Division stepped in, so we [the kids] had to
> go [leave the home]. . . . [W]e eventually moved back [home], slowly
> . . . tryin' to ease our way back in, you know, behind their [social
> services'] back . . . because they kinda eased up off us [decreased their
> supervision].
> *So what was that like? Child services stepping in?*
> It was [pause] unexpected, so we had to do somethin' very quick. . . .
> [I]t was pretty traumatizing. . . . They were tryin' to separate us.
> They were trying to separate us from each other. . . . [T]hey [just]
> showed up one day. I forgot who called 'em on us. . . . [He ponders.]
> [T]here was a [previous] letter or someone [just] came to our
> door. . . . I was 12–13.

Intervention by child services forced Khareem's family to make quick decisions about their living arrangements. In an effort to avoid state action, he and his siblings temporarily moved in with a relative. This was a ruse, as Khareem and the others gradually sneaked back to the home behind social services' backs. They had never truly intended to live with the relative. This was quickly seized cover to protect the group (family), to keep them together in theory at least while alleviating state intrusion. Interestingly, at this age (twelve to thirteen) that Tevin had faced real thoughts of losing his mother, had no one to take care of him, and shifted his focus to "making money." Khareem, on the other hand, was at risk of separation from his mother and having to confront social services. These were critical moments that by broad cultural standards found both young men vulnerable entering into less than conventional or desirable relationships (i.e., with OGs, child services). They had been forced to negotiate relationships and space for survival's sake, exposing their insecurities and jeopardizing their stability. It was through state intervention—eventually and perceivably good, bad, or indifferent—that their everyday lives, as they knew them, faced disruption.

Khareem and his family tried living below the radar. They feared having their family split and avoided being taken into state custody. Their family had been their one constant, and the threat of Khareem and his siblings being taken away by the state was "traumatizing." It symbolically represented *more* loss. It was like taking away the stability that they had acquired by now having a house. Child services now challenged the indelible role of their family, which had always been "all they had." Thus, this became space for resistance—a refusal to completely relinquish or sever ties with their only semblance of normalcy. They reportedly "made the most of" their living conditions. Khareem explained their resolve and their tolerance of the conditions: "[W]e made it work. . . . [W]e had some good times there."

Those "times" specifically spoke to relationships—the value they attached to interactions between family and friends throughout the neighborhood.

School and Work

> I was missin' a lot of school. . . . [W]hen I was at school, you
> know, I was bein' bullied. . . . It was hard to keep up. I was in
> special education classes, . . . so I was the outcast. . . . I wasn't,
> you know, up to par with the status quo. . . . They didn't know
> my situation. They just knew that I, you know, came to school
> with clothes that wasn't name brand, [with] hand-me-down, big
> clothes. . . . I was a[n] easy target.

Khareem's educational experiences were no better than his living conditions. School compounded his situation with isolation and bullying. He was absent a lot, the result of poverty and inadequate or lack of housing. He did not have fashionable clothes and sometimes had no money to wash the ones that he owned, which meant he either missed school or wore them dirty. All these difficulties occurred around the same time (over years) that the family were being contacted and visited by social services. While I cannot definitively connect the school to the report on Khareem's family to social services contacts, the timing is especially noteworthy. From home to school, Khareem's troubles continued to mount beyond his control. As an example, here is how he explained repeatedly missing the school bus:

> [W]hen we first moved into the house, we were [still] back and forth
> between places to live . . . because we were still tryin' to get the house
> fixed up, . . . [S]o we would catch a Metro Link bus to the place where the
> school said that they were going to send the yellow school bus to pick us
> up, but sometimes we wouldn't be able to make it. . . . [W]e wouldn't
> have the money [to catch the city bus to the designated school bus stop].

School proved too difficult for Khareem to manage. Once he was old enough, he got a job. He was finally able to earn his *own* money, but even that proved bittersweet. Here is how he described what happened:

> I was goin' to work every day. . . . I had to deal with the bills too. . . . It
> [his living conditions] was now *my* problem. . . . [T]hat's where most
> of my money was goin', . . . and to be somebody who's finally givin'
> [earning] money . . . [and I] can finally afford to buy some clothes that
> I never had. . . . [I]t's kind of sad to have to give it up, like your *whole*
> pay check to just make it. . . . I was under a lot of stress . . . and I was
> workin' . . . [at a job] which was racist and physically draining. . . .
> [C]o-workers and some of the customers were rude. . . . [P]eople seemed
> to come there and felt like they could just talk to you or treat you
> anyway. . . . [T]hey look[ed] down on you and the co-workers actually

look down[ed] on you too. . . . Just systematic stuff about the job that I noticed. . . . [I]t wasn't anything out front, you know. It was always you had to figure it out. . . . [He ponders:] "Hey, that was kinda racist."

With little education and experience, Khareem landed a low-paying job, one that even by industry standards was the lowest rung of positions at his workplace. The employees and customers reportedly treated him badly. He was working at a business mostly frequented by white citizens, as it was located in a predominantly white community. Khareem described encounters that awakened his sensibilities to overt and subtle racism. He was now becoming more apt at recognizing and connecting the nuances of oppression, in other places and back at home in his neighborhood.

Moving Out

I flipped, then moved out. I lost it mentally. I was havin' panic attacks. . . . [T]he people around me was just sayin', "Man, this is from all that build-up . . . from all that stuff that y'all goin' through and the trauma. . . . [I]t's finally just comin' out." . . . I've always been a pretty reserved person who's been able to take a lot, . . . so that comin' out was really dramatic. I didn't really know how to release that.

Khareem's transformation began with him "flipping out." His brokenness had physically manifested itself, as it does for others who face unyielding, overlapping disadvantage. This is expected and consistent with the fact that African Americans living below the poverty line are three times more likely to report psychological distress than those living at "over twice the poverty level."[11] It is also true when considering homelessness and mental distress that blacks are likelier not to receive any or adequate treatment.[12] There was seemingly no give for Khareem, and his not knowing "how to release" inspires us to reserve judgment and critically think about black citizens' responses when they are overwhelmed with hopelessness and living in desolate places. Some are exhausted, fighting from indigent vantage points. It is also the case that in direct action or while fighting for social justice generally, blacks face rigid, inflexible systems. Yet Khareem has managed to come full circle. At last contact, he had earned his GED and was attending college while working in a culturally centered environment. These are all things that he mostly attributes to having moved out when he had an opportunity to relocate to a nicer, education-focused location. Here is how he described what happened:

[I]n my head I'm like, "This can't be what life is . . . what life is about," so, obviously I moved out of the old house. . . . Somethin' told me to . . .

to move. . . . [It] was just like a saving grace because I don't think I would've survived [it].

"TRYIN' TO BREAK THAT CYCLE"

Meet Ted, age thirty-one.

A lot of people policing my neighborhood. You not from my neighborhood, so why you policing my neighborhood? You don't even know anybody on this street. So how can you say what's going on in this neighborhood . . . ? You don't know nothing about me or my kids. . . . It's a jungle out there and we just trying to make it day to day. You say you want us to plan for a future, but I can't plan . . . if I don't see it. . . . I'm [just] trying to break that cycle.

Ted's narrative primarily hinges on random thoughts, frustrations, breaking the cycle, and second chances. His mother struggled with drug addiction throughout part of his childhood. She spent time in rehabilitation centers, and after she was released she found it increasingly difficult to manage Ted. By his own admission, he was badly behaved in school. He was bored with it and recalled being told, "You gone be just like your daddy." He gradually turned to the streets. Ted had never had a real relationship with his father, who had been sentenced to life in prison before Ted's birth. Ted too has now been incarcerated. This consequence began with desperate decisions and behaviors stemming from yet another embattled childhood.

Childhood

By age thirteen, Ted had run away, stealing purses for money to buy food and engaging in similar behaviors, which initially landed him in the local juvenile detention center. He had become too much for his mother to handle. While there, he reportedly established relationships that ultimately made him even more susceptible to the criminal justice system. Here is how he described his experience:

[W]hen I went to juvenile [detention] it actually escalated my criminal history. . . . I met all these people . . . and we became a family.

His time spent in juvie appears to have done more harm than good. On the one hand, it afforded Ted a newfound "family"—similar to the G and OG alliances—that became an immediate means for buffering or coping with many difficulties. On the other hand, it broadened the tent for illegitimate opportunities, which increased upon his release and fast-tracked him for prison. This occurred in the absence of and limited availability of non-criminal, nonintrusive community services and resources, especially for disadvantaged youth. In an even larger neighborhood network, the vulnerable Ted thought to make good by selling drugs in his neighborhood and rationalized his decision:

> I tried to stay out of my momma's way so that she could take care of my sisters. I just didn't want her to have to abandon them for me. . . . I started selling drugs . . . taking care of myself since I was 13. As far as getting the clothes I want to wear, I have to wear these certain [brand of] clothes so they won't talk about me. . . . [O]nce I got those clothes, I was cool.

Tevin, Khareem, and Ted all hit critical junctures between twelve and thirteen years of age that set each of them on a life-altering course. Ted was trying not to burden his mother. There were things he wanted, such as new clothes, but he could not ask for or receive them without feeling that he would be setting the family back financially. He took matters—at least the parts he thought he could manage—into his own hands. Ted explained how he was teased at school: "I couldn't focus . . . because I was constantly ridiculed." Not all children in or near poor communities experience disadvantage the same way. Sometimes there are pockets of advantage (e.g., those with higher socioeconomic status or in areas experiencing gentrification), varying from family to family, within and across overlapping poor black neighborhoods. This makes a difference in attire, the condition of one's home, whether people own vehicles or not, and so forth. In addition, some children took part in a desegregation school program, whereby inner-city students were bused to predominantly white schools in the more affluent areas of St. Louis County. This makes differences even more overt, as sometimes race coupled with the appearance of low socioeconomic status creates an even clearer contrast between affluent white students and disadvantaged black ones. This too becomes added pressure and a reason for wanting to make fast money. Khareem attended city and county schools; Ted attended city schools and had dropped out by the tenth grade.

Ted discussed going to prison as if it were a rite of passage. He thought it was the place where one learned to be a man. He believed it to be an accomplishment of black masculinity, particularly as his childhood reference was mostly of black men in his community being disproportionately incarcerated. Now as an adult and with a family of his own, Ted's thoughts about prison and life in general are very different. He has reported earning his GED, part of his attempt to earn redemption. He communicated wanting to set an example for his children and not wanting them to fall prey to the criminal justice system, as being a convicted felon leaves him stigmatized and shut out of opportunities.

Second Chance

> [B]ecause of a mistake I made when I was 17 years old. . . . [H]ow
> can you hold a teenager accountable for his actions for the rest of
> his life? That one mistake . . . that judges me for the rest of my
> life. . . . [T]hey say there's a lot of doors open, but when you get
> to that door you don't fit the criteria. . . . I'm trying to be a better
> person, a productive citizen, . . . but when I get to the door, [the
> employer says], "[W]e ain't open." I have to survive! So how can
> I believe *you* if you keep lying. . . . I have facts [unemployment
> and poverty] to prove that you [are] lying to me.

I first met Ted while attending a community meeting, where I vividly
remember him all but begging for a job from a city official. He expressed
just needing a second chance, which resulted in information being
exchanged and a promise that someone would get back to him. I interviewed Ted a week later. He reported calling and emailing "his new city
contact," still with no response at that time. He said, "It's a constant lie. . . .
[S]o I [just] make up my own situation" (hustle). This is the "lying" that
Ted spoke of and the reason for his frustration with systemic forces that
seemingly refused to "work" with him, literally. Ted wanted to give back to
his community—one that did not even allow him to volunteer at some
places because of his felony conviction. As an example, he explained that he
had to be off parole for a certain period before he could volunteer at the
juvenile center. He stated, "I'm the person that went through what they
went through," and he believed that he could make the greatest difference
working with youth. Unemployed and feeling institutionally blackballed,
he perceived his situation (and others') to be nothing short of systemic
entrapment:

> [T]hey [the dominant, the powerful] want the crime to raise in a certain
> area. . . . [They] want it to go that certain way 'cause it's big business.
> Prison is big business. . . . if I'm investing in prison that means I want
> this [it] to be lucrative, . . . that means I need to apply certain things to
> make sure that this happens. . . . [T]hey [the powerful] know what to do,
> . . . and I feel like it's a lot of propaganda. . . . [T]hings are done on
> purpose. . . . [Y]ou say, okay, how can we stop the violence? Well, stop
> filling our streets with guns and dope. . . . [T]hat's just the bottom
> line. . . . I don't think it's that hard.

Ted drew correlations among prison, deplorable social conditions, and
persistent crime in disadvantaged black communities. His explanations are
consistent with prison as an industrial complex. He challenged nonviolence
rhetoric by referring to it as "propaganda." He redirected attention to

dominant contradictions: seemingly deliberate failures to enact policies and practices that could eradicate disorder and crime because certain industries benefit from them. Poor black citizens do not control the gun and drug industries or orchestrate the widespread dissemination of those products across communities. Ted reordered the narrative by first placing policies and practices—which seemingly protect the profitability of the aforementioned industries—at the crux of crime in the black community.

"Real Talk"

Ted repeatedly communicated his desire to provide better for his family. He and his wife were raising their children along with a younger cousin, and he wanted to move to a different area. His fifteen-year old son was robbed at gunpoint on the way to his bus stop. They took his shoes and headphones. Realizing the trauma his son now faces, Ted stated:

> You go to school for six hours a day, but you still have to come home. . . . [S]chool never prepares you for what you have to deal with. [Now] you [his son] distracted by that [the robbery]. . . . [Y]ou [he] can't focus on school work.

It is in this vein that he connected the robbery, his son's trauma, and distraction to the overall conditions faced by poor black citizens across neighborhoods:

> You [we] pray for the best because that's what you have to do. That's all you can do. Police ain't gon' protect you [us]. . . . Government not protecting us. . . . [Plus] how can I expect you [fellow black citizen] to care about my life if you don't care about your own? . . . We don't know who we are [or] where we come from.

This exchange sounds a bit pessimistic. In actuality, it is "just real talk": an unfiltered discussion about the state of some poor black citizens as Ted perceived it. He reframed his discussion in a historical black cultural perspective by highlighting cultural detachment—some black citizens not knowing who they are and where they come from, culturally—as (dis)order first associated with enslavement. He continued by situating and connecting actions from the onset of the nation to the present:

> A lot of people don't wanna deal with that reality. I can make it fairly simple for you, and this is just real talk. America was built on murder. . . stealing. I [just] don't see why people are so confused that it's going on today. It's the same thing.

Again, Ted provided context for (dis)order as it relates to historically preceding dominant actions (e.g., colonization, conquest) and the denial of them, as having long-lasting effects on people of color and social conditions generally and reciprocally.

Ted's interview seemed conversational and therapeutic for him. He had been visibly moved by different issues, even becoming choked up periodically. I wanted to be especially sensitive to his thoughts and experiences, affording him time and space to clear his head. It was the least I could do. His discussions were heavy, and I wanted him to be okay, particularly when he left the interview. Ted had come full circle emotionally while talking. From childhood neglect to protecting a family of his own, Ted described desperately fighting every day, clinging to cultural identity, and a relentless pursuit of redemption and freedom.

THEIR LIVES MATTER, NOW: HIGHLIGHTING LIFE OVER DEATH, POST-FERGUSON

Engaging in both small and large gestures and actions, many black citizens are diversely attending to black lives (e.g., Tevin, Khareem, Ted) across neighborhoods. Most do so legitimately and selflessly, receiving little to no attention and using their own limited resources. A few (i.e., the OGs) step in illegitimately, providing neighborhood support where there is a tremendous lack and great vulnerability due to structural inadequacy. Good, bad, or indifferent, alliances are forged among black citizens, especially those who are poor, to buffer the direct and indirect effects of disorder and crime across neighborhoods and in direct action. There is an empirical need to understand the role(s) of these relationships and arrangements (i.e., informal social ties and social control) that protect and serve the black community. This is especially true at the onset of and in midstream of a twenty-first-century black empowerment movement. Analysis should hinge on preserving lives and improving the quality of life for black citizens as a humanitarian mandate to be holistically attended to rather than only responded to because someone has been killed or has survived police brutality or interpersonal neighborhood violence. The true measure of whether black lives matter begins with the structural and institutional (re)ordering, (re)prioritizing, and accountability of discriminative policies and practices that persistently impede the quality of black life.

Tevin's, Khareem's, and Ted's lives matter, as do those of other black citizens. There are countless others like them that have unfortunately not been accounted for. They have seemingly only mattered posthumously, and even then, that has been through mostly snippets. With little to no context, the depth and significance of black experiences, especially of the poor, are not realized as constantly entangled in overlapping social forces. This work, however, addresses the totality of black lives as black citizens survived from childhood to adulthood and are able to share it. This is alongside of and directly in sync with the post-Ferguson movement and push, regionally and nationally, for racial advancement in the twenty-first century.

Since black men are likelier to face violent crimes than black women, this section highlights black men's specific encounters with the police.[13] In addition, as this project began with the death of Mike Brown Jr. and the beginning of a movement, I return to black citizen–police conflict, especially as Brown cannot describe his. Tevin, Khareem, and Ted were able and willing to share their experiences. This does not mean that interpersonal neighborhood violence is less important than conflict with the police, but only that participants generally held law enforcement to a greater standard—as commissioned state actors, paid to protect and serve. Here is how Tevin, who lives in the suburbs and keeps being profiled by the police, described what he thought of them:

> [M]y baby momma was in the hospital and [I had] just came from seeing her. It was like about 12 o'clock. I pull up, I guess somebody house had got broken into [a home invasion]. . . . I'm getting out the car . . . getting my baby out the back . . . He [police] pulled up, jumped out the car real fast, had his gun out. "Get on the ground!" I didn't follow directions at all because I'm not getting on the ground. First, I'm not getting on the ground at all in front of my child. I'm not getting on the ground because I just pulled up to my house. . . . I'm on the lease, so you can't say that I'm not supposed to be here. . . . [M]y car [plates are] good. My car [is] not stolen. I have full coverage insurance. What [are] you doing this for? Then as everything calmed down, he [police] did that because they said . . . a young black man . . . broke into somebody's house. . . . I'm a young black man . . . so they assumed that I did it. I had to put my baby back in the car seat and they put me in handcuffs . . . I had to wear the handcuffs for a whole hour until the sergeant came. . . . [T]he sergeant apologized to me multiple times. . . . But like I said, police, . . . they just do stuff for attention. . . . [T]hey got a badge, . . . they feel like, well, they can get away with anything and they can because the judge [court system] gonna always take the police side before they take our [black citizens'] side.

Simply put, Tevin could have died that night in front of his baby. He "did not comply" with police, which becomes a coded action denoting "threat" and the police "fearing for their lives." This can be translated into justification for police to shoot to kill—perceived by many in the black community to be a routinely convenient police defense in the absence of restraint. Like

Ted, Tevin is trying to redeem himself from having been incarcerated. He has relocated, works full time providing for his family, and still feels targeted because of his felony. He reported not hating the police, but expressed frustration about their profiling. Tevin was insulted and humiliated by the police. His resistance was about empowerment—he refused to be demeaned (get on the ground) in front of his neighbors and baby. He arguably took a chance, post-Ferguson, and not because he was guilty.

Khareem also faced police aggression, having a gun held on him as a child of middle school age. At that time he had no criminal history. Here is how he recalled his experience:

> [W]e [me and a neighborhood friend] were playin' with a toy gun. . . .
> [H]e [police] made a U-turn. . . and we put the gun on the ground, . . .
> had our hands [already] up 'cause we knew what was comin', so he still
> got out of his car with his gun drawn, . . . yellin' at us to get down on the
> ground, and we did. . . . [T]hey saw that it was a toy gun, they had us on
> the ground with their gun[s] drawn. . . . I'd say about ten minutes . . .
> with their guns held on us. . . . Put us both in handcuffs and . . . took our
> IDs. Ran our names just to see that there was nothin' on our records.
> They had to let us go 'cause we wasn't doin' anything. It was a toy.

As Khareem shared his account, I was reminded of Tamir Rice, at the crux of whose murder was a pellet gun. Ten minutes is a long time to be held at gunpoint; anything could have gone drastically wrong. Khareem had other negative encounters with the police, as a witness to other neighborhood incidents. Such incidents become part of the cumulative experiences of black citizens.[14] Ted also recalled numerous negative encounters with the police. He expressed distrust of them, along with wanting to see them interact respectfully across neighborhoods. Research shows that black citizens generally do not hate the police, but rather are adamantly opposed to differential treatment.[15] They want to be served humanely.

Ted's comments were extensive, linking or capturing other relevant issues or events. Of the three participants quoted in this chapter, he is the only one who spoke of specific incidents in Ferguson. Tevin and Khareem generalized discussions or statements regarding Ferguson. Yet Ferguson was a reference for all participants, directly and indirectly. Here is how Ted discussed police encounters and civil unrest in the context of the looting and burning of the QuikTrip:

> You got a lot of people talkin' about, oh, they [blacks] tore down their
> own neighborhood. Now they can't even go to the store. [He speaks
> hypothetically:] Well, can I [neighborhood black citizens] go to *that*
> store and tell the clerk, "Look, I ain't got no gas but I need to get back

and forth to work, I come in here all the time, can you give me some gas to get back and forth to work, I got you [will pay you] on Friday? . . . [Y]ou know, when I get paid?" So, why should I [we] care about an *insured* store? You [they are] *insured*. I don't care about breaking into your store, taking anything out of there.

Ted's assertion was not meant to encourage or condone crime in Ferguson or anywhere else, any more than Tevin's refusal to get on the ground was meant to inflame the exchange and provoke the police. Ted only provided context for how actions in Ferguson and beyond became part of the overall resistance. Despite widespread criticism and denigration of the arson and looting, his point is that resistance in this sense speaks to the economic exploitation of poor black communities. It highlights the fact that systems allow for everyone else (i.e., white, Asian, and Arab business owners) to benefit from black consumerism, with more benefits going out of the community than coming in. Reciprocity is lost in these relationships. Therefore, the "looting" and "burning" are not about the store, but rather symbolic of resisting capitalism that prospers at the cost of devaluing black lives and the quality thereof in run-down neighborhoods.

Narratives such as Tevin's, Khareem's, and Ted's matter. They are important for examining transitions from childhood to adulthood, pre and post-Ferguson. It is in this space that various forms of black resistance, empowerment, and social movement became points of reference in these participants' conversations, without my asking directly. For example, Tevin mentioned a friend who does things related to the Black Lives Matter campaign.[16] He spoke proudly about him, recalling his friend's transition from the streets to the movement. Tevin saw himself in his friend and seemed inspired, too. Khareem attributed his progress to learning about his black identity and tied his improvement to now sharing a home with someone who is culturally enlightened and Afrocentric. He also works with a black empowerment organization. Ted is empowered through community involvement. He attaches himself to programs, events, and activities throughout the city that specifically embrace and work to advance black culture and community. I met him at a community meeting. In short, all three indirectly credited black empowerment for influencing their personal progress. I cannot unequivocally attribute their progress to post-Ferguson civil unrest, but I do infer that based on their increased interests and awareness, they benefit from its momentum. With in-group racial (black) and residential (St. Louis) statuses, they are directly attached to and impacted by the movement as members of the region and through various forms of involvement. Opportunities for mobilizing and organizing have become plentiful regionally. The men are also indirectly connected and vested through persons that they know who are also inspired by and organize as part of the movement. All three use their newfound knowledge and inspiration to propel hope and improvements for their lives. As community leader/organizer, Chon stated:

> [The] police shoot people, people shoot other people but prior to Ferguson there was not mass communication about IT that drove IT [redirected it].

The Ferguson uprising is a pivotal point in history and a driving force for new directions. Its twofold agenda in preserving black life is in effect, and its impact is inescapable. This twenty-first-century movement has gained prominence and become a mainstay for social change in the black community.

OTHERMOTHERING AND COMMUNITY OTHERMOTHERING: FRAMING OUTREACH AND ACTIVISM IN BLACK FEMINISM

> I'm not out there to fight them. . . . That whole neighborhood needs a hug. That whole neighborhood needs love. That's just flat out. . . . [I]t's not what you do, it's how you do it.
>
> TRACY, age forty

Consistent with cultural tradition, this project found black women protecting and serving as "othermothers" and "community othermothers."[17] In othermothering, blood- or kinship-related women, such as grandmothers, cousins, and aunts, were "assisting blood mothers by sharing mothering responsibilities."[18] There is a longstanding cultural history of black women in America especially coming to be needed throughout the community in diverse circumstances. Othermothering is an informal network, extended from slavery, in which a "cooperative" approach was taken to childrearing, whereby all slave women were responsible for all slave children.[19] This is a tradition, one initially characterized by kinship but also extending to and including fictive kin relationships.[20] It has persisted well into the twenty-first century and captures "mothering" extended, irrespective of biological relationships. There continues to be a need, and now a varying expectation, within the black community—subtly and overtly—for black women to step in and assume roles as othermothers (e.g., feed children, babysit) as necessary. They do this when parents are unable to attend to their own children fully (as happened with Tevin, Khareem, and Ted). This is especially the case for those in impoverished places, where varying degrees of need call for resilience and extended women-centered alliances.

As othermothering provides "a foundation for conceptualizing women's political activism," the term *community othermother* has emerged as a sociopolitical derivative.[21] As an example, community othermothering has been associated with warning young black women about sexual violence.[22] Specific to this project, community othermothering is exemplified by black women employing varying degrees of socioeconomic and political influence, up to full "activist mothering."[23] Collins described this as "the type of power many African-Americans have in mind when they describe the 'strong black women' they hope will revitalize contemporary Black neighborhoods."[24] This power occupies the culturally entrenched space through which black women sacrificially and meticulously gain and employ capital and status in an effort to advance neighborhoods and, more broadly, the black community.

Community othermothers generally receive little to no "fanfare or recognition."[25] They operate selflessly alongside of othermothers, protecting and serving especially black interests. This study depicts community othermothers strategically and culturally maneuvering as resistance—providing buffers or counters to disorder and its effects. Collins describes these women as working "on behalf of the community by expressing ethics of caring and personal accountability. . . . [T]heir purpose is to bring people along, to—in the words of the late-nineteenth century black feminists— 'uplift the race' so that vulnerable members of the black community will be able to attain the self-reliance and independence essential for resistance."[26]

This project found women operating as both othermothers and community othermothers. Through a litany of circumstances they are found uniquely and empathetically allying and engaging with other black citizens, within neighborhoods and across communities (e.g., in protests and neighborhoods). This section specifically addresses community othermothering by three women: Tracy, Lauren, and Angela. Their efforts reflected and included both roles to some degree—from everyday simple gestures and exchanges (othermothering) in the neighborhood to socioeconomic and political positioning (community othermothering) that leveraged a particular kind of cultural influence.

Community Othermothers

Meet Tracy, age forty, and Lauren, age forty-two. They are uniquely situated in that they are entrepreneurs. They both have businesses in neighborhoods that are racked by drugs and violence. Although they both live in

St. Louis County, I included them in this project as if they were inner-city residents. They spend significant amounts of time in the city due to their businesses—arguably more than they spend at home—so it seemed reasonable to report their exchanges in this way. They are vested and trusted members of the neighborhood. The residents treat them as neighbors, and they reciprocally perceive one another as needed allies. Numerous other women also engaged as othermothers and community othermothers throughout this project. However, I specifically highlight Tracy's and Lauren's actions because they operate through entrepreneurship. Unlike the businesses Ted discussed—which extract and do not give back—they employ and tailor legitimate services unique to their neighbors and for the larger community. Although they are just economically vested in the neighborhood, their roles somewhat emulate those who live there.

As an example, here is how Tracy described how she navigates interactions with children in the neighborhood:

> [I]t's kids in the neighborhood who depend on me. . . . It's a little girl who comes through all the time and she has a odor, I want to bring her home so bad and just bathe her and do her hair so bad. . . . [S]he has to be eight. Seven or eight years old. I'm gonna give her nine at the most. . . . They [the little girl and another kid] go to the school [nearby], . . . and they tell me, "We didn't see you Monday." I give them candy every time I see them. . . . I'm supposed to be there [in the neighborhood] to make a profit, but that don't matter to me. Those kids need it [support]. . . . Yeah. And I call them, "Hey, friendy pie. What's up, friendy pie?" . . . It's so heartbreaking. . . . I know her mother because her mother walks her to and from school, . . . and if it's not her mother then it's a little dirty man that comes and gets them. . . . No car. It's raining outside, they just be walking in the rain. No umbrellas. They don't stop in [into the business] on those days 'cause it's raining. I be like, oh Lord have mercy, there go my friends [watching them]. . . . [T]hey like to play with me and joke with me. Give me a hug. . . . I hug those kids 'cause they want a hug. . . . I just give them a hug.

From wanting to fix "friendy pie's" hair to hugs, Tracy struggles as a community othermother with seeing her and other neighborhood children unclean. She perceives "friendy pie's" mother as not doing enough to care for her. She is pained by this, as well as by her own seemingly inability to step in and resolve the problem. In an effort to respect boundaries, Tracy attends to the neighborhood kids as best as she can—in perceivably safe and nonintrusive ways. These exchanges increase trust, as they are more agreeable than those of social services. Tracy gives them after-school snacks and hugs, as she "knows" both will make them happy. The kids know that she genuinely cares for them. They expect to see her whenever they pass through, for more treats, hugs, and playful conversations—that is, motherly affection—calling attention to those times when she has not been present.

There are several men who also wander into Tracy's businesses alone. They are unemployed, unhoused, and apparently drug addicted—sometimes simultaneously and interchangeably. Here is how she described her response to them:

> I do a lot of talking to the neighborhood . . . like the guys that steal. How y'all doing? Y'all being good? Y'all, don't be out there in no trouble; . . . be careful. Y'all, don't be bothering nobody. . . . I talk to them; . . . I pray with them. And they ask me to. [She repeats what they say to her:] "I'm not doing good today; can you pray for me?" And I do. . . . [W]e bow our heads and we actually pray. I pray with them; . . . they say thank you and they go on out the door.

Tracy is street savvy and watchful of the neighborhood. She is aware of neighborhood incidents, sometimes verified by those men. She knows when things have been stolen (e.g., her air conditioning unit). She suspects that one or two of the men may have taken it, since others have dropped hints about it. They sometimes do wrong things, wavering among various states of drug addiction, unhousing, and unemployment. Therefore, Tracey shows concern for them by encouraging and then sternly admonishing them, when necessary. She even periodically hires them to do odd jobs (e.g., take out trash, sweep and mop floors) to curb their bad behavior. She sends them off to clean up or straighten themselves up, explaining that they must be more presentable for customers. They oblige, as they are familiar with her personality. She communicates her expectations (e.g., "y'all being good") while forbidding bad behavior (e.g., "don't be bothering nobody"). They respond accordingly so as not to disappoint her as a community othermother. They share with her that they are not doing well and seek comfort from her. They respect her and believe that her prayers will help them. She rewards them with kindness and goodwill—praying and encouraging; otherwise they might not receive any.

Lauren is also community othermothering in the neighborhood surrounding her business. Aware of community needs, she has worked to provide safe recreational space for children. Here is how she described what she did:

> I tried to do a project to get a safe playground built here in the area, so I talked to families about why they don't take their children to the neighborhood playground. . . . I was able to get some feedback on why they don't take their children outside, why they don't take them to the neighborhood park.

Do you remember some of the things they said?

Absolutely. High gang activity, drug paraphernalia that was spread along the playground, just violence, fear of violence, stray bullets. I wanted to get a place that was wide open to the community, . . . that we [the business] would take responsibility for. . . . [T]he community would share the responsibility of keeping it safe and making sure that it, that it stayed safe and clean and free of debris. We [her business] would agree to maintain it. . . . I have customers who live in this community. . . . I wanted to have a safe place that, that the children could come, . . . a place that had equipment that was going to be maintained . . . provide an outlet, a physical outlet for them and that they could freely come to and share in the experience of play. . . . I'm here in the community. These are my neighbors, so I don't want to have like a separatist type, you know, attitude that I'm here to make money in your community but you can't use any of my resources.

The women-centered network in Lauren's disadvantaged neighborhood is partly her collaborating and maneuvering as a community othermother to provide safe, enjoyable space for the mostly single black mothers and children in her neighborhood.[27] She did not want to just profit from the neighborhood, but rather to reciprocally use her influence and the resources of her business to give back to them. She has other projects in mind to benefit the neighborhood. Lauren thinks of and treats children in the neighborhood as if they were her own and shares responsibility with surrounding neighbors as an extended family. Together, as best they can, they buffer the effects of disorder by providing the "experience of play" for children in a safe location, away from "violence, fear of violence, and stray bullets," with Lauren's business providing oversight.

Loss and Violence

My interview with Angela, forty-eight, was a bit delayed. She called and gave me a rough estimate of when she thought she would be available, saying that she had an errand to run. She had teddy bears to drop off. Since we had scheduled the interview, a child had been accidentally shot and killed across town, and I could hear the urgency in her voice. She had quickly gathered things that she needed and was on her way to the scene.

Angela is a community othermother. She religiously helps with street memorials for crime victims all over the city, participates in protests, and engages in other activities. This is in addition to organizing her own sociopolitical community events. She takes what little she has and makes it work, with donations and assistance from others.

Based on previous phone conversations, I had some inkling of how Angela operated and knew that I needed to be patient. I could tell that she was excited about speaking with me but could easily be called to duty in the community. This could be for any reason; nothing seemed to escape her. She operated as if she were an ex-officio mayor. She always seemed to have a plan or mission targeting needs in the community. It was no wonder that the day of her interview was no different. She called back a couple of hours later to confirm our meeting and to alert me that she was on her way. I worked while waiting for her. Roughly twenty minutes later, she walked in with a couple of kids and a tote bag. The kids went in another direction as she headed toward me. I could tell that she was relieved to be there but was still very emotional and really angry about the murder of a local kid. I could see her tearing up as we began to talk, and I asked if she wanted me to pause. She motioned as if to say "no, keep going" and then stated:

> I just got through dropping teddy bears off to somebody. . . . [T]hat child [is] gone [dead]. . . . "[W]hat do YOU [people] be thinking . . .?" I say all the time, OVER and OVER and OVER. . . . "[Y]ou gotta protect your kids," and people not getn it.

Black children's lives matter. Like all children, they are precious and innocent. They are the more vulnerable parties, just like senior citizens, in all-too-often tenuous situations that persist in isolated, black neighborhoods. Angela was extremely bothered, and throughout her interview she admonished her family: the black community. She spoke as if they all—babies to adults—were her children. She had instructed them "over and over and over" again, to no avail. She was visibly hurt and disappointed.

As a community othermother, Angela's connections and sociopolitical work run deep. It is as if she knows everyone and everything across neighborhoods and beyond, well into direct action. She is an "activist mother," and her efforts know no boundaries.[28] She "demonstrates a clear rejection of separateness and individual interests."[29] In the interview she described how she brings the community or "family" together when I asked her about her participation with local groups and organizing:

> *Have you ever worked with individuals or local groups to solve community problems?*
> Yes, [I] did stuff *myself*. The people in the community always help. . . . [I] had stop-the-violence events, . . . had a balloon release for people that loss their love ones due to violence, had a second annual balloon release for people that loss their love ones this year. . . . [It was] pretty crowded. . . . [W]e had different families [there], had a stage, . . . [had] a picnic table, BBQ; . . . released over 100 balloons; . . .

didn't have enough balloons 'cause there were over a 100 people there. . . . [It] turned out nice [and] was more crowded this year than last. . . . [I] just did something this past Saturday. . . . [I had] a stop-the-violence event, . . . [had] DJ, hotdogs again, bottle water, chips, dancers [a youth dance group].
Where are you doing these [events]?
Local parks and lots [vacant lots]. . . . [Just] pick a lot and take over.

As Angela spontaneously recalled events that she had organized, she appeared proud of her accomplishments. This was especially the case regarding the turnouts. They had increased, and she was glad that there was more involvement across neighborhoods. Part of her efforts hinged on engagement and awareness, which had seen improvement. This was so even if she was getting a relatively small turnout compared to other organizations. In fact, she seemed somewhat put off when I asked whether she worked with other organizations. Her tone when she said she "did stuff *myself*" implied that she did not "need" any particular organization or group to guide or determine her work across neighborhoods. She had ideas about registering her "own" organization and had the paperwork in her bag for getting started through the Missouri Secretary of State Office.

Angela's extended family—the black community—helps her with activities. This is part of her aim: to get them involved with local neighborhood projects. This does not mean that she is resistant to other community groups and will not work with them; she works with them regularly. She only wanted to make clear that she did not need their permission or lead to do anything. In fact, it may be that she is better aligned and able to address many neighborhood needs intimately. She has the wherewithal to navigate and negotiate many arrangements and relationships—without red tape—across St. Louis City and County neighborhoods. People trust her and see her as a resource, which speaks to her carrying around a tote bag filled with papers (e.g., applications, fliers), disseminating information pertaining to health-care programs, giveaways, educational programs, job training, and so forth. This is her way of keeping the community plugged in. Here is how she explained this:

I always keep a lot of literature. Like if I go somewhere, I'll pick up information to give to people like if something [is] goin on.

Angela can be found laboring on behalf of poor black citizens in countless ways across the St. Louis region. She mostly organizes events that provide comfort and assistance to all in the community who are aggrieved, whether or not police killings or homicides are involved. She sees grief of any kind in the black community as consuming and an added pressure for which she seeks to provide support. She community othermothers with little to no resources, and she reiterated to me "...I been doin' this stuff on my own... without gettin' paid" only to emphasize that she sees this as a personal responsibility and obligation to the community. Money is not her motivation; she expects none. More than anything, she seems to embrace facilitating unity.

Angela and I cross paths regularly. We are often at the same community events, ranging from nonviolence marches to direct action in Ferguson. I saw her a lot at protests following the Jason Stockley verdict.[30] I have been able to witness her firsthand, interacting with members of the community. I have even seen her arrive with food at events she did not organize. She and other community othermothers—other activist mothers I am familiar with—contribute to supporting a family. In instances when we have both been present, we happily greeted one another with a hug. She would then follow up immediately by informing me of various things transpiring throughout the region. I appreciated this information, especially as there were programs that I was unaware of but considered attending. This is now her way of "taking care" of me. She is aware of the work that I do and has always been excited about pitching in whenever possible. I too have inadvertently become part of her women-centered network.

CONCLUSION

Black lives matter *before* death. Their everyday existences are significant, especially as their quality of life has tremendous implications for their survival. It is for this reason that this chapter has provided case studies on three black men whose lives were shaped in deprivation and neglect. Everything about who they are reflects unyielding lack, in isolation. Their lives have emulated the resources and opportunities legitimately or illegitimately made available to them in the places where they have resided—disproportionately black spaces where the effects of barrenness and desolation (disorder) undercut social progress. Then, through a black feminist framework, this chapter examined three black women as othermothers and community othermothers. Through women-centered networks (i.e., othermothering and community othermothering) and cultural tradition, they step in to provide care and support through empowerment and activism across black neighborhoods and communities. It is not by mere chance or coincidence that neighborhoods and their residents get to experience this care, and it is also not by happenstance that blacks continue disproportionately to face layers of pervasive destitution.

There is a litany of factors that undermine a community; more directly, they affect black lives in their entirety. Traditional ideas about disorder and subsequent responses do not overtly depict social system and structures as inherently rigged against populations of color, black citizens particularly. However, there are hierarchal rankings that by virtue of social construction and power leave communities and citizens of color, especially the poor, purposefully situated as losing, and others (i.e., the dominant) as winning. Consequently, poor black experiences often reflect the "losing by design" portion of this arrangement, which affords populations of color little to no room to prevail or in some instances even survive. Nevertheless, some do prevail, by relying on a variation of informal alliances and actions, occurring interchangeably, that may compromise or advance their lives in various ways.

5. "We Are in a State of Emergency"

For several years I attended the "Stop the Violence" marches, rallies, and summits with Free Peace Community Inc. Each time my emotions were mixed, as I knew that I would be surrounded by more crime victims and grieving families (i.e., survivors and surviving families). I could vicariously feel their pain. Many had also been protesting police brutality. I wanted to support the families, their messages and missions, and the local organization that hosted events and resources for them. The marches were especially personal because they put me directly back in my childhood neighborhood—emotionally, mentally, and physically—reminiscing about how I had grown up surrounded by and exposed to violence. Despite being almost thirty years removed from those days, I was still very much affected by these events, as I could imagine the sound of gunshots ringing in the near distance. These are the long-lasting effects of disorder, similar to those that many at the march were experiencing daily, although for them the effects were directly exacerbated by violence, loss, and heartache.

Survivors and surviving families wore T-shirts, displayed pictures, and carried posters of their loved ones during the marches, as they did when participating in police protests. Differing slightly from protests, the marches afforded a platform specific to them, centering on lives lost to interpersonal neighborhood violence. The opening speeches at each march were filled with empowering messages from survivors and surviving families. They provided warnings, awareness, and even messages of hope for improving the state of poor black neighborhoods. As I marched with the families, I documented events as carefully and thoughtfully as I could. This effort was particularly important because my aim was to safely extend their platforms. Survivors and surviving families of neighborhood violence are largely invisible, as is their pain. They generally receive less coverage than black citizen–police protests do, so people are not as aware of their names and faces. They deserve significant attention and assistance. My hope here is to highlight their plight, increase much-needed nonviolent community awareness, and broaden support.

This chapter raises the significance of the voices of survivors and surviving families of violence through a post-Ferguson framework. As can be expected, black citizen–police brutality cases tend to garner significant attention; this chapter is instead framed by survivor families and survivors of interpersonal neighborhood violence. They have been afforded a platform for sharing their heartfelt thoughts and directives for the black community. Participating in crime prevention activities and programs is an example of how some black citizens in general engaged with local formal organizations. Some belonged to or benefited from neighborhood meetings and associations, town hall meetings, and local charitable organizations. Others were situationally affiliated with formal organizations. They were volunteers or donators and therefore were not members or benefiters. Generally, this project found that most participants were engaging in informal integration and participating less formally in local organizations. This chapter captures the few who were doing the latter because the black community faces a state of emergency in its fight to preserve and advance the quality of black life.

"SO MANY DIFFERENT PHASES"

Meet Nia, age forty-four.

I met Nia while attending a town hall meeting primarily centered on physical disorder: derelict properties and vacant lots throughout St. Louis City. This event had been organized by a state legislator and characterized as a "state of emergency" for the black community. I had a sign-up table there for my project. Nia stopped by my table; I introduced myself and briefly explained my project. She agreed to be interviewed later; however, before leaving, she began to tell me that she had an adult child who was missing. I ushered her off to the side of the table for privacy. She was looking for another platform on which to share her story. She was sorely hurting and did not believe that she was receiving adequate assistance from law enforcement or members of the community. I listened intently as she whispered her plans to organize in search of her loved one. Then, when I felt it was appropriate, I ensured her that I would call her so that she could freely and anonymously speak further about her situation. However, weeks had passed by the time I was able to interview Nia. By the time I called, her child's remains had been found, so she wanted to schedule an interview to express her reaction. Here is how she described her feelings when we met:

> I go through so many different phases. . . . Some days I want the person that did this to my child [dead], I want *their* parents dead and *their* kids dead, and [then I want] *them* [the murderer and the person's family] to have to sit here and feel what I feel. Then some days I feel sorry for [the murderer's] mom and don't want [her] to go through what I go through; . . . [It's] pain constantly, [it's] heartache.

Nia's sentiments reveal a broad range of emotions—from wanting revenge to showing compassion to the family of the one responsible. This reaction also speaks to the fact that neighborhood violence can inspire more violence (or thoughts of it). Citizens sometimes arm themselves for protection or, worse, attempt to dispense vigilante justice (e.g., taking revenge, performing acts of self-help as social control) as additional forms of informal social control.[1] Crime or violence between blacks is partly due to social isolation.[2] It is for this reason that black citizens sometimes step in—individually, informally, and reciprocally—to combat disorder and its effects in their communities. They often lack adequate assistance even from law enforcement (e.g., there are delayed calls, no-shows), especially those who are disadvantaged.[3]

Interpersonal Neighborhood Violence

As this project examined community disorder and its effects broadly in the wake of Ferguson's civil unrest, I worked to understand formal organizational efforts in combating interpersonal neighborhood violence, specifically homicides. Between 1999 and 2015, the Centers for Disease Control and Prevention (CDC) revealed staggering homicide rates for non-Hispanic blacks compared with rates for all other races.[4] In 2015 the homicide rate for the overall population was 5.7 deaths per 100,000 people, with 20.9 deaths for blacks, 4.9 for Hispanics, and 2.6 for whites.[5] For deaths by firearms in 2015, the rate for the national population was 4.2 deaths per 100,000 people, with 1.6 for whites, 17.3 for blacks, and 4.8 for Native Americans or Alaskan Natives.[6] Even with decreases in black homicide rates, the current rates, among other factors, provide a reason for declaring a state of emergency in the black community.[7] Black citizens are dying or being killed at unconscionable rates. The living contend with this realization up close and personal through both direct and indirect victimization and pervasive institutional neglect, especially in disadvantaged neighborhoods. Given the empowered responses of black citizens for preserving and improving black lives post-Ferguson, it has been important to know *if* and *how* such issues were emerging in and being addressed through formal organizations. This study found that these issues were being addressed both in and beyond protests. They are part of meeting agendas, particularly in high-risk areas that face the worst of concentrated disadvantage and isolation. Like police brutality, interpersonal neighborhood violence also needs immediate attention.[8] Gun violence poses an imminent threat to the black community, an issue that also calls for analysis. This is how Nia spoke about gun violence:

> Put these guns down! . . . You can fight somebody and then tomorrow say, "They wasn't worth it," [but] once you take somebody's life, you can't get that back. And seeing how little our community is, it [death] always overlap[s] to somebody that you know. . . . I want people to think before they react. I want more unity, more coming together.

Part of "coming together" for Nia has meant partnering with organizations in search of missing citizens. Let us turn attention to missing and exploited black citizens, as this too is a significant issue in the black community, found to be formally organized and occurring as part of the broader effort to address neighborhood crises.

Missing and Exploited Black Citizens

Nia discussed the toll that her child's disappearance had taken on her family while she had been trying to participate in various organizations as well as to assist others facing similar experiences. Here is what she said:

> I'm involved with a lot of organizations [that are trying to find] missing people because my child was missing for months. . . . If another person is missing, I go out and [help] search [for her or him]. People contact me, and I help give [them] the right steps because police and politicians don't [tell] you the steps you need to take in order for you to do what you got to do when you have a love[d] one missing. . . . It was stressful. It was a strain on my household. Now, I'm fightin' for justice. . . . I gotta put everything else on the back burner. . . . They [the police] haven't really been talkin' to me. So I have to stay on them. . . . See, a lot of us [black citizens] don't stay on them; we just give up [on the police handling and solving black cases].

Research has revealed race and gender disparities in searches for missing citizens. As of 2017, the Federal Bureau of Investigation (FBI) had reported 219,484 black citizens missing, compared to 387,104 missing white citizens, across all age categories.[9] For the period 2016–2017, the Black and Missing Foundation Inc. (BAMFI) and the FBI together found that missing and unidentified black citizens make up more than 30 percent of missing persons, with whites making up more than 60 percent.[10] However, missing black citizens are less likely to receive the media attention and in-depth coverage that missing white citizens, particularly white women, do.[11] This phenomenon has been referred to as the "missing white woman syndrome" (MWWS) or the "missing white girl syndrome."[12] These findings are consistent with Nia's suspicion that other missing persons cases had been prioritized over hers. She stated:

> I hate to play the race card, but a white girl went missing the same week, [and] they found her in twenty-four hours.

Others have made similar arguments, calling attention to the fact that missing girls of color generally do not receive media coverage proportionate to that given to missing white girls.[13] Black girls or women in particular are described as never having platforms similar to those given to the disappearance of white ones such as Elizabeth Smart or Natalee Holloway.[14] *New York Daily News* columnist and activist Shaun King noted: "We don't see prime time television specials on [missing black girls]. Their images don't become permanent fixtures on Twitter. Their names don't get hashtags or trending topics. National manhunts . . . don't ensue. Crying black parents pleading for their children . . . don't interrupt our sitcoms as breaking news."[15]

There is also disregard for and devaluation of missing black boys and men; taken together with the data on missing black girls and women, this exposes a newfound, unfortunate reality for Nia and her family. They had become increasingly isolated because there had been no determination made about whether their loved one was dead or alive, unlike the news given to some other survivors and surviving families. For months Nia and her family had been left stuck in a holding pattern in addition to having to deal with other complexities of their lives. Nia's life had already been shaped by difficulties ranging from the frequent jailing of her mother during her childhood to her own involvement in a gang as a teenager. She characterized herself as a "street girl." She described her teen behaviors and those of others who had behaved similarly as "kids just wanting to belong to something." She also reported having been sexually assaulted by an unnamed person in the field of criminal justice and used her own experience to argue about systemic contradictions. Despite the existence of information that debunked her claims, she blamed the system for hypocritically interfering with parents' right to discipline their children (the effects of spankings versus police brutality of them).[16] Although not exclusively used by black citizens, this claim remains a traditionally deferred to and debated issue, especially regarding state-sanctioned criminal justice contact with black youth (e.g., Tamir Rice, Mike Brown) post-Ferguson.

Empathy

I have been especially cautious when engaging with survivors and surviving families of violence, whether police or interpersonal. I once had a surviving family member curse me out over the phone. I was volunteering with a phone bank for a local group and called to invite him and his family to an antiviolence event that was extending a platform for them to speak. He took the opportunity to vent about what he initially stated was a lack of support from community organizations. I did not take his response personally; his anger was not meant for me. I am also not convinced that it was truly meant for the local organizations, as he suggested. His responses seemed to have more to do with his being devastated by the recent loss of his sister to gun violence. Consequently, I just held the phone, listened, and humbly responded when prompted to or to confirm that I was still on the line. He calmed down almost immediately because I mostly remained quiet, talked a bit longer, and then ended the call respectfully.

Survivors and surviving families experience unfathomable pain, and when I encounter them I immediately offer them empathy and respect. I can vicariously feel their pain "because [I believe that] we are all one" and "your pain is my pain," as had been stated by a speaker in the introduction to a stop-the-violence march and rally I attended. This speaker had continued by having us repeat to one another, "I'm not your enemy; you're not my enemy." It is in this spirit that I let Nia and the surviving family member and patron on the phone speak freely. I was able to gauge their emotions and expectations and determine my next actions with them in mind. They were vulnerable, so this approach minimized the possibility for clichéd, condescending, and unnecessary reactionary responses from me. I was sometimes rendered speechless, realizing that I could say nothing to alleviate the pain they were feeling. The patron on the phone had been traumatized by his sister's murder. I just happened to be the person who heard him out regarding senseless killings. His diatribe seemed harmless, and it was the least that I could do to simply listen. He seemed thankful, relieved, and calmer by the end of our phone conversation.

FORMAL PARTICIPATION

We've been fighting to stop the violence, to stop the crime. Something is radically wrong. . . . Black people gotta start mobilizing.

SURVIVING FAMILY MEMBER, Free Peace Community Inc.
"Stop the Violence" march

I have spent years documenting black citizen–police conflicts and subsequent direct actions. I have also attended and participated in other community events and actions sponsored by various formal organizations throughout the St. Louis region, which mostly addressed a range of concerns including, but not limited to, police brutality. These organizations were confronting various forms and degrees of disorder (both social and physical) in diverse ways. Attending these events gave me a chance to gauge the level of black citizens' formal participation or involvement with confronting other social issues compared to their participation in matters that centered on police clashes. In addition, these events afforded me opportunities to account for other social problems and possible formal group or neighborhood attempts to resolve (or not resolve) them. Such problems sometimes cannot be easily resolved because the disproportionately degrading conditions for black citizens do not begin and end with differential treatment by law enforcement. There are deep discriminative, overlapping forces at play that persistently work to stunt the advancement of black America locally and more broadly. Police brutality is merely a by-product of these forces, forever seething beneath the surface.[17]

As St. Louis came to garner national and international attention as the epicenter of a twenty-first-century social movement, it likewise was repeatedly dubbed the "murder capital of the country."[18] This dynamic was part of the reason I undertook this project. While we protesters were embedded in direct actions, black citizens were still dying from interpersonal neighborhood violence. This project afforded me an opportunity to examine community disorder by looking at interpersonal neighborhood violence as a corresponding threat and focus. Furthermore, through studying formal participation or neighborhood organizations, I can examine "the degree to which people participate in tenants' groups, neighborhood improvement associations, block crime watch[es,] and other community service organizations."[19]

Through this study, I was able to assess how interview participants reported their involvement with group, formal organizations (i.e., committed/frequent, not committed/infrequent) compared with the involvement of visible attendees (e.g., small or large turnouts) at various neighborhood events sponsored by neighborhood groups or associations.[20] I observed and accounted for various forms of formal participation in real time in different places across the region. I documented the age ranges of participants, the focus of group efforts and solutions, and the likelihood of black citizens involving themselves in formal participation across various groups. I also thought that this effort could provide me with more insight into the demographics of participants (e.g., homeownership) through participant observation, to compare with the insights I had gained through in-depth interviews and focus groups.

This project found black citizens participating in formal organizations as either committed and belonging to or benefiting from them. This observation included but was not limited to complex police interactions and reflected interpersonal neighborhood violence and other matters related to or deriving from neighborhood disorder. Regarding *belonging to* organizations, black citizens were long-term participants who were committed to, frequently involved with, and considered to be members of the group. They were contributors to or participants in meetings as well as initiatives or events in which they were committed to serve actively and frequently in some capacity. Regarding *benefiting from* organizations, black citizens' involvement with community organizations was limited to contacts made or association with them only to obtain needed assistance (e.g., a food pantry, Christmas giveaways, an adopt a family program, or back-to-school giveaways). Some black citizens who were committed members of an organization also benefited from it at times. For example, some of the members lived on fixed incomes. They were retired and sometimes benefited by getting food from food pantries. Even then, they cited neighborhood and community needs as their first priority and served their groups accordingly—benefiting themselves only as a secondary concern. There were also a few interviewees who did not identify as either belonging to or benefiting from formal organizations. They donated or volunteered sporadically, remaining unattached to a formal organization.

Belonging to Local Neighborhood Groups

> We gotta do better than what we doin' out here. We got to stop this violence. . . .We got innocent kids getting hit with bullets. . . . The proverb says it takes a village. . . . It take[s] all of us, and some of you guys need to get together and be mentors to these young brothers. . . . I'm on this street every day, every night. That's my job! I'm on *every* killing scene, whether it is the police or whether it is with us killing each other. . . . We gotta come together, and we gotta do more than what we doin'.
>
> ACTIVIST, Free Peace Community Inc. "Stop the Violence" march

Through in-depth interviews and focus groups, this study found that participants who were mostly older (senior citizens), homeowners, and/or professionals were committed to or *belonged to* formal neighborhood organizations (i.e., were members).[21] Those groups included but were not limited to "tenants' groups, neighborhood improvement associations, block crime watches, and other community service organizations.[22] As members, a few interview participants were committed to regularly attending meetings and contributing through various means such as assisting with problem solving and planning neighborhood initiatives and programs. They were also committed to donating, volunteering, or assisting in other ways—as best they could—to implement the neighborhood programs. For instance, Mr. MacArthur, age sixty-eight, is a retired homeowner who belongs to numerous neighborhood groups. When asked about volunteer work and neighborhood organizations, he mentioned that he has been volunteering with Newbridge Boys' and Girls' Club for thirty-five years. He then described his neighborhood meetings:

> *And so you all have neighborhood meetings?*
> Yes.
> *Ok, how often do you . . .* [He interrupts:]
> Weekly.
> *What is the attendance like?*
> Thirty-five people.
> *OK, and so what kinds of things do you talk about?*
> We talk about whatever's goin' on. [We discuss] if there's [been] any
> burglaries and strong-arm robberies, . . . [A]re the kids [in the
> neighborhood] feeling okay with the gang influx—like are they
> being recruited? Are they intimidated? Or how often do they ask
> NOT to go to school? Things like that. We need to start payin'
> attention to things like this. We need to start paying attention to
> when your child LOVE[S] goin' to school every day—you couldn't
> keep him in the house—and now all of a sudden, he don't wanna go.

Here Mr. MacArthur is describing conversations in which participants gauge possible problems in the neighborhood. It is through other members and sporadic individual exchanges outside of meetings that members sometimes become aware of problems in the neighborhood. This dynamic is consistent with research findings and informal integration. These discussions reflect connections that organization members have with neighbors who are more likely to bond individually rather than to become members of their organizations. Members personally relay the concerns of their neighbors at meetings. Then, based on the responses they get, they offer suggestions and attempt to resolve issues as a matter of safety.

Shelly, age fifty-nine, commented a little more extensively on her neighborhood group. Although she belongs to her block association, neighborhood reciprocity is clearly at play. Here is how she discussed her meetings, first defining *neighborly:*

[Being] *neighborly* means that, first of all, you interact, and you know who's on your block. We have a block association. We plan several events throughout the year together. We have our monthly or every other month meetings. We check on each other. We have a phone tree, and so we pay attention to what's happening on our street, and if there's anything that seems to be problematic, or criminal, or could be a hazard, we look out for each other. We call the police if necessary, or we call that particular person [the one affected or who has not been seen] and make sure everything's okay. I travel a lot, and so there are times when if I leave and my car sits in front of my house and doesn't move for two or three days, I have two or three neighbors calling me to check on me to see if I'm okay. That like never happened in my affluent suburban neighborhood.

Shelly's block association is apparently very structured. There seems to be a clear understanding of how members engage and what they expect from one another beyond attending meetings. She spontaneously provided this information, drawing distinctions. The fact that she called attention to her previous experiences in her "affluent suburban neighborhood" references her old home. She chose to move back to the city to be closer to her work, but there is a great deal of disorder and crime in her neighborhood. Nevertheless, she is satisfied with her new home. She has ties to her neighbors that for her have proven to be more valuable than neighborhood relationships in places that are more affluent and impersonal (i.e., the suburbs). She embraces the notion of being "neighborly."

Another participant, Johnny, age fifty-eight, listed numerous former and current organizations he belonged to and volunteered with. He described a couple of them:

There was a program called Neighborhood Joy. . . . They did drug marches. . . . They would go out into the neighborhoods and confront known drug houses and stand out in front [of them]. It's a program that no longer exists. . . . There [were] some forces that conspired to take it over. It was a brainchild of a very visionary person, . . . and the whole point around it was to turn elementary schools into one-stop shops for social services. . . . One of the by-products was this drug march thing. They were done like once a month on a Friday night after doin' some research and findin' out where the problem areas were and going to those suspected drug houses.
How did you all do the research? What was that like?
You know, observing certain places and listenin' to people talkin'. That kinda thing. And then the format of a drug march was—we'd start off, we'd carry signs, go to a place, and then we also had [a] police escort. We'd go to a place that was a suspected drug house, and we'd confront it, and this [action] led to some interesting confrontations.

What did those [confrontations] look like?

Well, first off, you have folks that, you know, . . . that really don't want attention brought to them. So then the first thing they wanna do is deny what's goin' on, but then they see all these people there, and all these people sayin', "Well, you know, we've heard blah blah this, and blah blah that," and then they see the police escort, so then they don't necessarily want to do anything . . . that's gonna get them [the drug house] into another situation. Ok, so it's basically a strong warning. . . . You know, you [they] see all these people, and you see the police escort; you know . . . it's [just] a very strong warning.

I had often heard about drug marches although I have not personally witnessed any. Interestingly, though, I could visualize one as Johnny explained it. He seemed to have been moved by them while simultaneously also being bothered that they no longer happened. Nevertheless, Johnny very much enjoys volunteering. With the same tenacity with which he participated in drug marches, he remains committed to being involved with neighborhood efforts. He is currently connected with a black cultural initiative full time, providing great services and resources for neighborhood empowerment.

Ward Meetings   I was once invited to a monthly ward meeting. It was a perfect opportunity to see what happened and compare it with the reports of some interview participants who had attended them in their respective neighborhoods. This one was scheduled for a Saturday morning at an inner-city local community center. There appeared to be roughly fifty or more residents in attendance, along with several local and state elected officials. As the meeting was convened, consistent with my previous findings, most of the residents appeared to be senior citizens. Once they began engaging in dialogue, based on residents' questions and comments, it was clear to me that most were also retirees and homeowners in the neighborhoods.

There was an interesting set of exchanges as the attendees were briefed on emerging community issues and received city and state updates from their respective elected officials. In turn, they were able to ask questions about various issues. Those topics ranged from increases in trash fees to having something done about derelict cars in their community. Attendees were concerned about and called attention to physical and social disorder. They listened attentively to each elected official as each responded with reports and explanations, from the local to the state levels. The most contentious exchanges dealt with a report on the rate increase for trash services, especially when attendees complained about not having their trash picked up when scheduled. Delays in pickups meant that they had more trash in their neighborhoods, and this was a problem for most. They wanted to know why they were now being expected to pay more for what they regarded as poor service. They also wanted to know where the money they paid for trash pickup was going, particularly regarding expenditures on city improvements.

While some residents asked hard questions, others mumbled—appearing to be disgruntled—and waited for responses. Their council member explained that the poor service was due to not having enough trash trucks to service the city. Several residents clearly did not accept that response. I remember one older woman in particular respectfully expressing her frustration, sharing that she knew of other neighborhoods (i.e., white affluent sections) that did not have that problem. She had learned from a friend—who lived in a more affluent, mostly white part of the inner city—that the latter's trash pickup was always on schedule. Timely pickups were apparently only occurring across town, and this attendee could see trash strewn about throughout her less-advantaged neighborhood. Others, upon hearing her comments, mumbled and gestured, being not only surprised but also livid. This account is typical of vicarious experiences or shared stories that cause black citizens to suspect that they are receiving differential treatment. At this ward meeting, attendees shared and compared their experiences with trash service across neighborhoods. Poor trash service appeared to be no different in their various neighborhoods, particularly for those black and disadvantaged. This problem is an example of many in which structural ineptness drives disorder and stereotypical ideas about black citizens: how they choose to live and the condition of their neighborhoods (e.g., dirty, nasty, filled with trash, rodent infested). The participants nevertheless trustingly calmed down and moved on to the next order of business as their council member further explained that their trash pickup fees were going toward purchasing new trucks and hiring more employees. I would not have known that trash pickup was a problem or a serious matter if I had not attended a neighborhood meeting and heard the residents' many complaints and concerns. Trash pickup problems are the result of a dysfunctional city government. They are an example of institutional disorder indirectly passed on to disadvantaged black citizens, giving the appearance that trash-filled neighborhoods result solely from their behaviors. I continued to track this matter beyond the meeting and later confirmed that more trash trucks had been purchased.[23]

Benefiting from Local Neighborhood Organizations and Organizing

> If we can't respect each other, who else is gonna respect us? If
> we don't love each other, who else is gonna love us? It's [death
> has become] our normal. We gotta break the chains. [There is
> some applause.] Our people [historically] fought for us. . . . This
> whole lot should be filled, this whole damn lot. . . . Every house
> on the block has felt this pain. . . . We need prayer. We need
> unity. . . . We hurtin'. This is what I do, . . . but it took my pain
> [my loss] to wake me up, y'all. . . . Don't let the whole St. Louis
> go through this.
>
> SURVIVING FAMILY MEMBER, Free Peace Community Inc.
"Stop the Violence" march

Through in-depth interviews and focus groups, this project mostly found that younger nonprofessional participants who were renters and who were connected with formal organizations generally *benefited from* them. They were connected with neighborhood organizations through charity rather than through membership. They did not seem particularly interested in formally connecting with other members of the community in official group settings. Instead, many seemed satisfied with making similar gestures and arrangements with neighbors individually, since these were more organic and did not call for participating in scheduled meetings and adhering to other requirements. Without saying so directly, these participants seemed to be satisfied with forming individual ties and responding to community disorder in more impromptu ways rather than through formal arrangements.

As an example, let us consider Malik, age thirty-one, who helped out as a nonmember and also benefited from another formal organization in his neighborhood. When asked about his community involvement, he talked about building a garden and receiving charitable items. Here is what he said:

> *Have you ever worked with community organizations?*
>   I did gardens . . .
> *Oh, . . . the community gardens?*
>   Yeah, I did one of them.
> *Have you ever participated in any "charitable" organizations?*
>   I used to go down . . . to this place right here named the Sun Center. . . .
>   It's mostly . . . to pick up food products, or they feed us[, and] . . . [we]
>   pick up clothes. They give us clothes to take home with us.

Participants disclosed whether they had received charitable help in different ways. Unlike obtaining participants' responses about belonging, it usually took my posing different questions, asking several times, to get concise answers or information about this topic. At other times, someone's involvement in neighborhood groups gradually emerged while we were discussing other matters. Malik, however, first mentioned working with community gardens and then benefiting from charity. Although he did not directly attest to his work occurring on a volunteer basis, his interview revealed that he engaged as a nonmember who was just simply volunteering his time and effort without being formally committed or belonging to the organization. I classified him as *benefiting* because his involvement appeared consistent and appropriate when compared with the efforts of other participants.

"State of Emergency" Town Hall Meeting   This meeting was attended by at least 150 members from the community who were looking to benefit from local organizations and resources. They hoped to strategize to revitalize their neighborhoods. Here is how an elected official described structural issues and their effects and then called on citizens to counter them:

> [He looks into the audience:] *This* is what community looks like!!! It's about being engaged and being able to find a way to change the dynamics in the community. We have *too many* vacant and abandoned buildings in our community. . . . [So] why are we here?!? Why have we gathered today?!? [Because] we are in a state of emergency. . . . The City of St. Louis owns approximately 10,000 buildings that are vacant and abandoned. [The city is] the largest landholder of abandoned properties, and we're here today to do something about that. . . . Now imagine a little kid walking up and down the street *every* single day, and all [she sees] is decay. Imagine what it does to the mind-set of that child. . . . [Her *mind* begins] to decay. It leads to a sense of hopelessness in those young folks. . . . And the only way we're going to change those dynamics [is that] we have to rebuild our community block by block [Audience responds: "Amen!"]. . . . I am counting on you all to do that with the resources that you [are] gonna hear [are] available today. I want you all to roll up your sleeves.

There are several things to note here. For starters, the opening speech began with the statement "This is what community looks like," then defined *community* as "being engaged," and urged finding ways "to change the dynamics in a community." The first statement is also part of a common chant used in police protests that reflect the overlap of issues in the movement: how semblances of black solidarity and collective action extend well beyond contentious black citizen–police relations to matters of discrimination and disorder generally. The messaging and move to mobilize become interchangeable and occur reciprocally—from the neighborhood to protests back to the neighborhood—urban to suburb. This happens because black mobilization to counter discrimination has been the agenda, regardless of the particular incident or event, post-Ferguson. The need to connect all forms of disorder as being structural and having generational effects is crucial. It affords holistic approaches for addressing discrimination and the devaluation of black lives, especially those disadvantaged. Contentious policing and interpersonal violence in destitute neighborhoods are not separate issues. Rather, they are collective manifestations, one after the other and on top of the other, of dereliction of duty from the dominant and local to national governments.

Urban or neighborhood decay reflects institutionally complacent devaluation, with real implications for children and others who are then contrarily expected to have hope and value life. Places where there are war-torn appearances give rise to war-torn responses. This dynamic is especially true since one has to alter her or his way of thinking and seeing the world generally in order to bear living in unyielding circumstances of deprivation. No number of timely trash pick-ups could solve the problem of 10,000 abandoned buildings, and similarly, no "broken window" alone accounts for these conditions.[24] Here is how one of the stakeholders and local leaders at the town hall explained this situation:

> I want to give a little backstory [about] how this meeting came to be. . . . People are tired; people are concerned. For as long as I can recall, the fate of our neighborhoods ha[s] been in the hands of outsiders. . . . These are developers who have controlled the land, taken ownership of neighborhoods and businesses, and created plans for the community, often without the community at the table. That needs to change.

This point was part of the reason for the meeting: to bring black citizens to the table. There is an understanding that life-changing decisions are routinely made *for* and *concerning* them, while *excluding* them. This situation has prevailed because it protects the interests of those most empowered—the developers and others. Consequently, the meeting aimed to change "those dynamics"—to educate local black citizens about how to buy back property from the city and take ownership of their own community. There were city officials present as well to offer guidance for acquiring property and provide information and connections for investing. This information ranged from purchasing homes, duplexes, apartment buildings, and vacant lots to the upkeep of them. Here is how a stakeholder or community organizer explained one of many processes for such change:

> Our hope is that today we can kick off a conversation around empowering individuals from within our community who are interested in

investing back into our neighborhoods. It is my belief [that] with a little guidance or [some] resources, more members in our communities can find financial independence and can do so through investing in the neighborhoods [that] we live in and care for.

Survivor and Surviving Family Activism As if from one family member to another (i.e., as fictive kin), survivors and surviving families share their losses, hurt, and possible solutions for combating neighborhood crime. Through heartfelt admonishments and instruction, survivors and surviving families become advocates and activists. A surviving family member used this "Stop the Violence" rally to benefit, or "teach," others in the community:

> We can look around at each other. We are all a part of a family. . . . Our roots [culture] run deep from state to state. We all are connected. We have to do better. We have to start teaching our children. We have to start teaching them to love from birth. . . . Our children must know . . . that [we] love them. That you are there for them. That you are their parent. You are not their friend. You cannot be a friend to your child. . . . You must be a parent. You much teach them discipline. You must teach them how to love their siblings, how to love their neighbors.

Through teaching, this surviving family member turned activist connected the audience through "family" or fictive kin sentiments and cultural "roots" in hope of improving conditions in the community. Formal participation in organizations provided survivors and surviving families with platforms and additional opportunities for activism. They provoked countering actions and empowerment on the heels of interpersonal violence. This outcome made injured or lost lives meaningful in life and in death. Survivors' and surviving families' heartfelt experience(s) and directives benefited themselves as well as others. They were therapeutic and provided new meaning and empowerment for pushing change by connecting and motivating others to do the same.

Formal organizations such as Free Peace Community Inc.; the Agency for African Share; and others that hosted neighborhood events provided support and resources for survivors of interpersonal neighborhood violence as well as for those who had been indirectly affected by it. These events often had numerous sponsors or collaborative partners from the community. They afforded more access and connections—somewhat like a fair—to black citizens locally. With music playing in the background and food and beverages provided, some local black business owners and leaders set up shop. There were tables and booths for attendees to stop and visit, having one-on-one conversations with black neighborhood stakeholders. By an event's end, we would always feel as if we had spent time together in fellowship as family.

People were meeting and becoming more familiar with one another—a reciprocal exchange that benefited both attendees and neighborhood partners. These events provided more exposure for existing and new black businesses to black citizens across neighborhoods and organizations and also introduced attendees and patrons to more local resources and vested networks. Differing from individual integration, formal events and gatherings provided more social capital and social and political community connections. They typically had paid staff and therefore were able to reach more people and garner more attention.

CONCLUSION

Although this project found some black citizens engaging in formal participation, they did so to a lesser degree than those participating in individual integration. This result is consistent with Ross and Jang's findings that citizens were likelier to form individual ties and counter disorder and its effects through informal integration than through formal participation.[25] However, black citizens who did engage in formal participation did so by *belonging to* or *benefiting from* them. Through belonging, they identified themselves as members fully immersed in their neighborhood organizations, groups, or committees and committed and actively working to further their agendas. Through benefiting, citizens admitted to deferring to neighborhood organizations or services because they needed assistance. These were resources readily available to the community. There were also those who operated in the middle, so to speak. They were not members, and they did not benefit from the organization(s). Rather, they involved themselves by occasionally volunteering or donating money to the group(s) formally, among other actions. Most participants who did not belong but formally volunteered or donated occasionally articulated their efforts as part of a pattern associated with individual, informal integration. They discussed volunteering and donating as a continuum of actions that they did on their own, similar to other individual efforts (e.g., greeting, alerting) throughout their neighborhood.

This study also found that more coordinated efforts regarding interpersonal neighborhood violence were made through formal participation. This engagement was somewhat comparable to the tenacity of protests but had smaller turnouts. There was also quite a bit of overlap. Some citizens or survivors and surviving families reported doing things to combat neighborhood violence on their own. They were also involved in black citizen–police direct actions and organizing and could be found embedded in nonviolent events throughout the city. However, there were greater resources and more support specifically intended for interpersonal violence issues attached to formal neighborhood or community organizations. They afforded a platform specific to survivors and survivor families of neighborhood violence. In addition, they had greater exposure through police protests, at least to the extent of being captured nationally and internationally wearing T-shirts and holding banners and signs with "stop-the-violence"–related messages.

Media focused more heavily on civil unrest; however, many protesters also paid attention to highlighting the lives that had been lost to violence generally despite the focus on police brutality. Therefore, direct action also positioned survivors and surviving families to highlight interpersonal neighborhood violence activism or advocacy, giving them more visibility in the movement for also sharing their lived experiences with the community. Others participating in or attending formal events benefited by gaining awareness, resources, and empowerment—necessary components for countering or campaigning against disorder and interpersonal neighborhood violence. Efforts to combat interpersonal neighborhood violence corresponded with black citizen–police conflict mobilization. They both sought to preserve black lives and advance their quality as institutional derivatives of disorder.

6. (No) Conclusion and Discussion

> Show me what *democracy* looks like. (THIS is what *democracy* looks like!)
>
> PROTEST CHANT

Imagine.

FADE IN:

DOWNTOWN ST. LOUIS—SOUTH TUCKER BOULEVARD, BETWEEN MARKET AND SPRUCE STREETS—DAY ONE, NOON
The Stockley verdict has been announced. I am at direct action occurring in downtown St. Louis.

On Friday, September 15, 2017, former police officer Jason Stockley was acquitted of the 2011 murder of Anthony Lamar Smith. It had taken years for Stockley to be brought to trial for first-degree murder and then weeks for him to be vindicated of all charges.[1] The protest community had anticipated this verdict and thus had been signaling the region for weeks that subsequent disruption would occur. Barricades had gone up around the downtown courthouse, and the governor had deployed the Army National Guard.[2] Activists and other black citizens perceived these actions as early indicators of an unfavorable decision. As the region had been on standby waiting for the announcement, likewise, local and state officials had been put on notice of black citizens' imminent responses. A little over three years after the fatal shooting of Mike Brown Jr. in Ferguson, the St. Louis region was again embroiled in the heat of civil unrest. This time we were roughly thirty minutes away from Ferguson in the city of St. Louis.

Here I was, back in direct action. Upon learning of the verdict, I had changed my clothes, left campus, and headed toward downtown St. Louis. That is where I spent most of the day, in the streets, between St. Louis city hall and the St. Louis Metropolitan Police Academy—accounting for black citizen–police interactions. I was anxious because tensions were running high. There had been periodic black citizen–police standoffs all day, with ongoing verbal exchanges and numerous citizens being pepper-sprayed. This is a visual I can never get used to. No matter how many times I witness it, it pains me to see a direct streaming of pepper spray into the face and eyes of protesters. As they buckle in pain, other protesters run in to clean their faces and eyes with milk or Maalox, as medics. In the end, this turned out to be an arduous day and the start of another chapter in an ongoing, relentless fight for social justice.

LAP DISSOLVE TO:

SAME PLACE—DOWNTOWN ST. LOUIS—SOUTH TUCKER BOULEVARD, OUTSIDE OF ST. LOUIS CITY HALL—DAY FOURTEEN, MORNING

It has now been two weeks of direct action since the Stockley verdict. This is a press conference called by a group of protest organizers. They are outside St. Louis city hall, standing in the street, surrounded by media. Each speaks about the movement. It is time for a Ferguson activist turned post-Ferguson elected official to weigh in.

> Touch one! (Touch all!)
> Touch one! (Touch all!)

[The protesters change to a different chant.]

> Say, I! (I!)
> I know! (I know!)
> I know that we will win! (I know that we will win!)

The official speaks:

> I like to thank those who have been out here. . . .Whether we had thousands, whether we had a couple of hundred, . . . one thing we gotta realize is that there's no legislation or list of demands that could be put forward to get you [those in power, the dominant] to understand, that "Ya'll gone stop killing us!" That's why we [are] out here in the streets. So when you're reporting [to media] and you get those questions from your listeners, asking, "What are their [activists'/black citizens'] *real* wants?" or "Do they *really* have strategy?" . . . [W]e absolutely got strategy, so we absolutely got demands but one thing we have to get set straight first is that, black folks will stop being disproportionately affected by this system. . . . [T]hat's why each and every person is out here, . . . because black lives matter and that's what they [those in power, the dominant] have to understand. So let's not keep talkin' about lists of demands. . . . [L]et's not keep talking about "let's come to the table". . . *WE'LL* set the tone, *WE'LL* set the time, and *WE'LL* set the place. . . .

We protested in Ferguson [in the streets] for 400 days straight, *400. Days. Straight!* So you take those *same* folks who were on the front-line, those *same* folks who got tear-gassed and pepper-sprayed together and you put 'em together and we learned. . . . [S]ome of us became elected officials, some of us became community leaders, some of us [now] work in different agencies. . . . We learned and not only did we learn, we expanded, we empowered, we educated! So now that 400 days we did in Ferguson, turns into 800 days, turns into 1,200 days. This[is] not a fly-by night movement; . . . rain, sleet, hail, or snow, . . . [W]e not going anywhere, so that's what *THEY* [the dominant/powerful] gotta understand. This press conference was to basically set the tone.—former Ferguson activist and now state elected official, post-Ferguson

SUMMARY AND FINDINGS

It has been well over three years since I first began ethnographic work centered in post-Ferguson direct action. I could not have imagined how incredibly taxing—mentally, emotionally, and physically—this process of gathering and examining data across two broad, evolving terrains (i.e., the protest community and urban/suburban disadvantaged neighborhoods) would be. The aforementioned speech reflects black resoluteness—the unfaltering strength of black alliance and commitment—and the trans-formative power of activism. My goal was to trustworthily and accurately examine and describe black citizens' post-Ferguson transformations throughout the St. Louis region. In real time this translated as my attempt-ing to chase, capture, and then analyze all aspects of a twenty-first-century black power movement in progress. This project evolved fluidly, often alongside the lives of many black citizens. I wanted to wholly document, examine, and explain those processes. This study reveals information for educating and advancing the entire black community.

The introduction to this book situates this project at the active scene of a homicide. It carves out a critical juncture—a placeholder for the loss of black life and raw emotions—within the first few hours following the shooting death of Michael Brown Jr. It attempts to connect and encapsulate readers in a meaningful way by walking them through the scenes of civil unrest in the St. Louis region—the starting point for subsequent broad direct action. Using intentionally vivid details of protest scenes and exchanges, I introduce an overarching twenty-first-century black empow-erment agenda hinging on combating widespread disorder: the social and physical disarray that leaves black citizens disproportionately victimized by police and other black citizens. This agenda was a two-pronged mission seeking to preserve black life and improve the quality thereof prior to and as a stimulus for the emergence and continuance of local grassroots and national/international organizations such as Black Lives Matter, Movement for Black Lives, and other mobilization efforts.

Chapter 1 provides a reflective account of my childhood experiences, capturing socialization and organization processes among black citizens in a portrayal of alliance and solidarity even among children that is rarely seen or understood outside of poor communities of color. I then discuss the twofold call to action following Brown's death and contextualization for the historical disparagement of black lives and black empowerment, as black citizens advanced a new movement. I further argue that the origin of the devaluation of black life as a widespread cultural norm is embedded in historical mechanisms. I critically examine and reassert the etymology and dominant construction of race and racial discourse—their definition, influence on politics, and subjective ascribing of all things black—as a construct for countering black advancement and maintaining dominant arrangements. This chapter provides a description of indelibly dominant processes that defer to discriminatory past ideologies in advancing new concepts for and backlash against black advancement (i.e., unbalanced criticism about black-on-black crime and the Ferguson Effect). I scrutinize these processes, offering their (de)construction as an educational resource for understanding inherently inflexible systems and structures.

In addition, I contend that it is because of long-standing white fear and belief in a racial threat that black citizens persistently and disproportionately face victimization. Likewise, it is through ploys of fear that the dominant asserts victim blaming, attempting without context to undermine the black effort. This project finds that black citizens, especially the poor, are also fearful and frustrated with their living conditions. They are aware of their vulnerabilities in two areas (victimization by both police and other citizens) and attempt to police or offset them, sometimes being unable to articulate their fear and frustration as a community. I also address identity politics as inescapably deferred to and counter the dominant's initial use of and reliance on it (i.e., slavery) for maintaining economic, racial, and political superiority. I push back against the dominant's subjective use of "identity" as politics to disparage black citizens (e.g., unbalanced criticism about black-on-black crime). I also highlight "scholar activism," provoking critical thought and examination of it as an often unadmitted, reciprocal alliance between academia and the community for forwarding collaborative projects, programs, and curriculum that advances twenty-first-century evidence and best practices.

Chapter 2 argues that disorder is racially and culturally subjective and protective of white interests. Since dominant definitions of (dis)order disproportionately encapsulate black citizens (their lives) as perpetuators of it, I argue for a culturally based reconceptualization of disorder. This study finds the traditional framework for disorder limited and unable to account for true order, beginning with and including the introduction of slavery. Furthermore, I argue that the fact that race and poverty are persistent correlations of disorder does not negate the need to include and examine their intersecting paths holistically through historically maintained, stratified policies and practices. We should be able to address disorder in communities of color based on the discriminatory "ordering" or purposefully structured arrangement of people and their communities as priorities (or not).

This project found that a racial/cultural reconceptualization is necessary for addressing broader forms of disorder in the context of black experiences and an empowerment movement. Since black lives matter and resistance work is ongoing, this study found racial discrimination to be an unaccounted for form of disorder. Similarly, this project found that victimization by police and other black citizens was a form of disorder excluded. They are the by-products of a racialized kind of "order," in which economical and racial disruptions (e.g., enslavement) came first and then spread similar conditions across new emerging communities (e.g., protest communities). This project, through impromptu discussion (i.e., in direct action), in-depth interviews, and focus groups, found that black citizens directly and indirectly identified historical or institutional discrimination as an initial cause of the physical and social conditions they contend with, conditions that set in motion all other forms of pervasive deprivation and broad cyclical and cultural derision for black citizens.

The project found that all three groups (i.e., protests, in-depth interviews, and focus groups) of participants also attributed some black citizens' inability "as a community or black collective" to rise out of subpar conditions to historical or institutional discrimination. Participants were a little less forgiving when addressing social mobility (or the lack thereof). Depending on the individual circumstances, they victim blamed and criticized one another, often out of racial frustrations (i.e., double consciousness, self-flagellation). It is in this space that context was sometimes lost, with black citizens articulating their thoughts about individual efforts as "we don't . . . ." Such casual "we" articulations further perpetuate stereotypical ideas of disorder as an inherently black trait. This project found it necessary to extend the concept of disorder to additional forms (e.g., discrimination) and spaces beyond neighborhoods (e.g., protest communities) in order to adequately address the totality of black life, post-Ferguson. Consequently, this study offers the post-Ferguson framework as a theoretical template for a cultural reconceptualization of disorder in the "black lives matter" era.

As this project presents a racial and cultural reconceptualization for disorder, I examined alternatives for policing disorder across black communities as black citizens identify and understand it. I carefully examined and scrutinized community policing as an overt contradiction when held up against the use of PPUs, post-Ferguson. This project found relationship building and forming alliances (e.g., social ties) to be crucial across all forms of policing (i.e., formal/informal), although this is more likely to occur in theory than in practice regarding formal policing, since black citizens feel they are treated like ISIS by the police. Black citizens were found to be facing the extreme ends of the police continuum for days and weeks on end under some of the most arduous conditions. It is in this context that black social ties became even more significant, as black citizens looked out for each other. They were found to be protecting and serving one another or at least broadly connecting through shared racial positions and relying on cultural codes and informal cues to manage one another's positions and safety. More specifically, this project shows that alliances are significant, particularly in poor black neighborhoods, as they offer solidarity and support in the absence of social services and other support. It is through established solidarity and relationships of reciprocity that trust is established and becomes conducive to regulating and navigating one another's behaviors across communities.

Chapter 3 reports that participants were very critical of the police and expected them to "do their jobs" by protecting and serving the community. When asked whether they thought black citizens policed themselves or one another, most answered "no" but then changed their answers to "yes" when I rephrased the question, asking instead whether "black citizens did things to protect and serve one another." They were generally very critical of themselves, but all denied feeling and mostly perceiving that other black citizens believed that police shootings were more important than interpersonal neighborhood violence. In fact, most of them explained that they thought reactions to these types of violence are different because black citizens hold the police—supposed professionals paid to protect them and not kill them—to higher standards. They often described police brutality as being like paying taxes for public executions, but even then they did not communicate hating the police; rather, they wanted equal protection and service from them.

Black citizens articulated definitive expectations of the police but only expressed informal reciprocity when it came to fellow black citizens. They considered policing one another to be an informal form of correction among family (e.g., fictive kin), but mostly thought of it as part of "protecting and servicing." Conversely, they expected professionalism and honorable behavior from law enforcement, who are commissioned and paid by taxpayers. In this case, the word *policing* did not need redefining.

Through in-depth interviews and focus groups—the study found that all black participants formed individual alliances through informal integration in their neighborhoods.[3] These were analogous to protest roles as marshals and specialized support. In sum, all interview participants reported or described having reciprocal ties with someone in their neighborhoods. This was so even though some of them repeatedly stated that they "stayed to themselves" and suggested that others did the same.

In this context, the use of ethnographic data is significant. It allowed for open-ended questions and answers, acquiring additional information that might otherwise have been misunderstood and lost in the analysis. Based on some participants' initial responses, it would have been easy to conclude falsely that black citizens had no allies, when they actually did. Clarity was provided through follow-up questions and extended discussions. Through protest exchanges, in-depth interviews, and focus groups, black citizens were found to be forging individual ties or engaging in informal integration. They did so in varying circumstances that resulted in trust and reciprocity as buffers to disorder.

Chapter 4 highlights case studies of three black men, whose in-depth interviews offered full life narratives from childhood through adulthood. This holistic examination of young black men, who are more likely to experience incarceration and violence than black women, included their timely testaments for making all black lives matter while citizens are alive. In this chapter I address fictive kin relationships linking men to legitimate and illegitimate relationships and actions in order to survive. For example, this chapter underscores the exposure and influence of male-centered street networks: the relationship between Gs and OGs. Similarly, I call attention to the considerable role of women-centered networks such as othermothers and community othermothers. Some women reported or described aligning themselves legitimately, traditionally, and culturally with vulnerable black citizens in their neighborhoods and community. Their accounts offer allegorical depictions of how some individuals "stay afloat." These women are moved to improve or transform their neighborhoods and communities broadly through gendered reinforcement.

All in-depth interview and focus group participants referenced or linked their experiences to Ferguson-related occurrences or semblances of them.

For instance, there were individuals who participated in direct action who perceivably dangled between legitimate and illegitimate lifestyles. Janet (see chapter 2) recalled being proud of the young black men "with sagging pants"—who wore dreadlocks, tattoos, and sometimes plain white T-shirts or no shirts—who had assumed newfound roles in direct action. They were managing their presentations, traffic, and other "protect and serve" matters, especially concerning women and children, despite stereotypes about their appearance that generally posit them as deviant. They also accomplished these changes even though they were more vulnerable to police brutality and interpersonal neighborhood violence. Some of them had been called out at rallies during the first week of civil unrest and charged by black community leaders to assist with the effort. They were present and seemingly motivated. They respectfully took their orders and obliged like foot soldiers. Their actions were mostly not captured by the media, which recurrently covered the few individuals who damaged and looted stores.

This study locates Ferguson and Ferguson civil unrest as a historical and transformative marker for individual and collective action—local, national, and international. Some local protesters are now full-time activists and community organizers. They are founders of not-for-profit foundations and grassroots organizations. Some have even run for political office and are currently elected officials. These endeavors are ongoing in St. Louis, particularly the post-Ferguson emergence of national/international efforts such as Black Lives Matter and Movement for Black Lives. Local activists and organizers collaborate in various ways with national/international projects, in addition to preexisting and persistent freedom work on the ground in St. Louis. This participation extends social ties nationwide, particularly as activists and organizers reciprocally deploy to other regions to assist with emerging conflicts. On occasion, a few have also traveled to other countries to support a similar agenda.

Finally, chapter 5 examines the role of formal participation among black citizens. Through in-depth interviews and focus groups, it gauges black citizens' involvement with formal organizations in their neighborhoods. Their participation ranged from memberships and commitments to neighborhood associations, to ward or town hall meetings, to neighborhood watch groups. Findings about formal participation revealed fewer citizens being likely to participate formally than informally. This study found that older or senior citizens, homeowners, and professional residents were more committed to formal group neighborhood efforts.[4] They were more residentially stable, vested, and aligned as committed and belonging members of formal groups than were younger, renting, and nonprofessional residents.[5] The latter were likely to form individual ties and engage through informal integration. Both approaches (i.e., informal integration and formal participation) occurred within and across neighborhoods.[6] In sum, all study participants were likelier to form alliances and buffer themselves through individual ties and informal integration than to engage in group, formal participation.

In addition, this project found that formal organizations were the vehicle through which more structured and publicized programs emerge that combat neighborhood crime and police brutality. I argue that black citizens care about and actively combat both, and that they appear to be treating one as more important than the other due to numerous factors—one being greater expectations for the police, who are paid employees of taxpayers, and another being the different venues that citizens engage in, formal versus informal organizing. Since black citizens were found to prefer to engage in revolutionary organic actions, they were less likely to take to formal neighborhood groups and associations. Therefore, they often wore T-shirts and carried banners about those killed in interpersonal neighborhood violence or in police protests depending on where they seemingly connected best. I found that black citizens attended venues that best suited them depending on their age, perspective, and overall philosophy.

For example, as a middle-aged, professional black woman, it is hardly likely that I would be a member of the same neighborhood group as and regularly meet to formally talk strategy with my grandmother and her friends. Further, it is unlikely that even if I lived in her neighborhood and chose to be a member of or committed to such a group, we would tackle the same issues or I could comfortably assert strategies that she and her friends could or would want to take part in. I certainly would not conceive of infringing upon or "taking over" such a group, as they would have retained years of ownership of it and I would see it as *"their* thing," fully realizing that this formal group association and membership is not as a sociologist. These are the dynamics to consider when formally accounting for "formal" neighborhood meetings. This example illustrates that there are various reasons for black citizens not joining formal organizations, and it should not be assumed that they are disconnected, untrusting, or don't feel safe enough with one another to participate or engage in them. Rather, they engage in ways best suited to their personalities, philosophies, and agendas and that comfortably provide for diverse attendance. Their engagement may then garner more publicity and attention in some instances and little to no attention in others.

Direct action functions more inclusively and progressively than do many formal organizations, despite its occurring as group or collective action. Direct actions tend to be composed of diverse populations, open to resistance, so there is a greater probability that connections will be formed and forward perspectives will be embedded across participants. Therefore, community leaders should be more cognizant of the need to frame programs and events that attract contemporary perspectives and approaches. This should also be understood as one of many explanations of why or how black citizens especially move to engage in individual integration and reciprocity rather than official, more formal group neighborhood meetings.

In sum, I found that neighborhoods were mixed, with both older, retired, homeowning residents and younger, nonprofessional renters, who did not necessarily mesh due to generational differences, among other factors, even though they wanted the same things: neighborhood safety and black advancement.

IMPLICATIONS

> What do we want? (Justice!)
> When do we want it? (Now!)
> What do we want? (Justice!)
> When do we want it? (Now!)
>
> PROTEST CHANT

This project began under some of the most tumultuous circumstances: on day one of Mike Brown Jr.'s death and at the start of the Ferguson civil unrest and uprising. It provides an ethnographic examination of blacks fighting for their lives, figuratively and literally. As blacks persistently and disproportionately face differential police treatment and high homicide rates (disorder) in their communities, they make extraordinary efforts to counter both against the backdrop of a twenty-first-century movement, by which I mean "networks of informal interactions between a plurality of individuals, groups and organizations, engaged in political or cultural conflict, on the basis of shared collective identities."[7]

This is black mobilization, reflecting a critical juncture at which the delineation and pronouncement of preserving and advancing black life became unavoidable discourse and recourse for all. Black citizens have empowered themselves through actions from diversely publicized mobilization efforts to hidden, everyday exchanges across mostly homogenous communities. Thus, this project found black citizens doing various things to protect and serve one another across communities. While they continually risked overlapping victimization—from police or one another—they persistently found ways to form alliances and negotiate space that perceivably minimized risks and hardships.

This project found blacks fighting back—most legitimately and a few illegitimately—as if they were a struggling family. They were fighting together to survive, often under duress—a result of persistently discriminative conditions (e.g., disorder) and despite the backlash of victim blaming from the dominant. Therefore, let us now turn to "the family." Through collective racial identity, black citizens trusted and referenced one another as fictive kin family members. They extended nonbiological ties and alliances to one another, emulating brothers, sisters, and so forth.

The Family

> Show me what a family looks like! (THIS is what a family looks like!)
>
> PROTEST CHANT

On countless occasions over many years, I have entered into protest spaces or community centers and events across disadvantaged neighborhoods and encountered "family." These are familial persons who turn into extended family members or acquire fictive kinship from direct action and community or movement work.[8] They aspire to advance black life and the quality thereof in various ways. Some do so as a full-time "calling," treating freedom work as a sacrificial life decision.[9] Their engagement often calls for intimate attachment(s) to community members and community work. As such, protesters, activists, leaders, and organizers often greet familiar persons in unity, through hugs and handshakes (e.g., grips and dap). They are known to one another, and their gestures are congenial testaments of solidarity. This is also the case with some elected officials at the local and state levels. Black elected officials are often intimately connected with and involved in direct actions, and they plan and attend community events. It is an expectation and obligation that they do so, as they are the empowered political voice(s) of many participating constituents. Familial trust and an informal measure of loyalty are extended to and expected from them.

There are instances in which "family members" may not know one another by name. However, their frequent contacts, shared associates, aligning behaviors, and comfort with the work result in recognition of them as trusted persons or family in the movement. For instance, some may not know my name or "know me, know me," as participant Angel from Focus Group 1 similarly intimated in chapter 3 about her neighbor.[10] However, they know my face; they know my flow or mannerisms as I interact with them, directly or indirectly. They also may know other activists and organizers that I closely engage with; this acts as somewhat of an informal vouching or checking system. They also may know that I am "out"—outside, out and about, attending and participating in all things "community" all the time.[11] They may know that I am a professor, researcher, author, or "home-girl"—identifying me by one or all of those categories—and therefore some show deference, regardless of the situation, which they expect to be reciprocated. I treat them the same way, as others sometimes similarly engage across neighborhoods and throughout the protest community.

There is an informal understanding and arrangement for engaging as an extended movement family. I liken these exchanges to what occurred in neighborhoods in which participants reported influxes of new neighbors. In some instances, they connected through familiarity—routinely seeing one another in shared space—although they did not know one another's names. They connected with and unofficially derived meaning and expectations from one another based on frequent visuals of each other in the neighborhood. This was at least enough contact to guarantee smiles, waves, or "hellos" or to develop some sense of comfort. This denotes degrees of connection—an acquaintanceship or fictive kinship through familiarity in the community but not as intimate as with some others. There has been a constant exchange of interactions—good, bad, and indifferent—for engagement among black citizens, whether or not they have been involved in direct action. Following is an example of how, following the Stockley verdict, acting as "family," an organizer encouraged solidarity among the mostly black protesters:

> They have taken our constitutional rights from us, they have taken our human rights from us. . . . [N]ow, it's the people's power. Say, "Power to the people." [Protesters repeat, "Power to the people!"] Now what we gone do, brothers and sisters . . . your unity is our success. We have to be unified. We got street brothers out here, front-line soldiers out here: . . . Six Deuce, GD, El-Ruckn. [Voices in the background say, "Alright. . .you hear me!"] . . . [W]e got college kids out here, . . . pastors out here. We got er'body out here workin together. . . . [O]ur unity is our success. They killin' black folks . . . [and] what I want us to do is stay unified. . . . I want everybody here to shake hands real quick. . . [W]e ain't here to talk. . . . DO IT NOW.

Imagine. Protesters were shaking hands, as well as hugging, smiling, and laughing together, as if in a church service. Notice how the organizer refers to protesters as "brothers and sisters." These are common terms of endearment and fictive kinship. This specifically translates to interactions with familial status within the black community. These exchanges occurred in front of the riot team and with media looming in the distance. Some of the police and media likely did not acknowledge the camaraderie, except to characterize it as a threat of "protesters gathering" and then to report on it disparagingly. This was expected, and part reason for certain media outlets and networks being shut out or not being embraced by the protest community.

Family Conflict and Silos   Movement work (protests and community organizing) is tedious. It is all encompassing and exhausting. It is a commitment that extends itself in all directions—sometimes leading to rifts within the family even while members are collectively fighting. Even within natural families there is an understanding that not everyone will get along at all times. Likewise, there are times when this applies in the movement, especially under relentless pressure. Disagreements occur within the family. Sometimes they emerge between individuals and sometimes within and across efforts and organizations. In any case, they should be understood analogously rather than as more space for derision within the black community. It is in this spirit that activist/organizer (Hakim) tried to explain emerging dissension within the family. Here is what he said:

> You lookin' at somebody who just swingin, like they don't know what's goin' on. Boom, boom . . . hitn ANYBODY and EVERYBODY. [He swings his arms.] And I tell people all the time, Ferguson [activists/ protesters], we swinging. . . . Look, I might accidentally hit you, Fam. It don't mean that I don't love [you].

Activists in St. Louis fight almost constantly and at great cost to themselves—swinging intensely—while relentlessly strategizing and working on many things at the same time. Since black citizens contend with all-around discrimination (oppression), the fight to alleviate themselves from its perceived effects is also all around them. Therefore, family members could inadvertently throw or catch a punch metaphorically (e.g., experience misplaced or misunderstood comments and actions), though no harm to fictive kinfolks in the community is intended. In some sense, this may be compared to friendly fire—with freedom fighters seemingly being treated as enemy combatants, at least to all appearances (e.g., facing armored tanks, the National Guard, and helicopters). The trauma of this struggle can leave black citizens discombobulated and subsequently disagreeing on some matters. Likewise, this can be the situation in poor neighborhoods apart from direct action. Some black citizens grind or hustle all the time—legitimately and illegitimately—to survive, sometimes injuring those in close proximity. I argue that this is how some blacks come to harm other black citizens. They act under insurmountable duress and in desperation in ways that may easily be conceived of as on-the-job hazards, to put it mildly (e.g., neighborhood drug dealers). They often take risks, attributing little or no value to their own lives or those of their neighbors. Institutional desolation and isolation breed despondency. As an effect, a few black citizens navigate neighborhood space in survival mode or by only living in the moment. This is how Ted, quoted in chapter 4, explained his previous state of hopelessness:

> [A]nything can get us [black men] killed. [We] don't really care about that. Don't nobody care about getting' killed [no more]. That's not a big deal, like so what? Why are we trying to live for a future that we don't see? What we building for? We livin' day to day. . . . We just trying to get through the day. I'm trying to pay this bill today. If I make $5,000 *today*, I'm gonna spend it *today* and make sure I take care of everything *today*. I'll figure out tomorrow later because tomorrow [is] not promised. . . . It's not and that's how we think.

Ted's comments provide significant insight into the mind-set of some residents who directly or indirectly resort to neighborhood crime and interpersonal violence. The fact that a few anticipate dying provides much food for thought when accounting for crime or homicide rates, which are correlated with persistently desolate neighborhood conditions and the overall lack of health and wellness of the community. I argue that as in some developing nations (e.g., in Rwanda), institutional exploitation and negligence in favor of dominant interests pits poor residents against one another at the local level.[12] It creates environments ripe for a few residents with no expectation of living beyond the moment to resort to pillaging and scrounging at the expense of the other(s).

Family disagreements may also emerge from philosophical differences. Protest and community organizers may have different ideas about how to advance black life. This is to be expected, especially as they are sometimes operating from different vantage points, with varying resources. On the one hand, some community organizers target and provide specialized assistance to black citizens. They may provide food pantries, job skills training, and other resources. On the other hand, protest organizers may lean more toward resistance work and preparing for ongoing direct action in the community. This does not mean one approach is better or worse than the other. Rather, they are distinct in how they analyze and strategize to provoke social change. This speaks to differences *across* community groups, between protest organizing specifically and community organizing broadly. They even overlap in some instances, and there can be diverse ideas *within* each group. Not all protest and community organizers unanimously agree about or approach black resistance or advancement in the same way. Examples are the dueling perspectives of W. E. B. DuBois and Booker T. Washington or Dr. Martin Luther King Jr. and Malcolm X.[13] All four men were significant to black advancement. Their positions and efforts were essential in advancing black life, whether individually or collectively. The same is true today. Since black citizens are not monolithic, their approaches and strategies are better suited when they correspond with each other, addressing different issues. Because some black citizens face tremendous disadvantages, there is a need for all hands on deck to work in various ways within the community. Even with a single vision—to resist discrimination and advance the totality of black life—diverse approaches should be embraced. Even when groups work somewhat separately (i.e., in silos) and collaborate only occasionally (e.g., supporting one another's events, engaging in joint programming), they are still family.

The fact that some leaders and organizers tend to work independently may also be influenced by gaining or losing funding and visibility. They sometimes compete for, secure (or not), and promote themselves differently because of these resources. These benefits become invaluable commodities and sometimes semblances of power and distinction between leaders or across organizations. Acquiring them translates into recognition and influence when leading and organizing in the somewhat thankless and threatening "struggle" to liberate or advance many. Furthermore, the need for money and visibility fuels particular kinds of maneuvering—even competition—that may create or intensify existing dissension within the black community. If leaders and organizations are not careful, competition and territorial approaches may distract or detract from black efforts. In some instances, through seemingly well-intended opportunities, black leaders and organizers and their efforts are hierarchically arranged or preferred politically, whether intentionally or inadvertently. They find themselves subtly and not always admittedly pitted against one another, directly and indirectly. This situation is also linked to endemic dominant oppression and disorder. It is conflict contingent upon increments of power, extended through economics and social capital. It is structurally similar to the previous analogy of developing nations (e.g., Rwanda).[14] Through long-standing historical socioeconomic and political competition, one faction or group is situated over or against another in a way that protects dominant interests (e.g., in Rwanda, the Hutus versus the Tutsis).[15] A case in point is that if it were not for the systemic oppression of blacks, there would be no urgent mobilization efforts or subsequent clashes. However, philosophical distinctions and lines that divide do not negate or eliminate informal understandings and extended familial relationships.

Political and Economic Advancement

[W]hat does freedom look like? We don't exactly know. . . . We just know that somebody got their foot on our neck and we tryin' to get that foot off.

KAVION, Ferguson activist

Disorderly communities are highly correlated with poverty, unemployment, educational disparity, renting versus homeownership, and other disproportionately discriminative and destabilizing socioeconomic factors.[16] These interactive issues are why some black citizens face relentless institutional and structural disadvantages. Kavion describes racial oppression and discrimination as so enduring that actual liberation is almost unimaginable. Black citizens fighting disparity in various ways is a constant. It is as if those who are poor are endlessly trying to escape or "get that foot off" their necks while contending with seemingly incessant negative conditions. Thus, they face unyielding restraint amid inflexible socioeconomic and political forces.

Black citizens holistically experience sporadic and incremental advancement, embedded in pervasive subjugation. This means that no matter the measure of progress, it comes attached to baked-in reminders of discriminative policies and practices (e.g., the arrest of Dr. Henry Louis Gates Jr.).[17] A continuum of racially charged narratives and fear tactics justifies and ensures bias and the degradation of black life. So then how do we preserve and advance black lives, particularly those laden with disorder? The solutions to improvement hinge on advancing the political and economic position of black citizens and community resources.[18] After all, as Skogan explains, it is through political decisions that neighborhood (re)structuring occurs.[19] "These decisions are made by governments and large institutional actors like banks, insurance and utility companies, and real-estate developers. The causes of disorder problems lie in part in what these powerful players decide to do . . . as a result of past politics and because they are overwhelmingly poor their redemption will depend to some degree on their capacity to extract resources from the broader community, through future politics."[20]

Politics   The fact that "powerful players" are making decisions without involving black citizens—those most negatively affected—speaks to the purposeful arranging and maintaining of race and space. This structuring persists as economically beneficial for the dominant and is consistent with the reason for the state of emergency town hall meeting discussed in chapter 5. Debatable decisions with far-reaching effects that are inconsiderate of black citizens suggest residents' interests do not matter. Black lives are tied to "a seat at the table." The fact that those impacted are not present at that table and part of negotiations is part of the reason and need for "Black Lives Matter" slogans, organization, and black empowerment efforts in general. Black interests and voices matter, whether expressed directly or indirectly. Neighborhood or community agendas should reflect this fact. There is a need for grooming elected officials or positioned individuals and for refusing support to those who do not consistently represent or protect black interests, regardless of political longevity or racial loyalty. The advancement of black lives should not be compromised, substituted for, or infinitely tethered to political alliances or relationships that do not yield systemic pushback and continuous inclusion and progress for black citizens, especially disadvantaged ones.

Neighborhood Divestment and Investment   Racial discrimination as disorder directly and indirectly discourages community investment. From residential segregation and isolation to transportation, systemic forces disproportionately create and maintain cycles of impoverishment and instability for some black citizens. An example is redlining, in which financial institutions persistently deny mortgages or rehabilitation loans to black citizens and disadvantaged black neighborhoods. This is not a new occurrence. It is a well-known practice in black neighborhoods across the country. In fact, a recent article in the St. Louis Post-Dispatch reported that African Americans are 2.5 times more likely to be denied home loans than non-Hispanic white citizens,[21] taking into account national practices and percentages. The article further states, "In 61 metro areas across the U.S., people of color were more likely to be denied conventional mortgage loans than whites, even when controlling for applicants' income, loan amount, and neighborhood."[22] This practice increases economic disadvantage for predominantly black, poor neighborhoods. It is one of many "drivers of decline" or erosion, including "government policy or investments, changes in the economy, demographic and migration shifts" and other widespread forms of discrimination.[23] As a result, places of color disproportionately become places of divestment, discouraging developers, businesses, and others from investing in them. Development, business, and investment are essential components for making neighborhoods vibrant and livable. Without these resources, they become desolate places in isolation. This translates to fewer employment opportunities and inaccessibility of basic essentials (e.g., lack of grocery stores).

St. Louis is hyper-segregated, which confirms and reciprocates biased attitudes and institutional discrimination.[24] Disadvantaged black citizens are subject to apartheid-like arrangements that do not occur by happenstance.[25] They are immersed in white fear and white in-group preferences that together impede residential integration.[26] Research shows that white citizens are the least favorable toward residential integration of all racial groups.[27] This is especially true among the affluent.[28] Likewise, whites are less favorable toward integrating specifically with black populations.[29] Instead, the dominant support policies and practices (e.g., white flight, gentrification) that attempt to separate, protect, and preserve white space.[30] As a result, residential segregation persists for predominantly black locations, in which black citizens are purposely partitioned and shut out of opportunities for community development. Poor black citizens especially live in barren places, sometimes with a deserted appearance and which have been declared "food deserts."[31] The Delmar Divide is certainly one example of overtly race- and class-distinguished places (and appearances), with advantaged whites living to the south of the divide and disadvantaged blacks to the north of it.[32]

Food desert refers to the fact that 70 percent of blacks residing in the city of St. Louis, and 63 percent of blacks residing in St. Louis County, do not have access to fresh food or mainstream chain grocery stores.[33] Access to fresh (healthy) food is a human right. Black citizens have a right to buy fresh food from mainstream supermarkets in their communities, rather than from neighborhood gas stations, convenience marts, and liquor stores. Again, black residents and empowered representatives need to be seated at the table. This means they should be presenting and contributing to community infrastructure and development agendas. This should be done alongside or represented by groomed or suitable candidates, elected officials, or other relevant persons who will counter institutional forces (e.g., redlining and "panic peddling").[34]

Black citizens should not be reduced to or forced to live in depressed neighborhoods. Black places are being purposely starved out, institutionally and literally, through actions ranging from the creation of food deserts to complete negligence. Residents are forced to move. Those who cannot are seemingly trapped, succumbing to abandonment as businesses dry up, residents leave, and properties reflect decay and dilapidation (i.e., physical disorder). *Real* "job creation and housing" are needed—the kinds that are accessible and competitive across all markets—for (re)building communities and combating disorder and its effects.[35] This also calls for other infrastructure investments, such as providing quality education, transit systems, parks and green space, and highways, all of which contribute to improving housing/property values.[36] These efforts should not be conflated with or replaced by urban renewal, or "Negro Removal" as some refer to it.[37] Gentrification and other plans often leave black residents physically (e.g., utilities are disconnected) or economically (e.g., they are priced out) displaced.[38]

Neighborhood Services   Black communities need more formal organizations or community service organizations and nonprofit programs to be embedded within their neighborhoods that are not politically selected and funded but rather are equitably funded and assessed, holistically and effectively tackling disparity. For example, funding a food bank or supporting one provides only minimal support, leaving other areas (e.g., unemployment, mental illness) unaddressed, which could correlate with the existence of the unhoused and hunger. In any case, such an approach only temporarily addresses a fraction of the overarching and underlying problem. While programs such as food banks are great, they cannot and should not have only one source of support or be stand-alone operations. They need to be complementary, part of all-encompassing initiatives in disadvantaged neighborhoods. There should also be more places that directly engage residents and assist with numerous issues (e.g., housing, job training, mental health/addiction, youth programs) at one location (e.g., in one building). In other words, there is a need for "one-stop-shop" services that are not overwhelmingly tasked for one particular organization. Rather, the all-encompassing services should be spread out across numerous nongovernmental organizations and agencies in each neighborhood, all receiving similar funding. This would keep people from falling through the cracks and being underassisted or not assisted at all due to an overwhelming number of cases and situations and a limited number of accommodating agencies or organizations. After all, it is through the lack of such triaged assistance that environments succumb to increased susceptibility to disorder and crime, resulting in aggressive policing. Let us now turn to the role of policing in disadvantaged black communities.

Policing   Aggressive policing—proactive or reactive—and disproportionate criminal justice supervision (e.g., arrests, incarceration) are not the answer for addressing community disorder. However, they have become an outlet or divergence—whereby black citizens and police become entangled in neighborhoods—due to structural issues such as displacement and dilapidation. In other words, just as black citizens rely on social ties to compensate for a lack of resources and other social services, the police are often tasked by their respective cities with many social service responsibilities. Despite the overall neglect of social services, the police should not be regarded as a convenient, though inadequate, go-to for addressing mental illness, addiction, the unhoused, and other issues. They are not trained to do this, and therefore jail and criminalization have become temporary fixes, with arrest being an ineffective response that only exacerbates matters. We cannot arrest our way out of inequity, inequality and structured inadequacy. The desperation of populations who may be dealing with those adverse conditions, combined with few or inadequately trained law enforcement, creates a situation ripe for havoc. Considered critically, why would police officers be expected to manage and handle situations for which they are obviously not trained? These often-difficult circumstances and conditions (e.g., addiction, mental illness, unhousing) call for specialized help or targeted care from professionals that is often well beyond the purview of law enforcement. Through this persistent arrangement, the police too come to be unfairly compromised. They are situated as "babysitters"—an actionable insult to black communities. It is as if the idea is to keep both parties—police and black citizens—busy fighting one another. The presence of untrained police, coupled with biases and differential tactics, creates an explosive situation, especially when the police are tasked with making impromptu life or death decisions for disadvantaged populations of color. This has become comparable to being on slave patrol, whereby poor white citizens found themselves policing slaves, providing the former with authority and respectability through the differential treatment of black populations.[39] Contemporary policing as arguably described, does the same. Policing is often low paying and comparatively low skilled, making it an acceptable, achievable, and respectable occupation for many who may be racially insensitive and detached from neighborhoods of color. This maneuvering continues as a result of the failure of broader structures and institutions (i.e., policies and practices) to become involved with tangible solutions.

Moreover, it is through incompatibly maintained policing expectations and directives that black citizens' distrust and lack of police restraint increase black citizen–police conflict. This refers to impromptu fluctuations—subjective decision making that catapults police from supposedly being community oriented to being paramilitary forces. With policing as a sliding continuum, black citizen–police interactions post-Ferguson have more to do with minimizing or eradicating the black threat or resistance. The Ferguson Effect is a red herring—particularly as police have historically been delayed or absent in responding to black communities.[40] More specifically, I am referring to when black citizens call for police help (a reactive, voluntary interaction), not when they are imposed upon by police (a proactive, involuntary interaction). When thus called upon to help, police have been known to show up late or not at all, compromising black life. Yet they have been proactively present in disparaging black life, aggressively policing law-abiding black citizens rather than the few actual offenders.[41] Again, this situation has persisted post-Ferguson, as black citizens counter discriminative treatment through a twenty-first-century movement.

Policing cannot be a one-stop-shop solution for addressing discrimination or community disorder, crime, and its effects. In many respects, the police agenda and tactics (e.g., brutality, PPUs) reflect and are also effects of disorder, and therefore the police engage in ways that exacerbate disparagement of black citizen neighborhoods and communities. The answer lies in institutional policies and practices that support community infrastructure and implementation of black interests and all-inclusive social services. Political sensitivity, inclusion, and accountability lie at the root of police reform.[42] The police are not separate from politics but are enforcers of it. They act in accordance with the government agenda, upholding and protecting its policies and practices. Moreover, it is through this arrangement that institutional neglect is maintained at the expense of black lives (e.g., they are subjected to brutality and victim blaming), through the inept positioning and scapegoating of differential law enforcement, and through the creation by policy makers of space for escaping culpability.

CONCLUSION, BUT NOT CONCLUDING!

You can't stop the revolution! (You can't stop the revolution!)

PROTEST CHANT

I argue that racial discrimination and systemic injustice are an undercurrent of (dis)order. It is with this understanding that we should prioritize behaviors and account for them. Examinations, conversations, and direct actions are ongoing. This is because how we think about racial discrimination and systemic injustice is subjectively and historically (dis)ordered at the expense of minorities. I liken this to protesters chanting, "You can't stop the revolution!" There continues to be an all-out resistance against systems that inherently leave marginalized populations—or at least those that are invariably vulnerable—to creatively fight and fend for themselves against the status quo in the twenty-first century. That said, it is not by coincidence that Black Lives Matter, the Movement for Black Lives, sister marches,

DACA efforts, the #NeverAgain movement (i.e., the Parkland High School students), the resurgence of the #MeToo movement, and innumerable local, national, and international organizations and initiatives have emerged, post-Ferguson.

The unrelenting visibility of state violence against black citizens' empowerment and mobility has resulted in widespread momentum for twenty-first-century resistance against "othering" policies and practices across all social paradigms. This project has attempted to account for that energy by contextualizing the totality of the black experiences in the St. Louis region—good, bad, and indifferent—especially because they are often captured in ways that work to undermine the advancement of black lives. That said, there are limitations, as this project, like interactions in protests and neighborhoods, became very fluid, and I was constantly negotiating in an effort to clarify messaging. Therefore, I now turn to the complexities that I experienced in capturing the nuances of black life, post-Ferguson.

Limitations

While black citizens, especially those who are poor, contend with widespread disorder, it is important to note that combating that disorder means broadening how we think about it and then addressing its implications through reconceptualizations of (dis)order. It is through the reconceptualization of disorder that we can begin to tackle and address the underpinnings of institutional discrimination—the policies and practices—that allow for the existence of failed economic structures and the sociopolitical practices that prevent improving black life and the quality thereof. In this reconceptualization, there are areas of the project that need to be revisited.

With regard to participants, the exploration of black life post-Ferguson would have benefited from more in-depth interviews with protesters. This would have provided more information on the effects of the movement beyond surface conversations while in direct action, comparable to what I got from those whom I met and interviewed outside of it. In addition, larger focus groups—with more males—would have allowed for more gender-diverse conversations and experiences.

Timing also proved extremely problematic, as direct action in the region is ongoing, which made data collection and the attempt to examine the data adequately feel unending. Furthermore, this project would have benefited from more time being spent with protesters/participants who were both protesting black citizen–police conflict and survivors and/or surviving family members of violence in their neighborhoods. This would have benefited the project with even more in-depth information, as these black citizens directly and vulnerably navigated both terrains in difficult circumstances. The additional information might have provided more insight into how black citizens navigate or manage actual incidents in both worlds (e.g., victimization by police, interpersonal neighborhood violence) rather than just the fear or threat of them. I account for some in this project, but only a few. Moreover, a project of this magnitude might have benefited from more time being spent with protest and community leaders and organizers of post-Ferguson programs and initiatives that emerged as a direct result of civil unrest, as well as from more suburban in-depth interviews.

Finally, through this project I found that there is room for devoting more attention to racial disparity and the visibility of missing and exploited persons of color and to the psychological trauma of survivors and surviving families, witnesses, and others who directly and indirectly experience interpersonal neighborhood violence.

Closing

> [T]his discussion just made me be really aware of a lot of
> things. . . . I *do* need to get involved with the people that's
> around me. . . . Because they are around and it's no way of run-
> ning away from the situation. . . . I talk to the young kids and
> then more like get to know them more, you know. [Then I] get
> to know my [other] neighbors, the people around the corner
> around from me. [I] get to know their mental state on whether
> they want to change or, you know, gonna do community
> service. . . . I need to get more active with the people.
>
> IESHA

This project has been a fight to the finish. I have fought to capture the movement—whose initial agenda called for addressing violence from the police and a few black citizens—in hopes of contextualizing and providing sensitivity to those who work tirelessly and thanklessly to improve the state of the entire black community. That said, I have settled with knowing that even if I never ended this project, there would still be too much left unsaid and too many underappreciated. Therefore, I hope others, like Iesha, will be influenced to begin or continue advancing social change through action.

Finally, this book gauges black citizens' social ties and participation—how they protected and served one another in vulnerable places. I found that they organized variably and creatively, as protesters and neighbors. They aligned themselves, contrary to disparaging narratives—which is part of the reason for exposing culturally inherent discrimination from the perspective of black citizens.[43] The depictions from "the ground" were often skewed and thus misleading in ways that did not always show respect to the black community. Therefore, as a takeaway, it is important to know that this movement "is leaderful, *not* leaderless" as one organizer put it. This project affirms that fact, and we should continue to think critically about black engagement and participation as *not* being monolithic or nonexistent, but rather as forever evolving, leading, ongoing, energizing, and diversely encompassing, despite broad, contrasting, and often denigrating depictions.

Notes

INTRODUCTION

1. Clarke and Lett (2014).
2. Clarke and Lett (2014).
3. *Direct action* is a broad term. In this study it describes or references all nonviolent actions or acts of resistance or civil disobedience. Protests are one of many forms of direct action, and I therefore use the terms interchangeably. Protests are forms of direct action; direct action can be protests, marches, boycotts, and so forth.
4. Boyles (2015).
5. Boyles (2015).
6. Explore St. Louis (2017).
7. O'Neil (2016).
8. Levitt (2010).
9. Huber (2010).
10. O'Neil (2016).
11. O'Neil (2016).
12. O'Neil (2016).
13. O'Neil (2016).
14. Better Together (n.d.); McDermott (2017a).
15. Better Together (n.d.).
16. Boyles (2015); McDermott (2017a).
17. Jones (2019).
18. United States Census Bureau (2017a, 2017b).
19. United States Census Bureau (2017a, 2017b).
20. United States Census Bureau (2017a, 2017b).
21. United States Census Bureau (2017a, 2017b).
22. Better Together (n.d.).
23. Better Together (2015).
24. Toler (2014).
25. Cusac (2009, 104).

26. Almeida and Lockard (2005).

27. Sampson (1991, 1988) (micro- and macro-analyses); Freire ([1970] 2007) ("critical consciousness").

28. This particular kind of activism was clear from the beginning. It was a twofold pronouncement of combating the victimization of black citizens. It is a balanced approach despite its victim blaming, with activists/organizers calling for black action focused on police brutality and interpersonal neighborhood violence.

29. Fox News (2015).

30. Fox News (2015).

31. Jones (2018); Ross and Jang (2000).

32. Skogan (2009); Marx and Archer (1971).

33. Ross (2011); Swaroop and Morenoff (2006); Ross, Mirowsky, and Pribesh (2001); Ross and Jang (2000); Furstenburg (1993); Skogan (1990); Wilson and Kelling (1982).

34. Swaroop and Morenoff (2006); Ross and Jang (2000); Anderson (1999); Suttles (1972); Janowitz (1967).

35. Brunson and Weitzer (2011); Dotollo and Stewart (2008); Bell and Nkomo (1998); Swidler (1986).

36. Swaroop and Morenoff (2006).

37. Patillo (1988, 755).

38. The quote is from Anderson (1999, 33). About OGs and Gs, see Jones (2018).

39. Pattillo (1988); Bursick and Grasmick (1993a, 1993b); Kornhauser (1978); Janowitz and Karsada (1974) (systemic model). Bursick and Grasmick (1993a, 1993b); Sampson (1991); Berry and Karsada (1977) (social organization).

40. Sampson (1991, 1988). See also Hazani and Nahari (2003) for multilevel analyses (social network analysis).

41. Skogan (1990).

42. Skogan (1990).

43. Skogan (1990).

44. Skogan (1990).

45. The terms *protester, activist, leader,* and *organizer* can sometimes be used interchangeably, representing the same or different person(s). Although I make distinctions in this project, I label participants based on their actions at the time of our exchange and their statements. That said, as a baseline, I characterize as protesters those protesting or engaging in direct action. They may or may not engage or participate intensely, as they may or may not be fully committed. Activists, on the other hand, I identify as committed to organizing and direct action. I considered them as being "all in" or vested in collective work and direct action. Leaders, as in protest leaders, are those acting in a lead position. They may be "leading" in a broad range of ways, from starting protest chants to making announcements. Similarly, this is the case for organizers, who may be actively organizing or known for doing so, and therefore, I labeled them as such in the discussion(s).

46. McMillan and Chavis (1986).

47. This book embodies a three-year ethnographic study that analyzes how blacks have protected and served themselves in post-Ferguson America—that is, during the immediate three years following Brown's death. It relies on 125 citizen exchanges from two distinct data sets,—the first from Ferguson-related protests, and the second from predominantly black neighborhoods with high rates of crime.

Data Set One was derived from civil unrest that provided seventy-five adult exchanges—direct and third-party conversations, observations, pictures, and field notes that I generally collected while embedded in countless direct actions in Ferguson and throughout the St. Louis region (e.g., various protest sites, marches, rallies, town hall/city council/grassroots organization meetings, programs, workshops, trainings, and emerging civic events). Data Set Two was drawn from crime prevention efforts that at times overlapped and ultimately were transposed with Ferguson (police brutality) protests, especially those following the Wilson indictment decision (i.e., the burning of Ferguson).

Data Set Two included forty-one individual, in-depth interviews and two focus groups consisting of nine participants (e.g., four urban and five suburban) from areas with high rates of aggravated assault, along with direct and third-party conversations and field notes generally acquired at gun violence summits, nonviolence marches, rallies, local businesses, churches, and community organizations throughout the St. Louis region. Taken together, this project's materials include direct and indirect, interactive, and often fluid exchanges with adult black citizens and countless participatory accounts gathered over years while attending police brutality direct actions and violence prevention efforts, which occurred individually or collaboratively, and sometimes simultaneously; I have documented both approaches throughout the St. Louis region. That is, there were times in the beginning of the unrest when I could focus solely on Ferguson efforts, and there were times following the indictment decision when I could focus more on community crime prevention. Then there were other times when events addressed both (e.g., the vulnerabilities of black life with police and black citizens) or took place at the same time. In those cases, I attended events and documented them as they emerged, regardless of the topic or issue.

48. I gained information from black citizens directly through impromptu conversations in the community, in-depth interviews, and focus groups.

49. Jenkins and Wallace (1996); Rose (1997).

1. BETWEEN A ROCK AND A HARD PLACE

1. Pierce (2007). Corkball is a variation of baseball, played predominantly by whites, that originated in St. Louis in the early 1900s.

2. Pierce (2007). This game could be characterized as "a serious men's game" and was often played with cheaper and more accessible equipment, such as a sturdy stick (e.g., a broom or mop stick) and a tennis ball.

3. Lartey (2017).

4. See Schaeffer (2014) for ongoing contradictions regarding social movements and change.

5. Hrabovský (2013, 68) (to scorch); Hrabovský (2013) (a curse); Ohlsen (2013) ("people of African descent").

6. Wander, Martin, and Nakayama (1999).

7. Wander, Martin, and Nakayama (1999, 60).

8. Wander, Martin, and Nakayama (1999, 17) ("identity signifier"); Ohlsen (2013); Johnson (2003).

9. Hrabovský (2013, 66–67).

10. Hrabovský (2013, 66).

11. Hrabovský (2013, 66) (philosophical literature); Ohlsen (2013, 7) (slave ships).

12. Entman and Rojecki (2000).

13. Entman and Rojecki (2000, 60, 61).

14. This footage is surveillance video released from Sam's Meat Market, showing Brown allegedly engaging in a strong arm robbery for cigarillos. As the mostly black protesters and citizens were waiting for explanations (more transparency) from the police regarding Brown's murder, these images were circulating.

15. Sanburn (2014).

16. Sanburn (2014).

17. Sanburn (2014).

18. The Ethical Society of Police (2018). A similar black policing organization on the national level is the National Organization of Black Law Enforcement Executives (NOBLE).

19. Breech (2014).

20. Wire (2014).

21. Crenshaw (1991, 1242).

22. hooks (1992, 10).

23. Brown and Ellis (1968).

24. Glaton (2015).

25. Johnson (2003, 10).

26. hooks (1992).

27. Boyles (2015).

28. NAACP Legal Defense Fund (n.d.).

29. NAACP Legal Defense Fund (n.d.).

30. Boyles (2015).

31. Griggs (2018). "While living black" speaks to the racial profiling of black citizens, as they are simply living and criminalized for engaging in everyday activities.

32. hooks (1992).

33. Lartey (2017); Massie (2016); Glaton (2015).

34. Foreman (2017); Lartey (2017).

35. Foreman (2017).

36. Williams (2017) (verbiage); Jenkins and Wallace (1996); Rose (1997).

37. Black Lives Matter (2018).

38. The most ardent activists in St. Louis articulate black efforts holistically and in the region, nationally, and internationally post-Ferguson as "a movement," "movement-work," "part of the movement," and so forth. They discuss and contextualize their roles and events related to the movement as "a calling" and infinite commitment.

39. Although Black Lives Matter is a thriving black organization, it is insulting to pigeonhole and treat black citizens as if they were part of a monolithic organization and incapable of tackling widespread issues through other memberships or approaches. There are countless local, national, and international organizations that similarly promote the preservation of black life through their missions and diverse strategies. This is also the case with individual black citizens, who often are unknown and yet work tirelessly in their communities to achieve similar objectives.

40. Williams (2017); Lartey (2017).

41. Braga and Brunson (2015) (*black* and *blackness*); Massie (2016) ("black-on-black crime").

42. Lartey (2017); Massie (2016).

43. Massie (2016).

44. Williams (2017).

45. Byers (2014). The Ferguson Effect is a highly contentious concept that created distractions during the civil unrest. In fact, use of the term was perceived as another disingenuous police tactic intended to distort and detract from their own discriminatory practices. (See chapter 2.) The term is an unfortunate ploy whose sole effect has been to redirect power by countering, redressing, and reassigning "black-on-black crime" and deviance as contradicting and delegitimizing black mobilization and advancement.

46. Boyles (2015).

47. Boyles (2015); Meehan and Ponder (2002).

48. Boyles (2015).

49. Hatcher (2014). *Town-gown* or *town and gown* refers to collaborative relationships of camaraderie and reciprocity established between university communities and the communities (e.g., local governments, businesses, organizations) in which they are located. Through these exchanges the communities collaborate to address issues affecting their shared populations—students and area residents—such as local crime, off-campus housing, and public transportation.

50. Huerta (2018).

51. Ray (2018).

52. Sudbury and Okazawa-Rey (2009, 3).

53. Sudbury and Okazawa-Rey (2009, 3).

54. Huerta (2018); Sudbury and Okazawa-Rey (2009).

55. Huerta (2018); Sudbury and Okazawa-Rey (2009).

56. hooks (1989).

57. hooks (1989).

58. Babchuk and Hitchcock (2013); Charmaz (2006, 35) (grounded theory ethnography); Battersby (1981, 93) (grounded ethnography).

59. Charmaz (2006, 35).

2. (DIS)ORDER AND INFORMAL SOCIAL TIES IN THE UNITED STATES

1. Kraska and Williams (2018); Kraska (2007).

2. Boyles (2015).

3. Brunson and Pegram (2018); Rios (2017); Boyles (2015); Alpert, MacDonald, and Dunham (2005); Chambliss (1994); Meehan and Ponder (2002).

4. Brunson and Pegram (2018); Rios (2017).

5. Collins (1990) ("community othermothering"); West and Zimmerman (1987) ("doing gender").

6. West and Zimmerman (1987, 5).

7. West and Zimmerman (1987, 5).

8. Skogan (1990); Ross and Jang (2000) (manifest socially and physically); Skogan (1990, 4) ("engender . . . fight or flight").

9. United States Department of Justice (2015).

10. Kraska and Williams (2018).

11. Mountz (2009, 332).

12. Alexander (2004); Eyerman (2004); Russell-Brown (1998) (racially atrocious events); Alexander (2004) ("indelible" mark).

13. Johnson (2003, 2).

14. Levine (1977).

15. Boyles (2015).

16. Boyles (2015).

17. Stewart et al. (2018); Ward-Brown (2016); Lumpkins (2008); Barnes (2008).

18. Skogan (1990, 21).

19. Sampson and Grove (1989, 777); Bursik (1984, 12); Kornhauser (1978, 120).

20. Triplett, Gainey, and Sun (2003); Byrne and Sampson (1986); Shaw and McKay (1942).

21. Skogan (1990).

22. Ross and Jang (2000, 404).

23. Sampson and Grove (1989); Kornhauser (1978); Shaw and McKay (1940); Thomas and Znaniecki 1920) (empirically measured); Shaw and McKay (1942) (explaining crime and delinquency).

24. Ross and Jang (2000, 404) (*weak social controls*); Skogan (1990) (perceptions of residents or community members).

25. Skogan (1990).

26. Skogan (1990).

27. Skogan (1990).

28. Dinesen and Sonderskov (2015).

29. Skogan (1990); Hope (1988).

30. Ross and Jang (2000); Pattillo (1988); Taylor (1996); Oliver (1988); Hackler, Ho, and Urquhart-Ross (1974); Maccoby, Newcomb, and Hartley (1958).
31. Pattillo (1988, 748).
32. Skogan (1990, 4)
33. Skogan (1990 5).
34. Boyles (2015).
35. Boyles (2015); Meehan and Ponder (2002).
36. Boyles (2015).
37. Boyles (2015).
38. Taylor et al. (2001) (family members' support); Marwell, Oliver, and Prahl (1988) (collective action and mobilization); Oliver (1988, 626); Feagin (1970) (urban friendship ties); Hannerz (1969); Stack (1974); Valentine (1978) (interpersonal exchanges).
39. Boyles (2015); Meehan and Ponder (2002).
40. Kraska (2007).
41. Boyles (2015).
42. Boyles (2015, 101).
43. Boyles (2015, 209).
44. Boyles (2015, 209).
45. Green (2000); Mastrofski, Worden, and Snipes (1995).
46. Bayley and Shearing (1996); Bayley (1994).
47. Websdale (2001) (unfavorable views of the program). Beanbag systems are "nylon bags of lead shot" aimed at citizens. See Kraska and Kappeler (1997).
48. Byers (2014).
49. Boyles (2015); Brunson (2007).
50. Boyles (2015); Brunson (2007).
51. Rosenfeld (2015) (Ferguson Effect); Boyles (2015); Brunson and Weitzer (2011); Brunson (2007); Brunson and Miller (2006a, 2006b).
52. Boyles (2015); Brunson (2007); Brunson and Miller (2006a, 2006b).
53. Kraska (2007).
54. Boyles (2015); Blalock (1967) (group threats); Boyles (2015); Smith and Holmes (2003) (racial threats).
55. Cordner (2000, 1995); Skogan (1994).
56. Kraska (2007).
57. Kraska (2007, 7).
58. Golden (2005).
59. Kraska (2007).
60. Kraska (2007).
61. Kraska and Kappeler (1997, 13).
62. The use of "broken window" here is a play on theory. See Kelling and Wilson (1982).
63. Kraska and Kappeler (1997, 13).
64. Durkheim (1893).
65. Martineau (1977) (dense, familial, and identifiable);Ross and Jang (2000); Pattillo (1988); Oliver (1988); Stack (1974).

66. Moynihan (1965).

67. Jones (2018); Swaroop and Morenoff (2006).

68. Ross and Jang (2000); Taylor (1996); Oliver (1988) (quantitative); Pattillo (1998) (qualitative).

69. Pattillo (1988) (item 1); Martineau (1977) (informal relationships); Ross and Jang (2000) (item 3, individual integration); Swaroop and Morenoff (2006) (item 3, neighboring).

70. Ross and Jang (2000).

71. Taylor (1996).

72. See also Sampson (1991, 1988).

73. Rountree and Warner (1999).

74. Rountree and Warner (1999, 790) (race, class, gender, or age); Sampson and Groves (1989); Bellair (1997); Warner and Rountree (1997) (mixed findings).

75. Wellman et al. (1983); Wellman (1979); Wellman and Leighton (1979).

76. Oliver (1988, 640).

77. Ross and Jang (2000).

78. Pattillo (1988).

79. Anderson (1999, 33).

80. Anderson (1999); see also Horowitz (1983).

81. Anderson (1999, 11).

82. Swidler (1986); Pattillo-McCoy (1998, 770); Bell and Nkomo (1998, 286); also Greene (1994, 1992) and Peters (1985); Brunson and Weitzer (2011); Duck (2015).

83. Jones (2018, 4, 6).

84. Jones (2018, 3, 116).

3. "A CHANGE GOTTA COME"

1. "WATCH Cops Physically Push CNN's Don Lemon" (2014).

2. I made the decision while documenting to stay clear of the media, unless relying on them as buffers for safety. This was mostly impossible; however, attempting to do so helped me remember my privileged role(s) (e.g., researcher) compared with the status of some at ground zero. This avoidance also helped me remain objective.

3. Foucault (1995, 63).

4. I also made a point of extending respect to and complying with the directions of trench workers—those frontline leaders and organizers who, whether or not they were involved in protests, were relentlessly leading, organizing, and strategizing community and movement work daily as "a calling" in life. They did this under some of the most challenging circumstances. Courtesy was not always extended to them, yet they selflessly and regularly put their bodies on the line for people.

5. "WATCH Cops Physically Push CNN's Don Lemon" (2014).

6. Meyer (2017).

7. Fowler and Chen (2017).

8. Individual, in-depth interviews and focus groups occurred outside of protests. Participant statements received during protests are not categorized as interviews but rather classified and discussed here as impromptu exchanges and conversations.

9. Focus Group 1 consisted of four participants, all black females. Three resided in the inner city and one lived in a suburban community.

10. Bisby is a pseudonym for a St. Louis suburb. I assigned pseudonyms to most locations, except when referencing Ferguson, places of direct actions, or public places throughout the region.

11. Lee (2014). *Unhoused* is an advocacy term used to describe various states of homelessness. The term *unhoused* is believed to be less denigrating and more integrative, as these people are still members of a community.

12. This project consisted of two focus groups: one representative of inner-city residents and the other of suburban residents. Both focus groups were composed of individuals who, regardless of where they resided at the time of the project, had lived in both urban and suburban places.

13. Currier and Byers (2014).

14. Currier and Byers (2014).

15. Boyles (2015); Brunson (2007); Brunson and Miller (2006a, 2006b).

16. Boyles (2015).

17. Participants from Focus Group 2 perceived police as being lackadaisical about catching suspected criminals in their neighborhoods as well as being thoughtless and inconsiderate of residents assisting their efforts. Among many other factors, this perception influenced their decisions to report or not report crimes. In some instances, they believed that by doing so, they would only be inviting more conflict without resolution.

18. Fivush (2010, 92–94).

19. Ross and Jang (2000, 402).

20. St. Clair (1998) (distress and disagreement); Fivush (2010, 90) ("being silent" and *"being* silenced").

21. Ross and Jang (2000).

22. Ross and Jang (2000).

23. Ross and Jang (2000, 409).

24. Ross and Jang (2000).

25. Ross and Jang (2000, 404).

26. See table 3.

27. Ross and Jang (2000, 404).

28. Ross and Jang (2000).

29. Ross and Jang (2000).

30. Du Bois (1903); Ioffe (2014).

31. Du Bois (1903) ("through the eyes of others"); Ioffe (2014).

32. Ioffe (2014).

33. Ioffe (2014).

34. Ioffe (2014).

35. Bivens (2005, 45).

36. National Alliance on Mental Illness (n.d.) (general population); American Psychiatric Association (2017) (treatment).

37. National Alliance on Mental Illness (n.d.).

38. National Alliance to End Homelessness (2018); National Alliance on Mental Illness (n.d.).

39. American Psychiatric Association (2017) (underinsurance); National Alliance on Mental Illness (n.d.); American Psychiatric Association, 2017) (misdiagnoses).

40. Jones (2018).

41. Michelle invites prostitutes and drug addicts to classes, realizing that they are likely not open to attending them. This is her way of extending kindness to them.

42. McVay, Schriraldi, and Ziedenberg (2004); National Institutes of Health (2018).

43. McVay, Schriraldi, and Ziedenberg (2004); National Institutes of Health (2018).

44. McVay, Schriraldi, and Ziedenberg (2004); National Institutes of Health (2018) (committing crime); Foundations Recovery Network (n.d.); National Bureau of Economic Research (NBER) (n.d.) (mental illness); National Institutes of Health (2018); McVay, Schriraldi, and Ziedenberg (2004) (criminalization).

45. Pattillo (1998).

46. Ross and Jang (2000).

47. Ross and Jang (2000).

4. MAKING BLACK LIVES MATTER

1. Ransby (2018).

2. Cloward and Ohlin (1960); Jones (2018); Rios (2017); Duck (2015). See also Robert Merton's (1938, 1968) strain theory.

3. Ross and Jang (2000) (network of reciprocity); Cloward and Ohlin (1960); Jones (2018); Rios (2017); Duck (2015) (response to strain); Cloward and Ohlin (1960) (lack of socially acceptable means). See also Robert Merton's (1938, 1968) strain theory.

4. Anderson (1999).

5. Cloward and Ohlin (1960). See also Robert Merton's (1938, 1968) strain theory.

6. *Hustling* refers to various ways to creatively make quick money, including both legitimate and illegitimate opportunities.

7. Gallagher (2011).

8. Park (2016).

9. Based on Khareem's accounts, his family may have slipped through the cracks by having water for an extended period of time without paying the bill. Once that fact was discovered, their water was turned off, and they owed an

astronomical amount. They continued without water for years because they were unable to bring the bill current.

10. Khareem could not provide details for some things. He was a child during the events described in some of his accounts and therefore may not have been privy to all decisions or specifics concerning their living conditions. Based on his accounts, they may have acquired their home through a $1 buy-back program. This is an arrangement in which citizens purchase abandoned homes in the city for $1 and thus assume all labor and financial responsibility for fixing it up.

11. United States Department of Health and Human Services (2018).

12. National Alliance on Mental Illness (n.d.); American Psychiatric Association (2017).

13. United States Department of Justice (2007).

14. Brunson (2007).

15. Boyles (2015).

16. From Tevin's description, his friend is not attached to the Black Lives Matter organization. Reportedly, he is innovative and does things to promote the theme.

17. Collins (1990, 192) ("othermothers"); Naylor (2005); Collins (1990, 146) ("community othermothers").

18. Collins (1990, 178); Troester (1984, 13).

19. Collins (1990, 181) ("cooperative" approach); Collins (1990); Dougherty (1978) (slave children).

20. Stack (1974).

21. Collins (1990, 189).

22. Collins (1990, 146); Clark-Lewis (1985).

23. Naples (1991).

24. Collins (1990, 193). My use of "strong black woman" in this context from Collins in no way minimizes or negates the disproportionate vulnerability and susceptibility of black women and women of color generally to exploitation, violence, and overall devaluation.

25. Collins (1990, 192).

26. Collins (1990, 208).

27. See Collins (1990, 208).

28. Collins (1990); Naples (1991) ("activist mother").

29. Collins.(1990, 192).

30. Currier and Byers (2017).

5. "WE ARE IN A STATE OF EMERGENCY"

1. Peterson and Krivo (1996) (violence as defense); Black (1983) (arm themselves and vigilante justice).

2. Peterson and Krivo (1993) (isolation); Wilson (1987).

3. Boyles (2015).

4. Murphy et al. (2017).

5. Murphy et al. (2017).

6. Murphy et al. (2017).

7. Murphy et al. (2017).

8. Hawkins (1993)

9. Federal Bureau of Investigation (FBI) (2017).

10. Black and Missing Foundation Inc. (BAMFI) (2016); FBI (2017). The missing population figures are from the 2017 FBI report across all age groups for black and white racial categories. The percentages reflect averages from both BAMFI (2016) and FBI (2017) across all age groups for black and white racial categories. The BAMFI white category includes missing Hispanic populations.

11. King (2017); Sommers (2016); Special to the Denver Post (2013/2016).

12. Sommers (2016, 278).

13. Jones (2017).

14. Special to the Denver Post (2013/2016); King (2017).

15. King (2017).

16. Gershoff (2013) (debunked her claim); Holmes (2014) (discipline their children).

17. Clark (2018); Boyles (2015).

18. Fenske (2015).

19. Ross and Jang (2000, 404).

20. See table 3 in chapter 3.

21. Ross and Jang (2000, 404).

22. Ross and Jang (2000, 404).

23. Moore (2018).

24. The use of "broken window" here is a play on theory. See Kelling and Wilson (1982).

25. Ross and Jang (2000).

6. (NO) CONCLUSION AND DISCUSSION

1. Long (2017).

2. McDermott (2017b).

3. See table 3 in chapter 3.

4. See table 3 in chapter 3.

5. See table 3 in chapter 3; Patillo (1988).

6. Ross and Jang (2000).

7. Diani (1992).

8. *Community work* or *movement work* refers to any task(s) or work associated with community organizing or mobilization efforts. This is activism language, terms and phrases commonly used in the same manner as job-related terminology.

9. *Freedom work* is similar to community work or movement work. These terms can be used interchangeably, but this term can be used specifically to refer to task(s) or work aimed at "liberating" people, especially black citizens.

10. The phrase "know me, know me" denotes comfortable familiarity only, rather than intimacy or intimate, personal engagement.

11. As used here, *out* means being outside or "out and about," traveling, and committedly involved in community events throughout the region.

12. Schaeffer (2014).

13. Moore (2003) (DuBois and Washington); Howard-Pitney (2004) (King and X).

14. Public Broadcasting System (PBS) (1999).

15. PBS (1999).

16. Skogan (1990).

17. Thompson (2010). Harvard professor Dr. Henry Louise Gates Jr. was mistakenly suspected of and arrested for breaking and entering into his own home in 2009.

18. Skogan (1990).

19. Skogan (1990).

20. Skogan (1990, 173).

21. O'Dea (2018).

22. O'Dea (2018).

23. Zuk, et al. (2015, 9).

24. Boyles (2015); Wilkes and Iceland (2004); Massey and Denton (1993, 1989).

25. Massey and Denton (1993).

26. Boyles (2015).

27. Boyles (2015).

28. Boyles (2015).

29. Boyles (2015); Farley et al. (1994).

30. Boyles (2015); Farley et. al. (1994).

31. Gallagher (2011).

32. Harlan (2014). "Delmar Divide" refers to a street, Delmar Boulevard, in the city of St. Louis. It is a major thoroughfare that runs east to west, separating the north and south sides of the inner city. As noted, this divide has race and class distinctions.

33. Holliday (2017).

34. Skogan (1990, 178) ("panic peddling").

35. Skogan (1990, 174).

36. Zuk et al. (2015).

37. Zuk et al. (2015, 10).

38. Marcuse (1985).

39. Boyles (2015).

40. Boyles (2015).

41. Boyles (2015).

42. Boyles (2015).

43. MacDonald (2017).

References

Alexander, Jeffrey. 2004. "Toward a Theory of Cultural Trauma." In *Cultural Trauma and Collective Identity*, 1–30. Berkeley: University of California Press.

Almeida, Rhea V., and Judith Lockard. 2005. "The Cultural Context Model: A New Paradigm for Accountability, Empowerment, and the Development of Critical Consciousness against Domestic Violence." In *Domestic Violence at the Margins: Readings on Race, Class, Gender, and Culture*, edited by Natalie J. Sokoloff with Christina Pratt, 301–320. Rutgers, NJ: Rutgers University Press.

Alpert, Geoffrey P., John M. Macdonald, and Roger G. Dunham. 2005. "Police Suspicion and Discretionary Decision Making During Citizen Stops." *Criminology* 43(2): 407–434.

American Psychiatric Association. 2017. "Mental Health Disparities: African-Americans." Accessed October 21, 2018. www.psychiatry.org/File%20 Library/Psychiatrists/Cultural-Competency/Mental-Health-Disparities /Mental-Health-Facts-for-African-Americans.pdf.

Anderson, Elijah. 1999. *Code of the Street: Decency, Violence, and the Moral Life of the Inner City*. New York: W. W. Norton.

Babchuk, Wayne A., and Robert K. Hitchcock. 2013. "Grounded Theory Ethnography: Merging Methodologies for Advancing Naturalistic Inquiry." Accessed April 25, 2018. http://newprairiepress.org/cgi/viewcontent. cgi?article=2980&context=aerc.

Barnes, Harper. 2008. *Never Been a Time: The 1917 Race Riot That Sparked the Civil Rights Movement*. New York: Walker.

Battersby, D. 1981. "The Use of Ethnography and Grounded Theory in Educational Settings." *McGill Journal of Education* 16(1): 91–98.

Bayley, David H. 1994. "International Differences in Community Policing." In *The Challenge of Community Policing: Testing the Promises*, edited by Dennis P. Rosenbaum, 278–281. Thousand Oaks, CA: Sage.

Bayley, David, and Clifford D. Shearing. 1996. "The Future of Policing." *Law and Society Review* 30(3): 585–606.

Bellair, Paul E. 1997. "Social Interaction and Community Crime: Explaining the Importance of Neighbor Networks." *Criminology* 35(4): 677–703.

Bell, Ella L.J. and Stella M. Nkomo. 1998. "Armoring: Learning to Withstand Racial Oppression." *Journal of Comparative Family Studies* 29(2): 285–295.

Berry, Brian J.L., and John D. Karsada. 1977. *Contemporary Urban Ecology.* New York: Macmillan.

Better Together. n.d. St. Louis nonprofit organization. Accessed July 28, 2018. www.bettertogetherstl.com/.

———. 2015. Public Safety-Police Report no. 1 Regional Overview, 2. Accessed April 15, 2019. https://static1.squarespace.com/static/59790f03a5790abd 8c698c9c/t/5c4d6324c2241b81fc30a05d/1548575553900/BT-Police-Report -1-Full-Report-FINAL1+%282%29.pdf.

Bivens, Donna K. 2005. "What Is Internalized Racism?" In *Flipping the Script: White Privilege and Community Building.* MP Associates, Inc. and the Center for Policy Assessment and Development. Accessed November 14, 2018. www.racialequitytools.org/resourcefiles/What_is_Internalized _Racism.pdf.

Black, Donald. 1983. "Crime as Social Control." *American Sociological Review* 48(1): 34–45.

Black and Missing Foundation, Inc. (BAMFI). 2016. Home page. Accessed November 14, 2018. www.blackandmissinginc.com/cdad/stats.htm.

Black Lives Matter. n.d. "Herstory." Accessed August 4, 2018. https://black livesmatter.com/about/herstory/.

Blalock, Hubert M. 1967. *Toward a Theory of Minority-Group Relations.* New York: Wiley.

Boyles, Andrea S. 2015. *Race, Place, and Suburban Policing: Too Close for Comfort.* Berkeley: University of California Press.

Braga, Anthony A., and Rod K. Brunson. 2015. "The Police and Public Discourse on 'Black-on-Black' Violence." *New Perspectives in Policing Bulletin* (May). Accessed September 14, 2018. www.ncjrs.gov/pdffiles1/nij/248588.pdf.

Breech, John. 2014. "St. Louis Police Group Wants Rams Disciplined for Ferguson Gesture." CBSSPORTS.COM, December 1. Accessed August 2, 2018. www .cbssports.com/nfl/news/st-louis-police-group-wants-rams-disciplined-for -ferguson-gesture/.

Brown, James, and Alfred James Ellis. 1968. "Say It Loud—I'm Black and I'm Proud." Songfacts. Accessed August 3, 2018. www.songfacts.com/detail .php?lyrics=10289.

Brunson, Rod K. 2007. "'Police Don't Like Black People': African-American Young Men's Accumulated Police Experiences." *Criminology & Public Policy* 6(1): 71–101.

Brunson, Rod K., and Jody Miller. 2006a. "Gender, Race, and Urban Policing: The Experience of African American Youths." *Gender & Society* 20(4): 531–552.

———. 2006b. "Young Black Men and Urban Policing in the United States." *British Journal of Criminology* 46 (4): 613–640.

Brunson, Rod K., and Kashea Pegram. 2018. "'Kids Do Not Make So Much Trouble, They Are Trouble': Police-Youth Relations." *Future of Children Princeton-Brookings* 28(1). Accessed August 27, 2018. https://futureofchild ren.princeton.edu/sites/futureofchildren/files/media/vol28issue1.pdf .

Brunson, Rod K., and Ronald Weitzer. 2011. "Negotiating Unwelcome Police Encounters: The Intergenerational Transmission of Conduct Norms." *Journal of Contemporary Ethnography* 40(4): 425–456.

Bursik, Robert J., Jr. 1984. "Ecological Theories of Crime and Delinquency since Shaw and McKay." Paper presented at the annual meeting of the American Society of Criminology, Cincinnati, November.

———. 2014. "The Informal Control of Crime through Neighborhood Networks." *Journal of Sociological Focus* 32(1): 85–97.

Bursik, Robert J., Jr., and Harold G. Grasmick. 1993a. *Neighborhoods and Crime: The Dimensions of Effective Community Control*. Lanham, MD: Lexington Books.

———. 1993b. "Economic Deprivation and Neighborhood Crime Rates, 1960–1980." *Law and Society Review* 27(2): 263–283.

Byers, Christine. 2014. "Crime Up after Ferguson and More Police Needed, Top St. Louis Area Chiefs Say." *St. Louis Post-Dispatch*, November 15. Accessed August 5, 2018. www.stltoday.com/news/local/crime-and-courts/crime-up -after-ferguson-and-more-police-needed-top-st/article_04d9f99f-9a9a -51be-a231-1707a57b50d6.html.

Byrne, James M., and Robert J. Sampson, eds. 1986. *The Social Ecology of Crime*. Saginaw, MI: Springer-Verlag.

Chambliss, William J. 1994. "Policing the Ghetto Underclass: The Politics of Law and Law Enforcement." *Social Problems* 41(2): 177–194.

Charmaz, Kathy. 2006. *Constructing Grounded Theory: A Practical Guide through Qualitative Analysis*. London: Sage.

Clark, Randall. 2018. "Cookie Thornton, Meacham Park, and Collective Experience: A Conversation with Sociologist Andrea Boyles." *St. Louis American*, March 19, Accessed April 16, 2018. www.stlamerican.com/news /local_news/cookie-thornton-meacham-park-and-collective-experience-a -conversation-with/article_036f2762-2b99-11e8-8ef9-3327299bd6a8.html.

Clark, Rachel, and Christopher Lett. 2014. "What Happened When Michael Brown Met Officer Darren Wilson." CNN, November 11. Accessed November 12, 2018. www.cnn.com/interactive/2014/08/us/ferguson-brown-timeline/.

Clark-Lewis, Elizabeth. 1985. *"This Work Had A'end": The Transition from Live-in to Day Work*. Memphis, TN: Center for Research on Women (2), Memphis State University.

Cloward, Richard A., and Lloyd E. Ohlin. 1960. *Delinquency and Opportunity: A Theory of Delinquent Gangs*. Oxon: Routledge.

Collins, Patricia Hill. 1990. *Black Feminist Thought: Knowledge, Consciousness, and the Politics of Empowerment*. Boston: Unwin Hyman.

Cordner, Gary. 1995. "Community Policing: Elements and Effects." *Police Forum* 5(3): 1–8.

———. 2000. "Community Policing Approach to Persons with Mental Illness." *Journal of the American Academy of Psychiatry and the Law* 28(3): 326–331.

———. 2014. "Community Policing." In *The Oxford Handbook of Police and Policing*, edited by Michael D. Reisig and Robert J. Kane, 148–171. New York: Oxford University Press.

Crenshaw, K., 1991. "Mapping the Margins: Intersectionality, Identity Politics, and Violence Against Women of Color." *Stanford Law Review* 43(6): 1241–1299.

Currier, Joel, and Christine Byers. 2014. "St. Louis Homicides up More Than 30 Percent in 2014 to Highest Total since 2008." *St. Louis Post-Dispatch*, December 31. Accessed October 18, 2018. www.stltoday.com/news/local /crime-and-courts/st-louis-homicides-up-more-than-percent-in-to-highest /article_1fedee5e-71df-5b12-8f1b-69ab62aab352.html.

———. 2017. "Heated Protests Follow Stockley Acquittal." *St. Louis Post Dispatch*, September 16. Accessed October 20, 2018. www.stltoday.com /news/local/crime-and-courts/heated-protests-follow-stockley-acquittal /article_c7ee91ad-e65b-5da6-84cb-0b478078c8cb.html.

Cusac, Anne-Marie. 2009. *Cruel and Unusual: The Culture of Punishment in America*. New Haven, CT: Yale University Press.

Diani, Mario. 1992. "The Concept of Social Movement." *Sociological Review* 40(1): 1–25.

Dinesen, Peter T., and Kim M. Sonderskov. 2015. "Ethnic Diversity and Social Trust." *American Sociological Review* 80(3): 550–573.

Dougherty, Molly C. 1978. *Becoming a Woman in Rural Black Culture*. New York: Holt, Rinehart, and Winston.

Dottolo, Andrea, and Abigail Stewart. 2008. "'Don't Ever Forget Now, You're a Black Man in America': Intersections of Race, Class and Gender in Encounters." *Sex Roles* 59(5–6): 350–364.

DuBois, William Edward Burghart. 1903. *The Souls of Black Folk*. Chicago: A.C. McClurg.

Duck, Waverly. 2015. *No Way Out: Precarious Living in the Shadow of Poverty and Drug Dealing*. Chicago: University of Chicago Press.

Duffy, Bobby. 2004. "Life Satisfaction and Trust in Other People." MORI Social Research Institute, March. Accessed March 16, 2019. www.ipsos.com/sites /default/files/publication/1970-01/sri_life_satisfaction_and_trust_in _other_people_122004.pdf.

Durkheim, Emile. 1893. *The Division of Labor in Society*. New York: Free Press.

Entman, Robert M., and Andrew Rojecki. 2000. *The Black Image in the White Mind: Media and Race in America*. Chicago: University of Chicago Press.

The Ethical Society of Police. 2018. "About Us." Accessed August 2, 2018. https://esopstl.org/about-us.

Explore St. Louis. 2017. St. Louis Convention and Visitors Commission. Accessed January 6, 2017. https://explorestlouis.com/wp-content/uploads /2011/06/St.-Louis-History.pdf.

Eyerman, Ron. 2004. "The Past in the Present: Culture and the Transmission of Memory." *Acta Sociologica* 47(2): 159–169.

Farley, R. 1970. "The Changing Distribution of Negroes within Metropolitan Areas: The Emergence of Black Suburbs." *American Journal of Sociology* 75(4): 512–529.

Farley, Reynolds, Howard Schuman, Suzanne Bianchi, Diane Colasanto, and Shirley Hatchett. 1994. "'Chocolate City, Vanilla Suburbs': Will the Trend Continue towards Racially Segregated Communities?" *Social Science Research* 7(4): 319–344.

Feagin, Joe R. 1970. "A Note on the Friendship Ties of Black Urbanites." *Social Forces* 49(2): 303–308.

Feagin, Joe. R. 1991. "The Continuing Significance of Race: Public Discrimination." *American Sociological Review* 56(1): 101–116.

Federal Bureau of Investigation (FBI). 2017. "2017 NCIC Missing Person and Unidentified Person Statistics." Accessed November 4, 2018. www.fbi.gov /file-repository/2017-ncic-missing-person-and-unidentified-person-statis tics.pdf.

Fenske, Sarah. 2015. "St. Louis Has the Highest Murder Rate in the Nation." *Riverfront Times*, October 1. Accessed April 16, 2018. www.riverfronttimes .com/newsblog/2015/10/01/st-louis-has-the-highest-murder-rate-in-the -nation.

Fischer, C. S. 1982. *To Dwell Among Friends: Personal Networks in Town and City*. Chicago: University of Chicago Press.

Fivush, Robyn. 2010. "Speaking Silence: The Social Construction of Silence in Autobiographical and Cultural Narratives." *Memory* 18(2): 88–98.

Foreman, James, [Jr.]. 2017. *Locking Up Our Own: Crime and Punishment in Black America*. New York: Farrar, Straus, and Giroux.

Foucault, Michel. 1995. *Discipline and Punishment: The Birth of the Prison*. New York: Vintage.

Foundations Recovery Network. n.d. "The Connection between Mental Illness and Substance Abuse." Accessed October 22, 2018. www.dualdiagnosis.org /mental-health-and-addiction/the-connection/.

Fowler, Nancy, and Eli Chen. 2017. "Protestors Go to Mostly White St. Charles to Deplore Stockley Verdict, Call for Freedom." St. Louis Public Radio, September 22. Accessed October 18, 2018. https://news.stlpublicradio.org /post/protesters-go-mostly-white-st-charles-deplore-stockley-verdict-call -freedom#stream/0.

Fox News. 2015. "Bill O'Reilly: Who Is the Biggest Loser in the Baltimore Riots?" *Talking Points*, April 29. Accessed January 3, 2017. www.foxnews .com/transcript/bill-oreilly-who-is-the-big-loser-in-the-baltimore-riots

Freire, Paulo. (1970) 2007. *Pedagogy of the Oppressed*. Translated by Myra B. Ramos. New York: Continuum.

Furnstenberg, Frank. 1993. "How Families Manage Risk and Opportunity in Dangerous Neighborhoods." In *Sociology and the Public Agenda*, edited by William J. Wilson, 231–258. Newbury Park, CA: Sage.

Gallagher, Mari. 2011. "USDA Defines Food Desert." *Nutrition in the News (Online)* 35(3). Accessed April 16, 2018. http://americannutritionassociation.org/newsletter/usda-defines-food-deserts.

Gershoff, Elizabeth T. 2013. "Spanking and Child Development: We Know Enough Now to Stop Hitting Our Children." *Child Development Perspectives* 7(3): 133–137.

Glaton, Dahleen. 2015. "The Big Lie: African Americans Don't Care about Black-on-Black Crime." *Chicago Tribune*, December 7. Accessed August 5, 2018. www.chicagotribune.com/news/columnists/ct-black-crime-glanton-talk-20151206-story.html#(.

Golden, Renny. 2007. *The War on the Family: Mothers in Prison and the Families They Leave Behind.* New York: Routledge.

Greene, Beverly. 1992. "Racial Socialization: A Tool in Psychotherapy with African American Children." In *Working with Culture: Psychotherapeutic Interventions with Ethnic Minority Youth*, edited by L. Vargas and J. Koss-Chioino, 63–84. San Francisco: Jossey-Bass.

———. 1994. "African American Women." In *Women of Color: Integrating Ethnic and Gender Identities in Psychotherapy*, edited by L. Comas-Diaz and B. Greene, 10–29. New York: Guilford.

Greene, Jack R. 2000. "Community Policing in America: Changing the Nature, Structure, and Function of the police." *Criminal Justice* 3(3): 299–370.

Greene, Jack R., and Ralph B. Taylor. 1988. "Community-based Policing and Foot Patrol: Issues of Theory and Evaluation." In *Community Policing: Rhetoric or Reality*, 195–224. Westport, CT: Praeger Publishers.

Griggs, Brandon. 2018. "Living While Black." *CNN*, December 28. Accessed April 15, 2019. www.cnn.com/2018/12/20/us/living-while-black-police-calls-trnd/index.html.

Hackler, James C., Kwai-Yiu Ho, and Carol Urquhart-Ross. 1974. "The Willingness to Intervene: Differing Community Characteristics." *Social Problems* 21(3): 328–344.

Hannerz, Ulf. 1969. *Soulside: Inquiries into Ghetto Culture and Community.* Chicago: University of Chicago Press.

Harlan, Chico. 2014. "In St. Louis, Delmar Boulevard Is the Line That Divides a City by Race and Perspective." *Washington Post*, August 22. Accessed April 16, 2018. www.washingtonpost.com/national/in-st-louis-delmar-boulevard-is-the-line-that-divides-a-city-by-race-and-perspective/2014/08/22/de69 2962-a2ba-4f53-8bc3-54f88f848fdb_story.html?utm_term=.6b6a2e8edb6d.

Harper, Barnes. 2008. *Never Been a Time: The 1917 Race Riot That Sparked the Civil Rights Movement.* New York: Walker.

Hatcher, William. 2014. "Cultivating Town and Gown Relationships for Cultivating Success." *PA Times.* Accessed October 13, 2018. https://patimes.org/cultivating-town-gown-relationships-development-success/.

Hawkins, Darnell F. 1993. "Inequality, Culture, and Interpersonal Violence." *Health Affairs* 12(4): 80–95.

Hazani, Moshe, and Galit Nahari. 2003. "Social Organization, Intergenerational Ties, and Juvenile Deliquency." *International Review of Sociology* 13(1): 3–20.

Holliday, Art. 2017. "Hundreds of Thousands of STL Residents Struggle to Access Healthy Food." *Five on Your Side*, November 1. Accessed November 11, 2018. www.ksdk.com/article/news/local/hundreds-of-thousands-of -stl-area-residents-struggle-to-access-healthy-food/63-487998853,

Holmes, Steven A. 2014. "Does Spanking Harm the Black Community?" CNN, September 18. Accessed November 4, 2018. www.cnn.com/2014/09/18 /opinion/holmes-spanking-black-community/index.html.

hooks, bell. 1989. *Talking Back: Thinking Feminist, Thinking Black*. Boston: South End Press.

———. 1992. *Black Looks: Race and Representation*. Boston: South End Press.

Hope, T. 1988. "Support for Neighborhood Watch: A British Crime Survey Analysis." In *Communities and Crime Prevention*, edited by T. Hope and M. Shaw, 146–163. London: HMSO.

Horowitz, Ruth. 1983. *Honor and the American Dream: Culture and Identity in a Chicano Community*. Rutgers, NJ: Rutgers University Press.

Howard-Pitney, David. 2004. *Martin Luther King, Jr., Malcolm X, and the Civil Rights Struggle of 1950s and 1960s: A Brief History with Documents*. Boston: Bedford/St. Martin's.

Hrabovský, M., 2013. "Concept of 'Blackness' in Theories of Race." *Asian and African Studies* 22(1), 65–88.

Huber, Joe. 2010. "The History and Possibilities of a St. Louis County Reunification." NEXTSTL, May 3. Accessed July 27, 2018. https://nextstl .com/2010/05/the-history-and-possibilities-of-a-st-louis-city-county -reunification/.

Huerta, Alvero. 2018. "Viva the Scholar Activist!" *Inside Higher Education*, March 30. accessed July 18, 2018. www.insidehighered.com/advice/2018 /03/30/importance-being-scholar-activist-opinion.

"I Won't Complain." 2008. YouTube video, posted September 2. Accessed November 13, 2018. www.youtube.com/watch?v=RZ_V5Jdoy2g.

Ioffe, Julia. 2014. "No One Treats African Americans Worse Than We Treat Ourselves: The Troubling Self-flagellation in Ferguson's Black Community." *New Republic*, August 19. Accessed October 20, 2018. https://newrepublic .com/article/119148/ferguson-renews-debate-among-blacks-politics -respectability.

Janowitz, Morris. 1967. *The Community Press in an Urban Setting*. Chicago: University of Chicago Press.

Jenkins, J. Craig, and Michael Wallace. 1996. "The Generalized Action Potential of Protest Movements: The New Class, Social Trends, and Political Exclusion." *Sociological Forum* 11(2): 183–207.

Johnson, E. Patrick. 2003. *Appropriating Blackness: Performance and the Politics of Authenticity*. Durham, NC: Duke University Press.

Jones, Mike. 2019. "City-County Merger Considered from a Black Political Perspective." *The St. Louis American*, February 28. Accessed April 14, 2019. www.stlamerican.com/news/columnists/mike_jones/city-county-merger -considered-from-a-black-political-perspective/article_6847e0ca-3aed -11e9-8acc-6ba7772f9210.html.

Jones, Nikki. 2018. *The Chosen One: Black Men and the Politics of Redemption.* Berkeley: University of California Press.

Jones, Roxanne. 2017. "Missing Black and Latina Children Are a Crisis for Us All." CNN, April 2. Accessed November 4, 2018. www.cnn.com/2017/04/02 /opinions/missing-girls-in-dc-jones-opinion/index.html.

Karsada, John, and Morris Janowitz. 1974. "Community Attachment in Mass Society." *American Sociological Review* 39(3): 328–339.

Kelling, George L. 1987. "Acquiring a Taste for Order: The Community and Police." *Crime & Delinquency* 33(1): 90–102.

Kelling, George L., and Mark H. Moore. 1988. "The Evolving Strategy of Policing." *Perspectives on Policing* November(4): 1–16. Accessed April 17, 2019. https://pdfs.semanticscholar.org/a614/21a27a6c4fa0e25962ef30e95a2 2371c1b9c.pdf.

Kelling, George L., and James Q. Wilson. 1982. "Broken Windows: The Police and Neighborhood Safety." *The Atlantic Monthly* (March). Accessed April 17, 2019. www.theatlantic.com/magazine/archive/1982/03/broken-win dows/304465/.

King, Shaun. 2017. "It's No Accident That We Hear So Little about Missing Black Girls in This Country." *New York Daily News*, March 22. Accessed November 4, 2018. www.nydailynews.com/news/national/king-no-accident -hear-missing-black-girls-article-1.3005609.

Kornhauser, Ruth. 1978. *Social Sources of Delinquency.* Chicago: University of Chicago Press.

Kraska, P.B., and Shannon Williams. 2018. "The Material Reality of State Violence: The Case of Police Militarization." In *The Routledge International Handbook of Violence Studies,* edited by Walter S. DeKeseredy, Callie Marie Rennison, and Amanda K. Hall-Sanchez. New York: Routledge.

Kraska, Peter B. 2001. *Militarizing the American Criminal Justice System: The Changing Roles of the Armed Forces and the Police.* Boston: Northeastern University Press.

———. 2007. "Militarization and Policing—Its Relevance to the 21st Century Police," *Policing,* 1–13. Accessed October 2018. https://cjmasters.eku.edu /sites/cjmasters.eku.edu/files/21stmilitarization.pdf.

Kraska, Peter B., and Victor E. Kappeler. 1997. "Militarizing American Police: The Rise and Normalization of Paramilitary Units." *Social Problems* 44(1): 1–18.

Krivo, Lauren J., Ruth D. Peterson, and Danielle C. Kuhl. 2009. "Segregation, Racial Structure, and Neighborhood Violent Crime." *American Journal of Sociology* 114(6): 1765–1802.

Lartey, Jamiles. 2017. "'Demolish That Lie': James Foreman, Jr. Takes on Black Lives Matter Backlash." *Guardian,* April 29. Accessed August 5, 2018. www .theguardian.com/us-news/2017/apr/29/james-forman-jr-locking-up-our -own-black-on-black-crime.

Lee, Peter. 2014. "Homeless or Unhoused." *Inside OSL (Organic Sack Lunches)* (blog), January. Accessed October 18, 2018. http://blog.oslserves.org/?p=38.

Levine, Lawrence. 1977. *Black Culture and Black Consciousness: Afro-American Folk Thought from Slavery to Freedom*. New York: Oxford University Press.

Levitt, Aimee. 2010. "The Great Divorce: Everything You Ever Wanted to Know about the St. Louis City/County Split." *Riverfront Times*, May 4. Accessed July 27, 2018. www.riverfronttimes.com/newsblog/2010/05/04/the-great-divorce-everything-you-ever-wanted-to-know-about-the-city-county-split.

Lewis, Oscar. 1959. *Five Families: Mexican Case Studies in the Culture of Poverty*. New York: Basic Books, Inc.

Long, Jason. 2017. "After Five Weeks, Judge Still Weighing Fate of Ex-Cop Charged with Murder." *Channel Five on Your Side*, September 14. Accessed April 14, 2018. www.ksdk.com/article/news/local/after-5-weeks-judge-still-weighing-fate-of-ex-cop-charged-with-murder/63-474694834.

Lumpkins, Charles L. 2008. *American Pogrom: The East St. Louis Race Riot and Black Politics*. Athens: Ohio University Press.

Maccoby, E. E., T. M. Newcomb, and E. L. Hartley, eds. 1958. *Readings in Social Psychology*. Oxford: Henry Holt.

MacDonald, Heather. 2017. "All That Kneeling Ignores the Real Cause of Black Homicides." *New York Post*, September 26. Accessed by April 16, 2018. https://nypost.com/2017/09/26/all-that-kneeling-ignores-the-real-cause-of-soaring-black-homicides/.

Marcuse, Peter. 1985. "Gentrification, Abandonment, and Displacement: Connection, Causes, and Policy Responses in New York City." *Urban Law Annual/Journal of Urban Contemporary Law* 28(4): 195–240.

Martineau, William H. 1977. "Informal Social Ties among Urban Black Americans: Some New Data and a Review of the Problem." *Journal of Black Studies* 8(1): 83–104.

Marwell, Gerald, Pamela E. Oliver, and Ralph Prahl. 1988. "Social Networks and Collective Action: A Theory of the Critical Mass III." *American Journal of Sociology* 94(3): 502–534.

Marx, Gary T., and Dane Archer. 1971. "Citizen Involvement in the Law Enforcement Process: The Case of Community Police Patrols." *American Behavioral Scientist* 15(1): 52.

Massey, Douglas S., and Nancy A. Denton. 1989. "Hypersegregation in US Metropolitan Areas: Black and Hispanic Segregation along Five Dimensions." *Demography* 26(3): 373–391.

———. 1993. *American Apartheid: Segregation and the Making of the Underclass*. Cambridge, MA: Harvard University Press.

Massie, Victoria M. 2016. "Why Black-on-Black Crime Isn't a Valid Argument against Criticizing Police Brutality." *VOX*, July 12. Accessed August 5, 2018. www.vox.com/2016/7/12/12152772/rudy-giuliani-black-on-black-crime-police.

Mastrofski, Stephen D., Robert E. Worden, and Jeffrey B. Snipes. 1995. "Law Enforcement in a Time of Community Policing." *Criminology* 33(4): 539–563.

McDermott, Kevin. 2017a. "Krewson, Stenger Back Latest Push for City-County Coordination." *St. Louis Post-Dispatch*, June 12. accessed July 28, 2018. https://www.stltoday.com/news/local/govt-and-politics/krewson-stenger-back-latest-push-for-city-county-coordination/article_22ddc131-a438-54f6-845e-2d7c07688df5.html.

———. 2017b. "National Guard Troops Were Put on Standby before Stockley Verdict." *St. Louis Post-Dispatch*, September 15. Accessed April 15, 2018. www.stltoday.com/news/local/govt-and-politics/national-guard-troops-were-put-on-standby-before-stockley-verdict/article_8b978ee9-80d8-5beb-9401-3933653f9b3e.html.

McMillan, David W., and David M. Chavis. 1986. "Sense of Community: A Definition and Theory." *Journal of Community Psychology* 14(1): 6–23.

McVay, Doug, Vincent Schriraldi, and Jason Ziedenberg. 2004. "Treatment or Incarceration? National and State Findings on the Efficacy and Cost Savings of Drug Treatment Versus Imprisonment." Justice Policy Institute, January 30. Accessed October 21, 2018. www.justicepolicy.org/uploads/justicepolicy/documents/04-01_rep_mdtreatmentorincarceration_ac-dp.pdf.

Meehan, A. J., and M. C. Ponder. 2002. "Race and Place: The Ecology of Racial Profiling African Americans." *Justice Quarterly* (19)3: 399–430.

Merton, Robert K. 1938. "Social Structure and Anomie." *American Sociological Review* 3(5): 672–682.

———. 1968. *Social Theory and Social Structure*. New York: Free Press.

Meyer, Lane. 2017. "News Reporter Almost Gets His Ass Kicked During Protests in St. Louis." YouTube video, posted September 15. Accessed October 17, 2018. www.youtube.com/watch?v=A9euriUzc1w.

Miller, Walter. 1958. "Lower Class Culture as a Generating Milieu of Gang Delinquency." *Journal of the Society for the Psychological Study of Social Issues* 14(3): 5–19.

Minino, Alrialdi. 2017. "QuickStats: Age-Adjusted Rates for Homicides, by Ethnicity—United States, 1999–2017." Centers for Disease Control and Prevention (CDC), August 11. Accessed November 4, 2018. www.cdc.gov/mmwr/volumes/66/wr/mm6631a9.htm.

Moore, Doug. 2018. "With Nearly Half Its Garbage Trucks Breaking Down, St. Louis Struggles to Collect Trash." *St. Louis Post-Dispatch*, July 18. Accessed November 1, 2018. www.stltoday.com/news/local/metro/with-nearly-half-its-garbage-trucks-breaking-down-st-louis/article_d17b4f44-a562-5164-9020-0fd3da3aa874.html.

Moore, Jacqueline. 2003. *Booker T. Washington, W. E. B. Dubois, and the Struggle for Racial Uplift*. Wilmington, DE: Scholarly Resources.

Mountz, Alison. 2009. "The Other." In *Key Concepts in Political Geography*, 328–337. Thousand Oaks, CA: Sage.

Moynihan, Daniel. 1965. "The Negro Family: The Case for National Action." The United States Department of Labor, March. Accessed April 13, 2018. www.dol.gov/oasam/programs/history/webid-meynihan.htm.

Murphy, Sherry L., Jiaquan Xu, Kenneth D. Kochenak, Sally Curtin, and Elizabeth Arias. 2017. "Deaths: Final Data for 2015." National Vital Statistics

System, Centers for Disease Control and Prevention (CDC), 66(6). Accessed November 4, 2018. www.cdc.gov/nchs/data/nvsr/nvsr66/nvsr66_06.pdf.

NAACP Legal Defense Fund. n.d. "The Significance of 'the Doll Test.'" Accessed August 4, 2018. www.naacpldf.org/brown-at-60-the-doll-test.

Naples, Nancy. 1991. "'JUST WHAT NEEDED TO BE DONE': The Political Practice of Women Workers in Low-Income Neighborhoods." *Gender and Society* 5(4): 478–494.

National Alliance on Mental Illness (NAMI). n.d. "African American Mental Health." Accessed October 21, 2018. www.nami.org/Find-Support/Diverse -Communities/African-Americans.

National Alliance to End Homelessness. 2018. "Racial Inequality in Homelessness, by the Numbers." June 4. Accessed October 21, 2018. https:// endhomelessness.org/resource/racial-inequalities-homelessness-numbers/.

National Bureau of Economic Research (NBER). n.d. "Mental Illness and Substance Abuse." Accessed October 22, 2018. www.nber.org/digest/apr02 /w8699.html.

National Institutes of Health. 2018. "Addiction and the Criminal Justice System." United States Department of Health and Human Services, updated June 30. Accessed October 22, 2018. https://report.nih.gov/nihfactsheets /ViewFactSheet.aspx?csid=22.

Naylor, Gloria. 2005. *The Women of Brewster Place*. New York: Penguin Books.

O'Dea, Janelle. 2018. "Lending Discrimination, Redlining Still Plagues St. Louis, New Data Show." *St. Louis Post-Dispatch*, February 19. Accessed April 15, 2018. www.stltoday.com/business/local/lending-discrimination -redlining-still-plague-st-louis-new-data-show/article_3e1a6847-799b -58d7-a680-651a0c1a2ea8.html.

Ohlsen, Flora O. 2013. "Defining Blackness-the Other." Master's thesis, Roskilde University-Malmo University. Accessed December 10, 2018. https://core.ac.uk/download/pdf/16199579.pdf.

Oliver, Melvin L. 1988. "The Urban Black Community as Network: Toward a Social Network Perspective." *Sociological Quarterly*, 29(4): 623–645.

O'Neil, Tim. 2016. "How the Great Divorce of St. Louis City and St. Louis County Got Started." *St. Louis Post-Dispatch*, August 22. Accessed January 3, 2017. www.stltoday.com/news/local/aug-how-the-great-divorce-of-st -louis-city-and/article_3e93fa29-7d01-570d-94f2-31eca08a9378.html.

Park, Jessica. 2016. "Is Homeless the Right Word for Those Living on the Streets?" *Hoodline News*, December 8. Accessed October 25, 2018. https:// hoodline.com/2016/12/is-homeless-the-right-word-for-those-living-on -the-street.

Pattillo, Mary E. 1988. "Sweet Mothers and Gangbangers: Managing Crime in a Black Middle Class Neighborhood." *Social Forces* 76(3): 747–774.

Pattillo-McCoy, Mary E. 1998. "Church Culture as a Strategy of Action in the Black Community." *American Sociological Review* 63(6): 767–784.

Peters, Marie. 1985. "Racial Socialization of Young Black Children." In *Black Children: Social, Educational and Parental Environments*, edited by H. McAdoo and J. McAdoo, 159–173. Newbury Park, CA: Sage.

Peterson, Ruth, and Lauren Krivo. 1993. "Racial Segregation and Black Urban Homicides." *Social Forces* 71(4): 1001–1026.

———. 1996. "Extremely Disadvantaged Neighborhoods and Urban Crime." *Social Forces* 75(2): 619–648.

Pierce, Charles P. 2007. "The Sport That Time Forgot." *Esquire*, January 29. Accessed October 6, 2018. www.esquire.com/sports/a1046/sport-time-for got-0600/.

Public Broadcasting System (PBS). 1999. "The Heart of the Hutu-Tutsi Conflict." *PBS NewsHour*, October 8. Accessed November 10, 2018. www .pbs.org/newshour/politics/africa-july-dec99-rwanda_10-08.

Putnam, R.D. 2007. "E Pluribus Unum: Diversity and Community in the 21st Century the 2006 Johan Skytte Prize Lecture." *Scandinavian Political Studies* 30(2): 137–174.

Ransby, Barbara. 2018. *Making All Black Lives Matter: Reimaging Freedom in the 21st Century*. Berkeley: University of California Press.

Ray, Ranita. 2018. "The Scholar-Activist Paradox." *UC Press Blog*, August 10. Accessed November 14, 2018. www.ucpress.edu/blog/37832/the-scholar -activist-paradox/.

Rios, Victor. 2017. *Human Targets: Schools, Police, and the Criminalization of Latino Youth*. Chicago: University of Chicago Press.

Rose, Fred. 1997. "Towards a Class-Cultural Theory of Social Movements: Reinterpreting New Social Movements." *Sociological Forum* 12(3): 461–494.

Rosenbaum, Dennis P., Arthur J. Lurigio, and Robert Carl Davis. 1998. *The Prevention of Crime: Social and Situational Strategies*. Belmont, CA: Wadsworth.

Rosenfeld, Richard. 2015. "Was There a 'Ferguson Effect' on Crime in St. Louis?" The Sentencing Project. Accessed September 1, 2018. https://sentencingpro ject.org/wp-content/uploads/2015/09/Ferguson-Effect.pdf.

Ross, Catherine E. 2011. "Collective Threat, Trust, and the Sense of Personal Control." *Journal of Health and Social Behavior* 52(3): 287–296.

Ross, Catherine E., and Sung Joon Jang. 2000. "Neighborhood Disorder, Fear, and Mistrust: The Buffering Role of Social Ties with Neighbors." *American Journal of Community Psychology* 28(4): 401–420.

Ross, Catherine E., John Mirowsky, and Shana Pribesh. 2001. "Powerlessness and the Amplification of Threat: Neighborhood Disadvantage, Disorder, and Mistrust." *American Sociological Review* 66(4): 568–591.

Rountree, Pamela Wilcox, and Barbara D. Warner. 1999. "Social Ties and Crime: Is The Relationship Gendered?" *Criminology* 37(4): 789–813.

Russell-Brown, Katherine. 1998. *The Color of Crime: Racial Hoaxes, White Fear, Black Protectionism, Police Harassment and Other Macroaggressions*. New York: New York University Press.

Sampson, Robert J. 1987. "Urban Black Violence: The Effect of Black Male Joblessness and Family Disruption." *American Journal of Sociology* 93(2): 348–382.

———. 1988. "Local Friendship Ties and Community Attachment in Mass Society: A Multi-level Systemic Model." *American Sociological Review* 53(5): 766–779.

———. 1991. "Linking the Macro- and Micro level Dimensions of Community Social Organization." *Social Forces* 70(1): 43–64.

Sampson, Robert J., and W. B. Groves. 1989. "Community Structure and Crime: Testing Social Disorganization Theory." *American Journal of Sociology* 94(4): 774–802.

Sanburn, Josh. 2014. "All the Ways Darren Wilson Described Being Afraid of Mike Brown." *TIME*, November 25. Accessed July 30, 2018. http://time .com/3605346/darren-wilson-michael-brown-demon/.

Schaeffer, Robert K. 2014. *Social Movements and Global Social Change: The Rising Tide.* Lanham, MD: Rowman and Littlefield.

Shaw, Clifford R., and Henry D. McKay. 1942. *Juvenile Delinquency and Urban Areas: A Study of Rates of Delinquents in Relation to Differential Characteristics of Local Communities in American Cities.* Chicago: University of Chicago Press.

Skogan, Wesley G. 1990. *Disorder and Decline: Crime and the Spiral of Decay in American Neighborhoods.* Berkeley: University of California Press.

———. 1994. "The Impact of Community Policing on Neighborhood Residents." In *The Challenge of Community Policing: Testing the Promises,* edited by D. Rosebaum, 167–181. Newbury Park, CA: Sage.

———. 2009. "Concern about Crime and Confidence in the Police Reassurance or Accountability?" *Police Quarterly* 12(3): 301–318.

Smith, Brad W., and Malcolm D. Holmes. 2003. "Community Accountability, Minority Threat and Police Brutality: An Examination of Civil Rights Criminal Complaints." *Criminology* 41(4): 1035–1064.

Sommers, Jack. 2016. "Missing White Woman Syndrome: An Empirical Analysis of Race and Gender in Online Coverage of Missing Persons." *Journal of Criminal Law and Criminology* 106(2): 275–314.

Special to the Denver Post. 2013/2016. "Why Do We Seldom Hear about Missing Black Children?" *Denver Post,* February 14. Accessed November 4, 2018. www.denverpost.com/2013/02/14/why-do-we-seldom-hear-about -missing-black-children/.

St. Clair, Robert N. 1998. "The Social and Cultural Construction of Silence." Louisville: The University of Louisville. Accessed October 2018. https://web .uri.edu/iaics/files/08-Robert-N.-St.-Clair.pdf.

Stack, Carol B. 1974. *All Our Kin: Strategies for Survival in the Black Community.* New York: Basic Books.

Stewart, Eric P., Daniel P. Mears, Patricia Y. Warren, Eric P. Baumer, and Ashley N. Arnio. 2018. "Lynchings, Racial Threat, and Whites' Punitive View towards Blacks." *Criminology* 56(3): 455–480.

Sudbury, Julia, and Margo Okazawa-Rey. *Activist Scholarship: Antiracism, Feminism, and Social Change.* New York: Routledge.

Suttles, Gerald D. 1972. *The Social Construction of Communities*. Chicago: University of Chicago Press.

Swaroop, Sapna, and Jeffrey D. Morenoff. 2006. "Building Community: The Neighborhood Context of Social Organization." *Social Forces* 84(3): 1665–1695.

Swidler, Ann. 1986. "Culture in Action: Symbols and Strategies." *American Sociological Review* 51(2): 273–286.

Taylor, Ralph B. 1996. "Neighborhood Responses to Disorder and Local Attachments: The Systemic Model of Attachment, Social Disorganization, and Neighborhood Use Value." *Sociological Forum* 11(1): 41–74.

Taylor, Robert J., Linda M. Chatters, Cheryl B. Hardison, and Anna Riley. 2001. "Informal Social Support Networks and Subjective Well-Being among African Americans." *Journal of Black Psychology* 27(4): 439–463.

Thomas, William I., and Florian Znaneicki. 1920. *The Polish Peasant in Europe and America: A Classic Work in Immigration History*. Boston: Gorham.

Thompson, Krissah. 2010. "Arrests of Harvard's Henry Louis Gates Was Avoidable, Report Says." *Washington Post*, June 30. Accessed November 11, 2018. www.washingtonpost.com/wp-dyn/content/article/2010/06/30/AR2010063001356.html.

Toler, Lindsay. 2014. "Thirteen Municipalities Fit into One Neighborhood." *Riverfront Times*, November 5. Accessed January 7, 2017. www.riverfront times.com/newsblog/2014/11/05/13-st-louis-county-municipalities-fit-in-one-city-neighborhood.

Triplett, Ruth A., Randy R. Gainey, and Ivan Y. Sun. 2003. "Institutional Strength, Social Control, and Neighborhood Crime Rates." *Theoretical Criminology* 7(4): 439–467.

Troester, Rosalie R. 1984. "Turbulence and tenderness: Mothers, daughters, and "othermothers" in Paule Marshall's Brown Girl, Brownstones." *Sage: A Scholarly Journal on Black Women* 1(2): 13–16.

United States Census Bureau. 2017a. "QuickFacts: St. Louis City, Missouri." Accessed July 28, 2018. http://www.census.gov/quickfacts/table/IPE120215/2965000.

United States Census Bureau. 2017b. "QuickFacts: St. Louis County, Missouri." Accessed July 28, 2018. www.census.gov/quickfacts/table/PST045215/29189.

United States Department of Health and Human Services. 2018. "Mental Health and African Americans." Office of Minority Health, last modified September 15. Accessed October 25, 2018. https://minorityhealth.hhs.gov/omh/browse.aspx?lvl=4&lvlid=24.

United States Department of Justice. 2007. "Black Victims of Violent Crimes." Report prepared by Erika Harrell. Office of Justice Programs, Bureau of Justice Statistics, August. Accessed April 16, 2019. www.bjs.gov/content/pub/pdf/bvvc.pdf.

———. 2015. "Investigation of the Ferguson Police Department." Civil Rights Division, March 4. Accessed August 15, 2018. www.justice.gov/sites/default /files/opa/press-releases/attachments/2015/03/04/ferguson_police_depart ment_report.pdf.

———. 2017. "Race and Hispanic Origin of Victims and Offenders, 2012– 2015." Report prepared by Rachel Morgan. Office of Justice Programs, Bureau of Justice Statistics, October. Accessed August 1, 2018. www.bjs.gov /content/pub/pdf/rhovo1215.pdf.

Valentine, BettyLou. 1978. *Hustling and Other Hard Work: Lifestyles in the Ghetto*. New York: Free Press.

Wander, P. C, J. N. Martin, and T. K. Nakayama. 1999. "Whiteness and Beyond: Socio-historical Foundations of Whiteness and Contemporary Challenges." In *Whiteness: The Communication of Social Identity*, edited by Thomas K. Nakayama & Judith N. Martin, 13–26. Thousand Oaks, CA: Sage.

Ward-Brown, Denise, dir. *Never Been a Time*. 2016. St. Louis, MO: 365 Productions. Video.

Warner, Barbara D., and Pamela W. Rountree, Pamela W. 1997. "Local Social Ties in a Community and Crime Model: Questioning the Systemic Nature of Social Control." *Social Problems* 44(4): 520–536.

"WATCH cops physically push CNN's Don Lemon during Tense Ferguson Protest." 2014. YouTube video, posted September 9. Accessed October 17, 2018. www.youtube.com/watch?v=Q1zVMEiEXwE.

Websdale, Neil. 2001. *Policing the Poor: From Slave Plantation to Public Housing*. Boston: Northeastern University Press.

Wellman, Barry. 1979. "The Community Question: The Intimate Networks of East Yonkers." *American Journal of Sociology* 84(5): 1201–1231.

Wellman, Barry, P. Carrington, and A. Hall. 1983. *Networks as Personal Comm- unities*. Toronto: University of Toronto, Center for Urban and Community Studies.

Wellman, Barry, and Barry Leighton. 1979. "Networks, Neighborhoods, and Communities: Approaches to the Study of Community Questions." *Urban Affairs Quarterly* 14(3): 363–390.

West, Candace, and Don H. Zimmerman. 1987. "Doing Gender." *Gender and Society* 1(2): 125–151.

Wilkes, Rima, and John Iceland. 2004. "Hypersegregation in the Twenty-First Century." *Demography* 41(1): 23–36.

Williams, Janice. 2017. "Majority of Americans Have 'Unfavorable View' of Black Lives Matter, Say Black Crime Is a Top Concern." *Newsweek*, August 3. Accessed August 5, 2018. www.newsweek.com/black-lives-matter-pro tests-police-646050.

Wilson, James Q., and George L. Kelling. 1982. "Broken Windows." *Atlantic Monthly* 249(3): 29–38.

Wilson, William Julius. 1987. *The Truly Disadvantaged: The Inner City, the Underclass, and Public Policy*. Chicago: University of Chicago Press.

Wire, Si. 2014. "Black St. Louis Police Officer Group Commends Rams' 'Hands Up' Protest." *Sports Illustrated*, December 3. Accessed August 2, 2018. www .si.com/nfl/2014/12/03/st-louis-rams-ferguson-protest-ethical-society -statement.

Zuk, Miriam, Ariel H. Bierbaum, Karen Chapple, Karolina Gorska, Anastasia Loukaitou-Siderus, Paul Ong, and Trevor Thomas. 2015. "Gentrification, Displacement, and the Role of Public Investment: A Literature Review." March 3. Accessed November 11, 2018. www.urbandisplacement.org/sites /default/files/images/displacement_lit_review_final.pdf.

Index

academia: town-gown relationships, 34–38, 75, 181n49
activist, use of term, 178n45
activist scholarship, 35–36
addiction: community services for, 170; life in black neighborhoods, 83, 94, 101–2, 103, 128, 129, 165; police role in dealing with addicts, 171; specialized neighborhood support for addicts, 92, 97–101, 106, 128; Ted, life story of, 117, 118, 120; Tevin, life story of, 106, 108, 109, 111; war on drugs, 62
Aeisha (specialized support by), 97, 101–2
Agency for Africa Share, 149
alcohol, neighborhood life and, 83, 169
Anderson, Elijah, 66–67
Angel (Focus Group 1), 82–84, 88
Angela (community othermother), 129–32
arrest, as replacement for social services, 100–101, 170–71
arrest of protesters: eye-witness report of, 53; five second rule, 70, 73; risk of, 42, 43, 71, 80, 89; snatch-and-grab arrests, 77–78; support for those arrested, 97
arson during protests, 51–52, 86, 123–24
Ava (neighborhood marshal), 92–93

Bell, E. L. E., 67
Benton (Focus Group 2), 84–88
Bess (Focus Group 2), 84–88
Better Together, 12–13
Black and Missing Foundation Inc. (BAMFI), 137–38, 188n10
black consciousness: "loving blackness" as political resistance, 29–30; conflict and silos within movements, 164–66; direct action and, 30–33; (dis)order, black cultural perspective of, 52–58; Khareem, life story of, 110–17; long-term commitment to activism, 153–54, 159, 161–62; othermothering, overview of, 125–36; philosophical differences in, 165–66; respectability, fight for, 96; social movements and black empowerment, 124–25; Ted, life story of, 117–21; Tevin, life story of, 106–11. *See also* blackness; black solidarity; fictive kin
Black Lives Matter (BLM), 168, 181n39; black consciousness and direct action, 32–33; early calls to action and, 26
blackness: cultural preferences for whiteness, 30; "loving blackness" as political resistance, 29–30; mistrust and threats of daily life for black